The
Third Position

by O.E. Nordahl

Copyright © 2015 by Oddgeir Eidheim Nordahl

All rights reserved.

First Edition.

ISBN 978-82-999749-2-9

O.E. Nordahl

oenordahl@gmail.com

Contents

PREFACE	7
INTRODUCTION	9
PART ONE: MAN	**13**
MEANING OF LIFE	**15**
SENSES	**18**
I. SENSE AND STIMULI	18
II. NORMALIZATION AND UTILIZATION	21
INSTINCT AND INTUITION	**23**
I. INSTINCT	23
II. DISTINCTIONS	25
III. INTUITION	29
AESTHETICS	**32**
I. PERCEPTION, HABITUATION, AND SELECTION	32
II. INSTINCTUAL DRIVE	36
III. COLOUR AND SIMILARITY	37
IV. SHAPE AND FUNCTIONAL VARIETY	40
V. ELIMINATION OF THE INEFFECTUAL	44
VI. BEAUTY AND IDEAL	46
VII. THE NATURAL AND THE ASSOCIATIVE	50
GENETIC REALITIES	**54**
I. GENETICS AND RACE	54
II. ADAPTATION AND HYBRIDIZATION	60
III. INTELLIGENCE, TESTOSTERONE, AND MISCEGENY	64
IV. PLUS ULTRA?	69
THE GENDERS	**73**
I. BASE DIFFERENCES	73
II. MAN IN RELATION TO WOMAN	77
III. WOMAN IN RELATION TO MAN	82
IV. MASCULINITY AND FEMININITY	85
V. REALITIES	89
VI. CAPABILITY	93

PART TWO: MIND — 97

FREE WILL — 99
INTELLIGENCE — 102
- I. MEASURE AND COMPARISON — 102
- II. EMPATHY AND FALLACY — 104
- III. CONSEQUENCE — 110
- IV. DECADENCE — 113
- V. IGNORANCE AND EVIL — 116

VALUATION — 123
- I. CAUSAL VALUE — 123
- II. SUBJECTIVITY AND THE SITUATIONAL — 126
- III. FAILURE TO VALUE — 130
- IV. MORALS, ETHICS, AND LAW — 134
- V. LOVE, HATE, AND ENVY — 138
- VI. MORAL POLARITY — 142
- VII. SHAME, FEAR, AND LAUGHTER — 146
- VIII. WISDOM AND OPINION — 150
- IV. THE GOOD AND POSITIONISM — 153

ASSOCIATION — 157
- I. MEMORY STRUCTURE — 157
- II. INVOLUNTARY ASSOCIATION — 159
- III. REVISIONISM AND NEGATIONISM — 164
- IV. PRESENTISM — 168
- V. COGNITIVE BIAS — 172
- VI. DISSOCIATION AND IDEAL — 177

SUFFERING AND HAPPINESS — 180
- I. THE PURSUIT OF HAPPINESS — 180
- II. SUFFERING — 182

PART THREE: A RECOLLECTION OF EVENTS — 187

THE SCULPTING OF MAN — 189
- I. CIVILIZATION AND THE ARYAN — 189
- II. DEATH AND RISE OF EMPIRES — 193
- III. THE GREAT CIVILIZATIONS — 196
- IV. THE NORTHERN MAN — 199
- V. ROMAN AND GERMANIC WAYS — 203
- VI. CELTIC MAN — 207
- VII. GERMANIC MIGRATIONS — 209
- VIII. MUSLIMS AND SLAVS — 211
- IX. THE VIKINGS — 213

X. THE NORSE AND THE NORMANS	218
XI. IMPACT ON THE WORLD	222
PLATO AND SOCRATES	**224**
I. THE POSITION OF PLATO	224
II. CRITIQUE AND COMPARISON	228
NIETZSCHE AND GERMANY	**233**
I. DESCRIPTION AND CHARACTERIZATION	233
II. FALSITIES AND CONTRADICTIONS	238
III. DIONYSUS, LOKI, AND DOWNFALL	245
IV. IDEALISM AND REALISM	247
V. PROPHECY OF A NEW EMPIRE	252
VI. ANTI-SEMITISM	256
THE CAUSATION OF THE WORLD WARS	**259**
I. PRECURSOR	259
II. BUILD UP TO WAR	262
III. AIMS AND TREATIES	267
IV. A WAR OF CONTENTION	271
V. HYPOCRISY AND PROPAGANDA	274
VI. DEFEAT AND AFTERMATH	277

PART FOUR: PROBLEMATIQUE OF PARTICULARS   283

SOCIETY AND LEADERSHIP	**285**
I. NATURAL INEQUALITY	285
II. HIERARCHY, CLASS, AND LEADERSHIP	288
III. GOVERNANCE AND SOCIETY	291
IMMIGRATION AND POLITICS	**294**
I. THE DESTRUCTION OF THE WEST	294
II. RHETORIC AND INFORMATION CONTROL	299
OTHER DESTRUCTIVE POLICIES	**304**
I. OVERPOPULATION AND POLLUTION	304
II. THE INSANITY OF NUCLEAR WEAPONS	307
III. DIFFERENTIATING IDEOLOGIES	309
MASONIC INSTITUTION OF THE JEW	**313**
I. THE RISE OF THE JEW IN EUROPE	313
II. THE OVERPRIVILEGED JEW	314
III. EXPLOITATION AND PALESTINE	316
IV. MANIPULATION AND DECEPTION	319
ATHEISM AND RELIGION	**322**
I. PAST AND PRESENT	322
II. ARIANISM AND THE REFORMATION	327
III. NEED AND USE OF RELIGION	330

LANGUAGE, WRITING, AND CULTURE	334
PART FIVE: NECESSITIES FOR THE FUTURE	**339**
A NEW STATE	**341**
I. A FIRST STEP	341
II. CURRICULA AND DUTY	344
III. THE FORMATION OF NOBILITY	348
IV. FREE ENTERPRISE AND THE STATE	350
V. BREEDING AND SOCIETY	353
VI. SHOULD AND SHOULD NOT	357
VII. THE MILITARY AND A NEW ORDER	361
NORDIC MATTERS	**364**
I. A COMMON NORDIC LANGUAGE	364
II. A NORDIC EMPIRE	365
ANGLO-AMERICAN COMBINE	**372**
I. PRELIMINARY AIMS AND NEEDS	372
II. UNIFICATION AND FEDERATION	376
III. AN ANGLO-AMERICAN WORLD	381
POTENTIALITIES	**383**
I. A STABILIZED WORLD	383
II. A NEW HOMELAND	389
III. COSMIC SURVIVAL	395
CONCLUSION	**399**

Preface

In my thirtieth year I wrote this book. It is a summary of the beliefs that I have had all my life, and that I am now fully able to explain and put to paper. It was drafted in the summer of 2014 in my fatherland of Norway, and it took me the rest of the year to complete it. Make no mistake, this book is the product of a lifetime of dedicated study. An autodidactic study that I found much more useful and enlightening than the meagre and pointless college education I finished at the age of 20. A study first and foremost in history, which I see as my main strength, and that I have spent a better part of my life reading. Later in life I turned to philosophy. With Plato, Schopenhauerian methods and insights, and definitions carved out by Nietzsche, I have armed myself. The conclusion reached is none other than that of fascism. This may be quite a blunt statement to some people, but this truth that I see is that the values of noble man, and the aristocracy of old, has its closest familiarity today with fascism. Fascism, which is nothing but the modern progression of these old values—and values always change in accordance with progress. And so, for this reason, and the one of semantics and avoidance of association, we are better off calling it the Third Position. A political viewpoint that is neither left nor right, but syncretic.

My aim is to tell this truth that I feel no one sees or even knows today, and the importance and urgency of it has impelled me to take action. I will offer as much of a complete insight into my point of view as I can, and in as a short and concise way possible without leaving out sufficient arguments and reasons for how and why conclusions were reached. Philosophical books, or books in general, tend to have either too much explanations for the very obvious and easy to understand—making the reading tedious and uninteresting—

or they abruptly come to conclusions and leave the reader wondering how they got there. Certainly, though, we are all prone to the failure of having objective clarity, and I am sure that I will commit these faults just mentioned.

Every part and process of this book was done on my own. That includes the writing, editing, etc. Also, bear in mind that English is not my mother tongue, although I do consider myself just as proficient in it. Whether any of this will be a source of praise or lambasting is yet to be seen. This book was earlier released in two parts in e-book format. I may give out editions later on with further elaborations or expansions if I find that I may have left something out, or I might cut away material found superfluous—if material is found repetitious, however, it serves the purpose of hammering in the points needed to be made. The message is otherwise set in stone, as I see it extremely unlikely that I would, or could, change my stance after having it all my life, and not having had any doubts about it, either.

I hope that I can make some changes and contributions through this work. The world has become hyper-individualistic and egoistic, and as a consequence people are extremely nihilistic and apolitical. If I can bring about any social or political change at all, I may consider this work a splendid success.

Introduction

This book will probably be seen as a political work, but it is also, in my eyes, very much a philosophical work. It aims to give answers to a lot more than politics, after all. Answers that are nowhere to be found today, or answers that no one dare to give because they are taboo and not politically correct, and in some instances they are even illegal to just talk about. A whole system surrounding the workings of life and nature will be built from the ground up, dialectically following the concatenation of thought in each query down to its root to find the cause of it. Some of the questions answered in this book are: Why and how do we value and determine right or wrong? What is beauty and aesthetics? What is empathy and emotion? What is hate and love? What is good, bad, and evil? What does learning and experience, and indoctrination and propaganda, do to us? Why do men and women behave as they do? What impact do genetic differences have, and why are they so important? What is man's place in nature and his connection to it? What are the consequences of modern politics dominated by liberals and socialists?

One of the main grievances people have today in the Western world is why altruism is forced down our throat—this helping of all others in the world—and some even question why we should help those in our own lands and nations at all. The policies I am referring to are open door immigration, the taxation of the citizen to pay for social benefits, and the foreign aid we hand out, which is also paid for by the working citizen. To give away to everyone what they have not earned and do not deserve is nothing but unchecked socialism. It is equalization at the expense of the strong and capable. But worst of all is when the ones helped are not even our kin or countrymen. These many altruisms and socialist practices are the most common political

Introduction

complaints today, and rightly so: it goes against the principles of nature itself. In nature it is the strong and capable that thrive and live on, after all. And it is only natural that you help out your own, first and foremost—those of your blood and those closest to it—instead of those which you have the least in common with. Western man today continues to lift up others around the world that only take care of their own in return. This is pure lunacy, and it is the exact same thing as actively working against your own, and working for those that are hostile to us and only serve themselves—the definition of treachery.

This way of nature—a natural perspective—has been my view of life as long as I can remember. I have also been a steadfast atheist all my life; I have always seen the superstitious nonsense for what it is. Science and nature, and a truthful representation of it, has therefore always been of the highest importance to me. I say truthful, because I do not consider the current political agenda and scientific community honest at all. Political correctness is their master and they are much too afraid to speak the truth. Science today is only accepted if the findings are in thread with, or promotes, the current political agenda. This is not how it should be. Political agenda should follow and change according to science and nature, and not the other way around.

The modern moral world is overwrought with frantic compassion and pity. Society today praises and empowers the weak and the smaller groups, and they dominate politics because of it. This entails helping any kind of minorities, or just anyone that is not a Caucasian male, frankly. Helping pitiful beings that would otherwise fail, or are just too lazy and dumb, to survive unaided. Women have long since gotten all their rights, yet they want even more today—more than men have—and in doing so, that equality they purportedly wanted goes flying out the window. And the minorities now play the racist card to no end, and get positive discrimination like affirmative action and several other types of benefits without any justification for it. Employment equity they call this, and women take advantage of this as well. What these people do not realize is that not giving someone a job or opportunity, because they have poor results and no prospective qualities, is not racism or discrimination, it is reality.

The guiding principle should be how nature and life functions: the strong and superior elements must be allowed to continue, and the weak and inferior must not. What's done today is to encourage and sustain this latter, thereby reversing nature and what is natural. For what? Because it is "evil" to do otherwise? One may as well call nature evil then. I will provide an account of why this thinking exists, how it has come to this, and why it is still practiced.

In short, this book is an attack upon the left-wing and the religious, and a defence of the old right, in many ways, and also that of atheism. To fully understand and benefit from this work it is expected that you have a general knowledge of history and nature, and it is also helpful to have had familiarized yourself with basic philosophy, e.g. Plato's dialogues. This book is built in such a way that one could start reading any chapter and section of it, and still be able to gain insight into the matter at hand. However, one will have a better comprehension and grasp of it by reading it in sequential order and in completion, obviously.

Part One: Man

'Man is the measure of all things." – Protagoras

Part One: Man

Meaning of Life

"What is the meaning of life?" people ask. But what they are really asking is: What is the meaning of my life? What is my purpose? They want to know how to live their lives according to what they want and dream, and they seek direction and guidance. And preferably a simple recipe to follow, or a quick and easy answer. But the truth is that there is no answer, because if you go by individual taste and desire, or simply by trying to measure a worth or meaning to a life by itself, then you cannot find one. There is no answer to such a silly question. It is like asking about the meaning or purpose of the cow, and finding answer in her milk, meat, or that she would calf so we would get more. But in doing so, we have already started to attribute the worth of the cow not to herself, but what her benefit is to us and what we gain from her—another fallacy of the ego. Ask yourself what all ancestors of that which is living today has in common and you will find the answer: procreation and the continuation of life itself—the survival of life—which is the only true purpose of it. This primordial factor, the need and urge to procreate and multiply, and to build upon the former expressions of itself, is the first and eternal drive of life. And it will continue to be strong, because if this will and willing to life and survival is weaker in some expressions of life, then that life will fail to compete with everything else that exhibits a stronger will to survive, and thus ultimately die out. The strongest will to live will always ensure its own continuance and dominance—at least where artificiality is not imposed. And so, the weak willed are simply weeded out in nature. As such, the will to life and survival had to be, and was, there from the very start and beginning of life. And because of this competition of these wills in nature, it will always ensure its own existence. Whether this applies to humankind still is a different matter, though. This question of "what is the meaning of life" is nothing but a direct consequence of intelligence, really. Only a thinking creature would ask such a question. It is nothing but an affliction of the mind caused by a greater awareness of its surroundings: to look for meaning or purpose in the existence of the Universe or life, just because they are there and have come into being.

And so, that is the meaning of life: Survival. The continuation of life. The type of life you have and the expression of it. Which would necessarily include those closest to your kind. That is why the meaning of life can never be found in just an individual or in yourself. Not true meaning, anyway. It always has to include some extension of what you are either in mind or matter. This extension meaning the expression of life that is most alike and similar to that of yours. And what is this extension of the self and the same but procreation? Even the most solitary of creatures on Earth still seek out their own by that need and drive—this will to survive. If they had not possessed this drive to do so, then they and their kind would obviously not be here. We extend ourselves and our lives by doing so; a bloodline that continues is the closest thing to immortality one can get. This drive to perpetuate the self is present in all of life. Even the weakest willed of creatures. The will to life is, after all, the sole trait that all previous life had in common. And undoubtedly the strongest. Life then, intrinsically, has the need to continue its own life. That is the nature and function of it. So, what is the meaning of life? Life itself. And if not that of your own, then at least in some capacity or benefit to those expressions of life closest to your own. That may be hard to understand in these individualistic times of self-gratification and hedonism, but such selflessness is quite common in nature, because not everyone has the capacity or privilege to procreate, and obviously were not meant to. Like those too weak, unworthy, or simply unable to. For example, not every ant in the ant colony is necessary for the function of biological reproduction, but they are still vital to the survival of the colony and their kind as a whole. The worker ant and most ants in the colony—generally speaking of course, and not gamergate colonies and the likes—are hindered biologically to reproduce. Natural selection made this behaviour ingrained in such a way by exclusion and extinction of colonies not behaving in that manner and therefore not benefiting from it. And just like them, we humans may find ourselves close to extinction if we do not start prioritizing and working for the survival of the colony instead of just ourselves. If the colony does not survive, then the few, the most capable and fittest, are unable to continue on with their way of life on behalf of the rest.

Senses

I. Sense and Stimuli

The two most common things in all life are sense and stimuli. They are the bases of life, really. In order to extract nourishment and nutrients from our environment, these functions are needed in some manner. In short, they enable life to struggle and compete in nature. Most senses are based on the common factors of Earth itself, but some are adapted according to the more peculiar factors of the rarer habitats. One such common factor is light, which is the single most important thing for all life on Earth—either directly or indirectly—and as it pervades all but the darkest of places and deepest of depths, it is natural that the eyes are one of the most common of senses. As most life on Earth live under such similar conditions, they have ended up with similar senses. I will explain how the senses work and what their function is within this frame of commonalities:

The first and primary function of the senses is to detect magnitude. Meaning a pressure, expansion, intensity, or quantity of some kind. Like with pressure on the skin and on the nerves, or the way the ear detects the faintest squeak to the loudest scream from differences in sound pressure. Or the way that strong or slight smells and tastes are detected. And in the case of the eye, it is quantity of light. Too little or too much quantity on the senses lie at either end of the spectrum. As too little may do no harm and makes your senses unable to sense anything, then on the other end, in having too much, may cause harm and cause your senses to be flooded with information, making all sensory input indistinguishable. Just how small amounts are detectable is very different in animals, and man is one that is quite average in all of them by comparison. Dogs have a delicate nose to track and find prey by smell. The keen eyesight of birds enable them to pinpoint prey on the ground from great heights. And the snake tastes himself around in life. Apart from his heat sensing ability, that is. The owl has better hearing to hunt properly at night. And in the case of touch, I may as well make man the example. For his nimble fingers, and ability to detect fine and course textures, enable him to build sophisticated tools and anything else his mind conjures up. We see, then, that creatures are very different as to how minute amounts they can detect. On the other end of this extreme are the large amounts, and there is really not a fine tuning there, because if the amounts are exceeded, then it usually involves pushing the senses to a point where the nerves die from a pressure or too much quantity. Hard to prove this in the matter of taste and smell, though. In the case of the eye, you can go blind if exposed to very intensive light, or too much of it (prolonged periods). Too much skin pressure will damage the nerves, and ultimately damage the tissue itself. The ear is even more sensitive, as that is its function, because sound pressure is very faint overall. This sensitivity leaves it more susceptible to damage than most other senses.

Then there is the character of information. Sensory quality. This is the frequency of sound—pitch—to the ear, frequency of light—colour—to the eye, the difference of particles to the nose and to taste, and heat or cold to that of touch. This measure of differentiation is important, because it helps us determine what character a situation or thing has. The quality itself is not necessarily harmful in the same manner as quantity, as long as it is within the norm of our physiology, but it can help us to detect if something is bad in some way: Strange tastes to avoid poisons. Or a smell to detect rot and decay. Unnatural or uncharacteristic colours to identify the good or the bad. Heat or cold in order to protect our skin and bodies. In sound we have the high pitch sounds that are usually associated with small things. And the larger they are, the heavier and deeper sounds they make. The difference of frequencies—the different tones in pattern—help us to identify different animals, phenomena, and that of speech in humans. But a frequency in sound is something that can damage the hearing. Another indication of the delicateness of that sense itself for sure.

There is a third function of the senses. This is one of location and locating. With our many sense nerves, we are able to estimate direction through a pattern of an increase or decrease, or a change by comparison. With smell, we can pinpoint the direction it comes from, or at least change our search accordingly when the smell is fainter or stronger. With taste, we can detect where in the mouth the thing we taste is. With hearing, the intensity of sound and the difference in its exhibition allows us to detect the general direction it comes from. Especially if constant or repetitive to allow for comparison. And the location of touch is very important. It enables us to identify a danger to precise areas so that we can attend to it. Or avoid something and move away. And if something moves along your skin, you can estimate direction by the comparison of previous locations to find a pattern in its movement. Location in the eye is something of a different character. The eye, as a sense, relies more on distant and outward changes and differences. These differences are what the eyes locate and find, which means that our method of locating by sight is something sensed, and even learnt, by having two eyes which give us that three-dimensional sight that can differentiate through comparisons of distant movement and that movement in our eyes and of our body. How our sight benefits from learning and knowledge is seen in many ways. For instance, judging distance is one that humans have to specifically study and be trained in to become better at. This rather small example illustrates how connected, and important, sight and mind are to each other, and how the more intelligent mind utilizes this sense better.

II. Normalization and Utilization

As our senses originated in Earthly environments, they developed and equalized in accordance to them as well. Life incapable of certain high or low levels of adaptation, in terms of a certain tolerance or sensitivity, will die out as a result, or do not come to life at all. In other words, there is an optimal adaptation according to each place of habitation, and on Earth, in general, which is the result of the imposition of all the factors in that environment on life. Meaning that the flora and fauna constitute a part of it as well, because of the way they affect life there. Such as how plants produce oxygen, and in this way it has actually changed the atmosphere of Earth itself. And how dead plants and life developed into, and constitute, the layer of dirt and earth on the surface of our planet. Things like these are therefore a condition of life in the same way as the habitability of Earth itself, and thus an intrinsic part of the many habitats here, such as the oceans, grasslands, deserts, tundra, and polar regions. And not just these prime factors of oxygen and dirt, but a great many other ones as well.

The sensory organs—apart from this imposition of normalization on them just mentioned—are perfected according to the need of the animal for its survival. An animal that rely on its hearing for food, for instance, will enable those of that kind with a more attuned hearing to do better in their life, and this will contribute greatly to their overall survival. This is how evolutionary perfection and specialization starts. What of men then? We dullards in the world of senses. We have little acuity or affinity in any senses, really. We are just quite average. Although, we are far from the worst, as some would have you believe today, and our senses are more than enough attuned for our lives. There is also something we have that far outshines what any other animal has: a large and sophisticated brain. It may not be a sense organ, but it is an organ, nonetheless. An organ that orchestrates all the senses, and collects the stimuli and identifies them, and connects them together by memory. An ever learning organ, and therefore the greatest one of them all. A fantastic device to interpret and thereby enhance all senses. Where the stupid and the animals are bewildered, our clever mind will make reason and sense of what they cannot. What need is there of extreme senses or physicalities when you can calculate, plan, and device a way? The brain—highly adaptable as it is—builds on ever more advanced knowledge, and readily adjusts itself and accept these strange things at a quick pace. Especially at young age. And how readily we take up these notions, all notions, even when we are almost completely ignorant of their inner workings. Unaware of how they function, or all of their functions. Or even what the use and purpose of them are at all. Although, even animals are capable of being readily accepting. Tameness we call it. Opposed to nature it is, in a sense—wariness being so crucial to survival in the perilous and unforgiving wilderness. And perhaps tameness is just as crucial in the jungle of human life.

Part One: Man

Instinct and Intuition

I. Instinct

When we speak of instinct, we speak of something that comes natural to us. Something ingrained that is a part of us and usually of some importance. Like a killer instinct. Or an instinct for survival. There is little definition as to what it really is, however. It is described as something that takes a hold, or has a hold of us. As opposed to that which is in our control and of our intelligent reasoning. Instinct usually involves a physical act that is done without much thinking. Like a reflex, but still not quite the same. A reflex is something that is mostly unavoidable, as it is the body protecting itself and keeping itself out of harm. The raising of the hand to protect the eyes, for instance. Or the retraction of a limb in danger of harm or already in harm. Or the bladder alleviating itself in times of fear in order to prepare for fight or flight. We have the innate sense of size, and thus strength and power, through our vision. A respect for larger height and size is natural to all animals. It is ingrained in life itself, really. We all scurry away if some large object were to head our way. One may say that this is intuition, but intuition is restricted to that of the mind, or drive of body conveyed by mind. And even though we may identify intuition in seemingly unintelligent creatures, it is restricted to memory and intelligence of some sort. Instinct, however, is something that is reminiscent of an urge, or a sense of a need or right action for the body; something we sense in and of ourselves. In modern society it is usually something that is seen as primal and uncivilized. Instincts are perceived as animalistic, and man very often thinks himself better than both animal and nature. Man can indeed hold back on, and control, what would instinctually feel right, though. He can starve himself for a purpose, or he can commit suicide instead of following his instinct for survival. We speak, then, of a mechanism that is given to us by nature, but is not necessarily needed or wanted anymore. The animal instinctively eats and eats, but man knows of the consequences of over-eating, and so he refrains from it. We suspend or repress our instincts, because we are able to deliberate on the results of an action and therefore control ourselves. We think before we act.

Instinct, at core, is the needful drive of life and the living. And as instinct is different from animal to animal, and even between the different races of men, we can simply conclude that it is the physical expression of the body and the genes, and what comes most natural to it. When a lion hunts prey and bites into it, he does so because he knows himself. A lion has a strong body and claws for tackling, and a big mouth and teeth, and he senses these strengths through living. He developed a taste for blood early on, and his aggressive nature powers that urge as well. A horse has strong legs for running away and therefore kicks. And he eats grass. A preference for grass is something the horse feels naturally. His taste and smell is adapted to like grass, and his body feels good when eating it. The long process of a certain way of living throughout many, many generations has made them like and do these things. With omnivores it is the same, but with wider specializations and adaptations. Bears, for instance, can change their diet to whatever suits them best, or what they find easiest to get. A bear can start hunting prey on land, and even humans, or it may continue eating berries and salmon. His body and nature allows for this diversity. Such as it is with man. Man is the most diverse animal there is.

In other words, we are restricted, or better to say built, for certain actions. The body senses this through the very complexities that it consists of, such as biochemical reactions to touch, smell, and hearing, or the physical naturalities of certain strengths and builds for different things like hands for gripping, or claws for tearing. In other words, instinct is just a general term of how a life-form should or could live according to how it has evolved. Instinct is therefore a very bunkum term, as it says nothing, really. And because it is so general and widely used without restraint, it can very easily be abused. One may say that humans are killers by instinct, or one may say that they are peaceful and non-violent. Any of it may be true because man is so diverse. Instinct was used before—and still is—to describe something that people did not understand. Sort of like assigning the cause of thunder and lightning to Thor. Or Schopenhauer's will, and the thing-in-itself, to all the things that we did not have a description or evidence for—all unknowns that we sense are there in some inexplicable way. As such, it is merely a trickery of words. All inclusive terms like these are old-fashioned and outdated. We may still use instinct as a word, but if we are to do so, then we have to define what it is in each animal or plant, and only then can we describe what is instinctual to each accordingly. And not throw the term around so freely and rhetorically as is done today.

II. Distinctions

Life is fragile, in many ways. In animal conservation today we see that when animals are bred in captivity, and then are let out into the wild, they will very often fail to adapt and survive. This is due to the fact that much of life, such as mammals and birds, are very intelligent and has therefore evolved in conjunction with being taught how to survive. The big cats learn to hunt by observing, and eventually join in at young age. The elephants will travel around in groups with their young, and will imprint on them regarding where to go, and when to go. The birds will learn migration through knowing what good places they found, and then return to. Information is thus a selective process in itself. When a good choice is made, it lives on. And the more intelligent a life-form is, the better choices they make, usually. However, this is exactly what makes life so fragile at times, because if some such knowledge is lost, and that life depends on doing what it has done for a very long time, then it may take quite a while before this behaviour is capable of being learned anew. If ever. The elephant released from captivity and let into the wild will not know where to go, and he will also not have a protective pack. This is not to say that instinct and intelligence will not prevail. The animals can see and sense a dry period coming on, or a wet season returning. They also have other animals which they can follow and imitate in order to survive as best they can. A water hole draws one creature in that sees or senses it. Like seeing a bird hovering over it, for example. And so, one animal attracts another. This works because animals are built around other animals, in a sense. Life attracts life. And as it does, it also affects life. The behaviour of the prey embed itself in the genes of the predator, and vice versa. For instance, the speed of the cheetah spurs on the evolution of the speed in the gazelle. This is a very concrete and easily seen example. Things are not always that easy to unravel, though. Nature is finely woven, and we have seen what consequences an introduction, or loss, of a species may have. The genes are at times very set in their way, and the expression of them, the instinct, may fail when not suited or adapted to something.

Behaviour is sometimes called extended phenotype, and one may very well call this instinctual, as it is the expression of genes as to what comes most natural to it, coupled with environment, what is available, etc. The beaver instinctively likes the water because he is built for it, and he will do what he can to extend this habitat, as most creatures do. And so, he builds dams. He uses his best tool for this, which is his sharp and strong teeth. It is his only tool available for cutting up wood. One can include intelligence in these matters, but not necessarily. Insects and other creatures of very low intelligence—I'm not saying they are stupid, though—always use their greatest assets in times of need. These assets may be stingers, big and sharp legs, or spit. Anything. We can conclude that they subconsciously know themselves and their strengths, and will use these whenever need be.

In many animals we have noticed divergent behaviour from normalcy. The cheetah is usually seen as a solitary hunter, but we have found that some cheetahs hunt in packs, and when they do this, they can hunt even larger prey than they are able to when alone. These cheetahs have found another way of survival, in other words. And while we consider the cheetah today a hunter that relies on speed, then a change of behaviour such as the one mentioned—a behaviour that is more successful or more convenient—can change that. Its impact is such that those who hunt according to this new tactic may become more successful, and this could then supersede the old behaviour by its survival or by a show and tell to others cheetahs. And then their speed might become a redundancy too, with the larger and stronger built individual cheetahs becoming more successful in this new tactic, which would eventually change the entire species. Consequently, the cheetah may evolve into a big built pack animal if this behaviour takes hold.

Through this example, we see a clear difference between instinct and learned behaviour. The cheetah who hunts solitary might not be instinctual. It could just be an occurrence due to practicality. Instinctual behaviour is something that is not as easily changed as that. Instinct is something that is there despite of everything. Easiest it is to explain if one couples it directly with survival: A behaviour that is or has been absolutely vital, and is still expressing itself as one to a great extent. A behaviour that comes from the genes and adapted to behave as such. We do not say of the dog that it is in his instinct to kill. We say this of the wolf frequently, though. We can state this confidently, because dogs are usually tame and obedient. That is their normal behaviour. And vice versa of the wolf. But we do recognize the ability of the dog to kill, because we often train him to do so, and also due to the fact that he was a predator back in his wolfish days. This is how it is with predators. Man and his killer instinct, for instance. There are residuals. But as stated before, with intelligence comes the ability to discern what to do, and what not to do, and the instinct can and will be repressed, and eventually weeded out to an ever greater degree. We did this very effectively before with the death penalty for severe crimes, such as murder. In doing so, we actually cleansed the gene pool of predatory behaviour—this killer instinct. It would have dissipated in the long run, though, because nature and life, and thus genes, will continue on with what is done. Man has become more and more pacifistic, ergo he will evolve in accordance with that. However, this type of weeding out is not as effective as that of natural selection, or intelligent selection, as was done with the termination of killers—elimination, that is. I think I may confidently state this behavioural and environmental adaptation as a fact of life, because it has finally been shown that genes switch on or off according to a use or impact upon them. We also know that when we train our bodies and minds a certain way, it will affect the offspring in some fashion. And so, there is a slight plasticity in DNA. The much used "I was not meant or built to do this or that" is therefore not true, and is nothing more than a bad excuse. If we strive, we can become better, and we will pass it on.

III. Intuition

Intuition is doing that which comes most naturally to us mentally, without the aware and intentional use of reason, information, and the conclusions thereof. Intuition is very similar to instinct, in that it is a spontaneous act. To say whether or not intuition is based upon knowledge is hard to say conclusively, but it is certainly not hampered by it. We always conclude what should and should not happen. Most animals act on some sort of intuition. Let's say that a cat were to hop onto a tree branch. The cat then infers that the tree branch will hold it, because it judges according to familiarity: It has hopped onto other such branches before. Branches that were just as long, or just as thick. It also knows that on the end it is thinner and more flexible. And so, it is a very primal knowledge. It is a base experience of the world, or the physics of the world. However, the cat jumped onto the branch and the branch broke. But a man, and presumably a well-educated man, might have seen that the branch would not be safe. Either there was a rift or break there that could have been seen with such knowledge beforehand, or maybe it had been half sawn off. In any case, the irregularity would have been seen by someone able to tell the consequences of such small and otherwise unnoticeable factors. Did the cat learn from this experience? Probably not, because he did not, and cannot, identify such patterns as easily as a more intelligent and informed creature would. But he may have become a bit more cautious for when the next moment arises in jumping onto a branch. Had the cat noticed some flaw in the branch early on, he would have been more cautious and perhaps tested it a bit. He would not have jumped, and instead would have treaded paw by paw onto it. He would then see that there is a rift when the branch bends, and that it breaks where it is. And so, there may be eventual learning. But the harder and more difficult it is to discern these pitfalls in nature, the easier they are to stumble into. If a human falls for them, it is more shameful. This is because it is expected that someone with higher intelligence than an animal ought not to fall victim to such accidents, and that he failed to avoid them when most other people did. This comparison of others is how we find normality. We always compare like to like in nature. This is aesthetics. This is done in order to detect a fault or flaw in that which should otherwise be normal or ideal. We will get to that in the next chapter. My point is that if one has a faulty intuition, or a faulty instinct for that matter, when compared to others, then one may be inferior in some way.

To intuit, then, is part of our ability to act spontaneously. Which is rooted in survival, really, as it is the need for a quick and accurate assessment when time is of the essence. Or expecting something to happen, or doing something that would provide an outcome expected. The cat did not properly intuit that the branch would leave him falling; at least his instincts twirled him around and enabled him to land on his feet. Intuition is thus a very primal thing. It is the animalistic nature of living in the moment—spontaneity. The world of man, however, has become more and more calculating and deliberate throughout time in concurrence with the increase of intelligence and knowledge in man. This increase made him able to foresee consequences, which is why he plans ahead accordingly. His reliance on pure intuition is less; he does not live in the moment, and is less spontaneous.

When we speak of women's intuition, then it is her spontaneity we speak of—this irrational and mindless nature: carelessness and a lack of regard for the future and the consequences. It is the identification of this primal and primitive nature in women, when we say they act purely on intuition. Or some lack of intelligence or knowledge, to be perfectly blunt. This unintelligent behaviour is the same as animal intuition, and it is not some trait exclusive to women—and not to men—and not necessarily this badge of pride they want it to be, either. One of the main reasons why a woman acts on intuition is because she is so bound to nature due to her inherent drives. I will elaborate on this in the chapter *The Genders*. Men can also be as irrational as some of these women, but they cannot be excused of it, because we do not expect, and we do not want, this trait in men. When a woman acts on intuition, it is part of her charm and her nature. Is this a good excuse? Perhaps not. But there is an attraction to it, nonetheless. Opposites attract, after all. Man likes the wildness and animalistic grace in woman. As opposed to his own nature that is ordered and artificial.

Aesthetics

I. Perception, Habituation, and Selection

We have many words for the feeling and perception of sense stimulus. We use these words in many aspects of our lives, and even use them interchangeably. The use of any such word is directly linked to how we perceived the stimulus—there is a good or bad characterization for each one. If we bite into a lemon, we call it bitter and sour. Both negative adjectives and usually bad notions. We do not eat raw lemons for that reason. If we were to characterize something as bitter or sour in the world, it would be something we'd wish to avoid in some way. A peach, on the other hand, we call sweet and delicious. There are always the things we would like to get or have, and the things we would like to avoid—the good and the bad. This is fundamental to our valuing. This dual nature of how the living valuate is also the reason for the polarity of thought in man, such as this/that, either/or, black/white, love/hate, good/evil, and false dilemmas and fallacies. We fall into the trap of outright acceptance or rejection because it is in our nature. Not counting instances of actual causality, of course, which will lead to a positive or negative outcome.

Most things come in between this polarity, however. Throughout life we continually dull ourselves by experiencing things; in both the good and the bad we build up a certain tolerance, or dullness. A peach may become rather common, or a lemon may not be as bad as earlier experienced. And so, we are not as taken in by an experience, due to having had them many times. We have become desensitized—habituated. But from the very first outset of things, one will derive a direct appreciation (valuation) through the senses. Some things are naturally good, or just an appreciated thing. The fresh air, the shining sun, and nature are such things. Very often we take these for granted, even though they are a good to us. This is because we are normalized to them. Our senses are normalized to our world. Most natural sounds come within a range that is neither too faint, nor too loud. Most tastes are detectable. Our eyes and our skin are adapted to the sunlight. We are all a product of the tolerated limit, or having a progressed evolutionary finesse of sense, within the confines of our environment and the interactions within. This is also why we usually take the world—our perception of it—for granted.

The adaptation of life is one of sculpting and shaping of, and into, the environment and all that this entails. A fruit emerged in plants so a seed will be eaten. Like a sweet fruit or some such that a species may have a special taste for. These differences and attractions come about in a number of ways. A flower will get a colour from a selection, or a mixing through hybridization, or even just mutation. Contrarily, through continual breeding within an entire species, a uniformity will emerge. Where there is divergence—and there almost always is—there will be differences. These differences may even occur within the same species of very close and similar genetic makeup. What we call phenotype. This is due to the great number of genes that allow for a number of manifestations that can and will occur if the criteria are met and the factors are there. Explained in simple terms, it means that DNA will have a number of active and inactive genes that will trigger on or off. Either seemingly at random, or from some bodily response or genetic predisposition. How this works is still largely mysterious to us today. Even when it comes to the expression of the phenotypes among the different human races in our very studied and researched human genome. And it is highly unlikely that if one solves this problem in one species or genetic makeup, that one will solve it across the board in genetics altogether. In any case, we have only started to scratch the surface of the foundations of life. Life is just so extremely diverse and complex. And even more so when one takes intelligence and behaviour into account.

With phenotypes, one can breed selectively to increase the chances of an occurrence. We have done this with roses, for instance. One cultivates similar expressions, e.g. reddish roses, to bring out more of it, or to stabilize a genotype. One can stabilize a genotype from a phenotype by breeding like with like. This way, the active genes will be passed on in greater strength—seen through their visual expression, after the fact—than it would in non-selected types. Ultimately, this will breed out all "irregularities" until gone or greatly suppressed. One can also mix differences to create hybrids—types that will look very atypical due to the irregular, or artificial, mix that was done. Man has done this selective breeding and hybridization for several thousand years now. Most notably in domesticated animals. We see this very clearly in the dog, where we have done this for so long, and in so geographically different and isolated areas, with much hybridization along the way, that we ended up with these huge varieties we now have in terms of size, fur, colour, shape, intelligence, and behaviour. This is man taking control of nature and then shaping it however he wants.

To do this we use the same bases as nature does when it selects. We use our instinctual senses and valuation. We experience immediate responses, and most of the time we assign a value to it that other life would. A lot of animals do have a similar reaction to smells, for instance. Smells that were naturally selected to be enticing to animals in order to attract them, and the reason for this is almost always linked or directly coupled with survival. Like the flowers and their spreading of pollen by nectar feeders. Or the delicious fruits, and the animals who feed on them and afterwards shed the seeds in a fertile covering, so that the plant will have a much better and faster start in life. Because of this, more and more enticing devices in plants and animals will emerge—in other words, they will improve—because of the natural selection of something better. Something sweeter, for example. The preference in and of collective nature lets ever greater and more fantastic things emerge. Things that benefit either a select or larger group. It was the gradual and continual selection by all life to become ever better that made the world so good to us. But it also is so at base, really, with these optimal conditions for life. Such as the cool temperatures between freezing and boiling, which is an optimal and foundational condition that allows for life—as we know it—to occur in the first place. And then that sweetness of life itself comes into being. Plant and vegetation that make oxygen, provide food, etc. And the luring mechanisms through sweet fruits, smells, and lovely visual displays. Or the protective/preventive ones, such as poisons, or foul smells and tastes. And just like nature, we humans also select. We select from a function or value. And since we are bound by the same foundations of environment as the rest of life, then we are susceptible in the same manner. Or act in similar accordance, it is better to say. The environment and conditions of life normalize all living things in it, and makes it common where there is commonality. Life normalizes nature collectively, because of the symbiosis in nature. Such as the flies, the bees, and the birds that all spread pollen. This is because the plants that had smells and tasty nectar for the largest number of creatures, and therefore utilized the largest number of creatures—more creatures that proportionally spread more pollen—thereby increased their chances for survival and their dominance over those that didn't or were not able to generalize. However, using the word able implies that plants work toward something like that intelligently, which they do not, and it is better to say that the randomness and mutations that offered increased survival did. And those that did not, died out. It is like this with animals as well, but not in the same manner, because animals can change their diets, habits, and behaviour. For some animals this takes a very long time, but for others, such as mammals, this is easier; a lot of mammals are omnivores.

II. Instinctual Drive

We see that on both sides of this normalization of senses—through environment and natural selection—there is the harmful and the beneficial. We can, however, explain it easiest if we start from the basis of how we sense. From instinct or intuition we can sense what we should have, or should be. When it is too dark, or when hearing is muffled, you feel a confinement or an enclosure of sorts. You can sense it, or that lack of sensing at least. You feel that something is not what it should be. This is very similar to numbness and pain—the two extremes of sense stimuli. When one feels a numbness or pain, one is driven towards an elimination of them. Like how we are driven by our hunger, or our sexual urge. And this sexual urge—that is a physical pressure in men—can be equated with a sensing. For instance, the lack of sexual release in men can lead to the condition colloquially called blue balls. This is pressure having built up to such a point that tissue is overstretched. Hence, the pain. Because of this, we may infer that there is a gradual build up and increasing pain, which then drives a creature to seek change or alleviation. It is the same in the other end of the spectrum. A lack of, or a numbness, may also drive one towards a pain or sensing. In other words, the body seeks equalization; a normality: not too much, and not too little. I'll venture that the insect is thus driven by these physiological stimuli, when working towards or out of the pupa, for example, in order to find its state of normality. All these strange behaviours in insects when they change their forms—strange to humans at least—is a physical drive, and when such physical sensations drive you towards a thing, or doing a thing, we may call it instinct. Many of these pupa transformations, and other such strange shapings in insects, is likened to birth, and for good reason. It is like the womb that only does the one thing it can do, when it has reached that final stage—it gives birth. And the baby, too, will be soft, round, and malleable, but later in life it will stretch out and stiffen into a grown human. A shaping that is driven by human urge, necessity, and desire—not counting genetic maturity, or that of age. For instance, a lifelong athlete will be of a different shape than a sedentary intellectual. The athlete in the shape of his body, but the intellectual may have actually changed the structure in his brain through greater usage. They have both strengthened and changed their body according to what they did and how they used it, and their will and instinct was the driving force behind this. A (mental) will that is more or less an outcome of environment and situation, and higher intelligence or athletic disposition can be seen as an extension of the instinctual (genetic).

III. Colour and Similarity

I have mentioned that there is a basis in nature when it comes to beauty. One that is there due to natural selection and survival. Plants entice animals with colour and shape. But what are these colours and shapes? How does one colour affect us? There is a normalcy to be seen here as well. Where the sky and water is blue, and the plant-life is green, then unusual, or not so unusual, colours are found when they are useful and needed. The flower will have sharp and bright colours to signify to pollen-bearers that it is there. But the insect may be green to blend into the surroundings, in order to not get eaten, or to have an advantage when hunting prey—what we call camouflage. We see that nature is colour coded like that. It does this to indicate what is there, or that it is there; a call to attention. Or not, when not beneficial. The colour coding and markings themselves may vary a great deal from place to place, and from life to life. A snake, for one, may have very bright colouring, in order to scare away predators. Bright, unusual colours are used to make themselves known, be it plant or animal. When used in plants, it is seen as one of mutual benefit, because a plant that indicates that it is there most likely thrives on the attention, and to guarantee that to happen it usually has some sweet and enticing lure. A plant can show that it is there and provide food without being harmed, or much harmed, by it. But an animal is either wholly, or not at all, a food source. Animals usually do not provide partial and mutual benefits in the same way as plants— not when it comes to individual life, that is. Also, defenceless and still as plants usually are, they are therefore not seen as a threat, either. And since animals are not in such a harmonious state with other animals as the plant is—meaning that they are not dependent on pollen or some such—then an animal that is highly visible due to colour or markings is an animal that is not hampered by it, and most likely very dangerous because of it. This is not always the case, but this is the subconscious reasoning in animals, nonetheless. We avoid animals that are fearless and wander about, and with a great and strange display of colour and shapes to boot, because we conclude that if it can do that, and has done that, without any consequences thus far, then there must be a reason why. And most animals do not want to find out that exact reason—unless they're desperate. Not all animals with these colours and markings are dangerous, though. Some have only evolved in parallel to other species that do merit some fear or avoidance. And these disguisers and mimickers take advantage of that, and it came about that way. They have survived trough a similarity of a feared and avoided animal of some kind. The greater resemblance one animal has with the other, the greater its chance for survival may be. And as a result, a closeness of resemblance and behaviour is selected by nature itself. One cannot judge solely by appearances then. There may be other qualities and values beneath a surface or behind an appearance—as it is with these mimickers. And also in all of life, in general. There may be a deceptive veil that hides or obscures what we see in others, or in things in nature. And even ourselves. A person may be resigned to not being good at something, without having even tried it, because he has been told that he is not good at it, or just by having been discouraged or uninterested to try altogether. Perhaps the person discouraged was scrawny and therefore dismissed without being given a chance. Whatever the case may be, know that hidden talents and qualities may be found in the least likeliest of places. And often are. Thus, appearances may be deceiving. Which is why we repeatedly use this term for both good and bad, seen and unseen, characteristics in humans. A liar and cheat may put up a good front, and an honest and kind man may be brash and forthcoming. It isn't easy to tell which is which sometimes. This is all part of nature.

We know that colours evoke certain responses. The cooler blues and greens elicit harmony, because they are part of the world we are adapted to biologically, and we do get used to them through living in this world as well. Red is the most unnatural—the colour of largest contrast or polarity—and that is why it is the most distressing one. Yellow and white are seen as life giving due to the sun. But any kind of bright colours seen in animals—that stand out from the green foliage—are usually perceived as a threat or warrants some avoidance—in concordance with the reasoning about animals who display themselves fearlessly. A purple is unnatural, but it has the cool blue and alarming red in it, and is therefore in between. Colour coding is thus universal. Or Earthly to use a better word. But our responses to colour may become associated and normalized differently through intelligence, due to their frequent use and prevalent portrayal in an artificial manner, such as in human society. That way, we can make an association regardless of what we would otherwise see or feel naturally.

The primary function of colour perception is simply to help us differentiate. We evolved that way because it helped us survive. It benefited nature and life. And when it didn't, it was discarded for its use, or not taken up at all. These colour blinded were therefore left with differentiation through luminance instead—tones of grey. Which is enough in certain situations, as these shades of grey do the same trick as a shape would. In places where there is little light, then colour is of no use, obviously. And this is why the nightly creatures, and that which resides in caves and depths, tends to lack the colour display seen in well-lit places. Shape and form can be the best disguise when done properly. How we distinguish between things, or our inability to do so due to close similarity—seen in these mimickers previously mentioned—is an indicator of this. These mimickers are first and foremost mimicking a shape, because colour and chameleonic traits do little good without the resemblance of what you are "trying" to be. And again, this is also because some animals do not see in colour. Like these nocturnal animals, and these animals in dim and dark places. In other words, there are more animals that differentiate through shape than colour, and this is one of the reasons why nature selects more by the former.

IV. Shape and Functional Variety

When nature selects shape in life, it selects according to a value and worth. And there is a universality in this selection. Things that produce pain and poisons are hard due to their capability in piercing skins. Correspondingly, defensive layers are also hard. Like the turtle or encased fruits—protecting what's inside. Animals even build and take up shelters in such similar shapes to protect themselves. Or they use tools that pierce. Or if sharp, then to cut and slash. These things we have an innate sense of through our body—our instinct. Most animals have some version of all these tools and attributes: we have a skeleton or exoskeleton for protection, with our skull being the most protected for that most important attribute; we have nails and teeth that are sharp; we have sharp, or pointy, bones on hands and feet that we use defensively; etc. But we humans are not as extreme in our attributes as other animals tend to be, and this is because we don't rely on them as much as we rely on our intelligence.

In view of this, we can classify all the bodily expressions and genes by a worth or value. This form, function, and use—these values—is why convergent evolution happens. Nature select values and attributes because of the need or benefit in having them, and when this occurs, they also evolve in accordance with comparable criteria—a similar beneficial action, and that of the commonalities of environment and on Earth. These attributes then start to specialize, which is the process of optimization or perfection. Attributes with a dedicated use or purpose will reach the highest possible state of perfection or optimization in this common environment due to the competition of nature and natural selection. The actions involved, such as biting or gripping, will have limited variables when it comes to how useful or energy efficient they are in the things they are used for, and when there are few variables, there is little difference, which is why convergent evolution leads to similarity. Or to rephrase, similar use and function will result in a similar form, since there is little or no leeway for optimal and efficient form and function in a thing when it comes to a singular, specific use. To reiterate then, attributes and genes are there because of their value and worth. But it may not always be as simple as that. Aesthetics may linger. The many expressions of aesthetics we have today may be a leftover from previous times and uses, and may no longer be of use, or even have any function. This also means that they may not be possible to explain from a contemporary view. And without complete and total knowledge of all previous situations, then one may never know. I will illustrate with the example of the hypothetical pack cheetah I spoke of earlier. If this cheetah were to change behaviour and become more like the lion, it would most likely conform to a greater use of pack attributes. It may evolve greater mass, such as stronger bones and larger muscles, in order to better cope with attacking larger animals. Within a pack it will need the use of tactics and cooperation instead, and it may then lose the attributes needed for speed. All of this can take a very long time, and if we were to see a pack cheetah before its evolution into a more fitting pack role, we would speculate as to why it looks more suited to hunting smaller prey by itself than large prey in a pack. This we may assume about much else of life that exists today as well, because as long as a trait is not detrimental to survival, then it may be retained. The tail bone in humans, for example. We retain a bone that may or may not be of some use that was originally there because our ancestors had tails. Our teeth is also a good example. We have a set of teeth that is more carnivorous than herbivorous, with our sharp incisors that rend and cut meat, and our long canine teeth to sink into flesh to grip it, pierce blood vessels, and rip tough and sinewy flesh apart. Thus, these canines are leftovers from a time and place where there was some need or worth in them. Not that there may not be any worth to them today, but it serves as an example of this retention of features that goes on in nature.

The horn beetles are naturally selected for their ability to tip their sexual opponents from trees in order to get to the females. And when we see that the beetles who have the longest reaching horns will win out in sexual competition, we realize that the trait that secures continued procreation will win out itself. Just like that, nature finds a tool and builds on it. But since nature is not selective or conscious, it may continue a behaviour until it becomes detrimental to the species altogether. This is called maladaptation. However, if a horn gets too large and cumbersome to drag around, then the smaller variations may live on, and so it does find an equilibrium in most cases. The specified meaning of maladaptation is a lack of rigidity or universality. Specialization in a food source, or a surrounding, will be a negative if things were to change or go away. Some species balance the edge so finely that if the slightest of change were to occur, then they would be severely threatened and may even die out. For example, there is the Irish elk whose extinction is popularly attributed to its pair of much too large and cumbersome antlers. And—as a contemporary example—the panda lives on very nutrient poor bamboo, and it needs to consume vast amounts of food to keep itself and its one offspring alive. A very fragile existence indeed. The greatest threat to the panda today is human encroachment on lands, but if the bamboo would have a very bad growth year, or there came about an infestation of leaf eating insects or some bamboo disease, then the panda may very well die out. Such things are the most prevalent cause of extinction throughout time. Man has certainly contributed, but it is not even close to that of nature. It is the way of life, really. New species emerge, and then they spread out to areas they did not inhabit before, and as a result they change the hierarchy and cycle of life in an ecosystem. Like that of disease, fungi, etc., that cause biological breakdown in the host. Anything, really. Things evolve and mutate, and then they gradually or very suddenly change the status quo. Life finds a way to live on and expand. These biological pioneers are doing it as a means to survival in the same way as those affected will also adapt, and then the genetic expressions that do best will live and continue on. Point being that any and all changes in the smallest or largest of life will affect nature as a whole.

Variation and mutation happens all the time. One might even say that all individual life is a variation—and in some cases even mutation—because they are not completely alike or similar to their source. Life strives and struggles on in whatever form it is in, and it becomes whatever it needs to be, or what it does, in order to survive. This is the will of life. Although, these are just the drives and effects—or the instincts it is better to say—that was inherited from an earlier expression that managed to survive because of it. What wants to live, and survives, passes on that wanting. Nature finds a way. Any way. That is why one should always try something before making a decision or valuation. Through trying, a new or different strength may be found and recognized. New differences in offspring are possible due to constant variation and mutation in life, and when this happens, behaviours will change according to these attributes. It may then spread with the continued reproduction of such differences or through learning—divergence of a species has begun. If you give up before trying and testing your skills and abilities, then you have failed according to the most important rule of life: to strive and compete; to test the worthiness of your strengths and let them live on. To push oneself is a good. Know your limits, though. That is just as important.

V. Elimination of the Ineffectual

The animal recognizes values, qualities, and worth in the many expressions of life. And with man being the most intelligent of animals, we recognize better than all. The larger and more colourful and complex a thing is, the greater impression of sophistication, and being very advanced and developed, it gives. This is quite logical, since it takes time to form great complexity and variety. A very, very long time. And as there is greater acuity in higher intelligence, then increased intelligence creates greater complexity as a result. This is because higher intelligence raises the level of understanding. Meaning that intelligence lessens an impression and astonishment in what it would otherwise do in that of lower intelligence. Intelligence thus raises the bar ever and ever higher. This is obvious when we look at man, but this is quite apparent in nature as well. Birds illustrate this with their great display of feathers, behaviours, and nests to impress their mates. Dolphins, too, have very advanced behaviours. As do many other intelligent creatures.

The expression and comprehension of aesthetics is measured and compared through the use of intelligence. Which is valued because it enables its own success in nature, since it (the brain) learns and adapts better than all other physical attributes. In other words, because it was successful and therefore important, then those methods of sexual selection that selected it lived on. Meaning that not only did a complex brain organ live on through its own determinant genes, but so did the genes—through their expression in the organism in conjunction with each other, and as a whole—that manifested the behaviour resulting in that sexual selection of intelligence and its emitter. But a greater intelligence does not necessitate a greater display of aesthetics, even though it tends to. When intelligence rises so high that it becomes aware of the importance of intelligence itself—the brain actually becoming fully aware of itself and its functioning, and of all the factors that were required to get to this now (self-)actualized ascendancy to prescience—then it can start to consciously select according to more precise criteria, such as the measuring of IQ and knowledge. And not according to the vagueness of these indirect ones like aesthetics.

As these aesthetic behaviours are there to show a value or worth, then another value and worth present for sexual selection may supplant those purely aesthetic ones. This is seen in the predatory animals, for instance. Their sexual selection is one of violent competition, or of dominance. The lions, wolves, and other four legged creatures are competing with bloody outcome to determine their worth. They show physical worth because they can and must. As predators, they are built for it—it's in their nature. We also see this in other strongly built creatures, such as the hoofed animals. These ruminants are usually big boned and live in packs with a dominant bull. Their survival is through having a big stature and build, and dangerous cranial outgrowths in the form of horns and antlers that allow them to protect themselves against predators. And these great strengths and tools of theirs is obviously therefore utilized in sexual competition as well: they butt heads, and fence with their horns. Birds are more fragile and that is why they have found other means. As do other competitors in nature—they compare and display without the use of force. The animal will almost always use its greatest asset and strength. This is part of the specialization that occurs in nature. Man has specialized his intelligence up to now, and to greater heights than all other life on our planet. He now dominates Earth.

VI. Beauty and Ideal

The specialization seen in animals and nature evidences a clear recognition of strengths and attributes through a knowledge and awareness of the self. And with this recognition, there is also the recognition of normality. Thus, we know, and then compare. In a species, an attraction and love of oneself and the similar is through the value that one places on living life suited to it, and the body is the senser and emitter of those things. In other words, your instincts—

the behaviour emitted through one's physical and genetic expression—is the judge of a love, and as such it is the love of yourself and everything that is similar to it, or resembles it. That is why the most unfamiliar of animals, and life, elicit much less empathy in us. Such as insects, reptiles, and fish, to name a few. We lack empathy for them, because we cannot familiarize ourselves with them. They may not have the eyes, or facial expressions, sounds, etc., that a mammal would have. If they have these other shapes and forms than what we are used to, we call them strange and alien. Conversely, likeness and similarity is the source of measure in what we like and appreciate. Or what we call beauty, if it is something very much liked. When we recognize other humans, we recognize a close similarity to ourselves. Our sexual drive—meaning anything from procreation to stimulation—will therefore be associated with those of other close likenesses. This is the basis of sexual beauty. However, associations may nevertheless form from experiences with sexuality, in general. And this is usually set at early age, or in early sexual age.

Similarity is also a normality. A normal function. One experiences and recollects a normality through encounters with other humans from early age and throughout life. Good and normal features from a large group of comparison, and therein we find what the best and most regular/normal ones are. This is how the ideal is built. On a side note: when all associations are dissociated, it forms a pure Ideal, as will be mentioned in the chapter *Association*. With a normality also comes a symmetry. Most animals and plants are symmetric. Only a few have asymmetrical attributes, and these are usually a part of a specialization. Such as a larger claw on one side, for example. These will still conform to a normality in a species, though, and will be judged in the same manner as a larger or smaller antler would. They are functional attributes, and thus they are valued. However, if a human would have something very asymmetrical, then they would be an aberration compared to the ideal of other humans. There is only a very small occurrence of total or overall great normality in people. And in life, in general. Although, to a smaller degree in the latter case, because nature is more subject to ideal selection, and it has a far greater weeding out of flawed, irregular, and abnormal traits than humans have. Most people have many flawed features of some kind. Ordinary people have some normal, and even some ideal features, but nevertheless do not possess a great, or major, quantity of them. This small occurrence of having a lot of normal features is what we call beauty and being good looking. We may even call them perfections. And this is a good word to use, because they are in a sense perfect—they have little or no abnormal features. They may have smooth skin, a slightly muscular and slender body, facial/body features that are not too large or small, or not too far apart, or not too close, etc.

We want proportions that are just right. Or right according to the ideal. These ideal things can be distinctive features that may be indefinable, or they may be some much sought after, positive traits. A tallness or a muscular build in a man is favourable. If this is greater than what is average or normal, it would not be an aberration, because there would be some value in it. This is because it is masculine beauty and they are male traits, and having more of them as a man is something good. For this same reason, a very dominant and unflinching male can also be seen as a good. These idealistic features work in the same way with woman. She may have larger than normal breasts and hips, but this is female beauty, as it may be an indicator of a good birth-giver and mother. Larger hips eases birthing, and larger breasts should have larger mammary glands, and thus more milk for the children—giving them an advantage early on in life by having access to greater quantities of nutrition. The ideal indicates something that is superior or better than the normal. Ideality is therefore a collection of the best features in a thing, even if they are not a normal occurrence. But having too much or too many of these ideal features may be perceived as an aberration and ugliness in itself, because it may differ too greatly from a normality—it differs from the similarity of ourselves and our kind. If one defines beauty as someone or something with a lot of normal features, then a great beauty would have that and then an ideal feature or two so it stands out a bit. To stand out in nature is important, because it eases the selective process. In animals we see this clearly. And in humans we see this more and more than ever before. Stranger, more invasive and odd features are used every day. Like tattoos, or a great quantity of piercings and other decorations of the body. The more extreme it is, the more it reveals something about our society: there is too much normality, and we have a problem differentiating. If there is nothing to differentiate, then there is little or no impression on the mind, and this leads to thinking that there is not much reason to mate with someone who is just like everyone else. Sexual selection always wants to find the best, or better, specimens any way it can. This current extremeness is a consequence of individualism. The great nihilism in people, due to the loss of faith and function in, and of, state, work, religion, and society, made us compensate for the loss of those expressions and values with purely aesthetic forms. Meaning that where we once valued people according to their talents and abilities through work and achievement—and we even had bloody competition in love and war—we now have reverted to a state of natural selection compared to that of birds, or even lower, due to the loss of physical or mental competition and elimination. We have become peacocks that dance around, make noises, and flaunt our feathers and adornments to indicate a value or worth.

VII. The Natural and the Associative

Like begets like. That is nature then. But not necessarily always. In a society where people are rich and fat, then a beauty or ideal would be seen in a slender person. This is because we recognize a single value: to be able to moderate oneself. It may be completely the other way around in a poor and competitive society, however. In a tribe or village where food is sparse, then food and any extension of food thereof, such as fatness, will indicate power. A fat creature in these cultures, and in nature in general, where life tends to be meagre and harsh, is therefore seen as a good and healthy thing, because it is proof that they are successful, and it also means that they are prepared for a potential hungry season or event. Pregnancy brings with it an increased appetite, and in turn a woman will usually put on weight because of it, and so this is also seen as healthy. But in modern society today, where people in general are much too fat and have too much food and leisure, then even the natural fat of a pregnancy is despised. The association has taken over completely and disregards any normal perception of it. In any case, we see in both societies that fat has a connection with a function or a consequence—there is recognition of the value and worth in it.

With beauty as function and value, we can detect beauty in a mental or metaphysical capacity as well. When we say that someone has beauty on the inside, then that is what we mean. As metaphor, in other words. We are actually saying that we have found a value in their personality or intellectual capacity. The ugly is the opposite: something not of value or of poor function. A gaunt body is usually always an ugly feature, because of that lack in muscle and fat, which indicates poor fitness and health, or just a sickness, in general. However, as said earlier, if a value has taken a certain hold—fatness perceived as undesirable and unhealthy—then even extreme thinness may be seen as attractive. This shows itself in many ways, and helps those alike to find each other through the show of common interests, for instance. This is due to an association made by higher intelligence, though, and as such is learned. A hate of something, e.g. certain politics or religions, will also associate all symbols, and everything associated with it, into an ugliness. This is because there is found no value in it. It may not be actual ugliness, but it may elicit feelings that will nevertheless make it something bad by association. This associative aesthetics should not be compared with regular aesthetics. The latter being derived from a natural point of view. Which is one of natural function and natural occurrence. Like the sun that is always there, and is almost always seen as a good. Or the value of a function in certain forms and shapes. Such as sharpness and the direct inference of what it does: to cut and prick. This is very basic in nature and all animals recognize these instinctually in some way or other. Most of human aesthetic sense is also is based on this, because of the integral part it has in our world and in our Universe. It is everywhere and everything. It is eternal.

In aesthetics it is sometimes difficult to pinpoint a direct correlation to a specific thing. In a building, we can see the shapes of roundness giving it softness, or a sharpness or height giving it a powerful and threatening feeling. A sound, or collection of sounds, will give off a feeling according to their natural occurrence as well. A deep base, and being long and far between, is something of a largeness and imposing nature. And the small, and their beeps and squeaks, give us the tiny and quick. This is natural because it conforms to what is normal in nature. The large and heavy make a deep impact and therefore a bass that reverberates. And the tiny and small make a high pitched noise with little or no echo. Also, that which is sharp and large is threatening, and that which is round and small is friendly because of its inability to do much harm.

The feeling of awe and astonishment comes from associative aesthetics. If you enter a cathedral, it may raise your hairs out of amazement. People are usually not able to point to where this feeling comes from, and the religious tend to say that they feel the presence of God in such situations. But what is actually happening is that one intuitively assesses everything about a thing immediately. Like the work involved, or the beauty of the composition. And even any associate feelings and ideas thereof. Such as God, and all that one would associate with God, church, and religion. Or if you were to see the building of a school that you once attended, then you would automatically associate the feelings about the time you had there with the sight of the building itself. This is associative aesthetics, because it is directly linked to memory, and thus intelligence. This, coupled with a sensory overflow, multiplicity, complexity, or the unusualness of it on the senses through space, lighting, echo, etc., as is found in large halls such as in churches, makes for a massive combined impact on both mind and body. Only man takes full pleasure in something like that. An animal would be rather oblivious and indifferent to it. The impact upon men is different according to individual values, but also according to their intelligence and knowledge. The man who has built such buildings, and seen them before, may be less affected by such feelings, because he knows the process of building it, or he has experienced it so many times that it has dulled him somewhat—he has become accustomed. But the intelligent man may be more aware of what it took to build something, and he can therefore see the difficulty and complexity in it where a less intelligent man would not. Or that intelligent man may not be so impressed at all, because of his knowledge and insight into the process of it. In most things, however, men perceive beauty much in the same way. Mount Fuji with its shape and snow covering, and its majestic solitude and height, will move most men in some way, and usually in the same way. Its imposing height evokes a feeling of the time and effort it would take to traverse it. And we also reflect on the power of the Earthly forces that sculpted such a thing. We marvel at the intricacies and complexities here on Earth, and the most sublime of it all is life itself. Everyone can and will find a beauty of some kind in the world, and if one ceases to do so, and no longer finds any beauty, then no value is seen in life at all.

Genetic Realities

I. Genetics and Race

To say that that we are all human is a gross oversimplification. "We are all of the same species", they say today. And although that is true, it is nevertheless not what they mean when they say it, because they state it as some sort of argument that we are exactly the same. Those kind of people also call it the "human race" and use the term race and species interchangeably, because they are completely ignorant about evolution and taxonomy. What caused such thinking and belief was the spouting of the propaganda that we are all one equal and similar human population. Which is far, far from the truth, and just goes to show how completely ignorant, or dishonest, people are today about what constitutes a species. It also illustrates the failure or intended failure in educating people about evolution and nature, and this is probably why the teaching of evolution has failed in the U.S. as a whole. How can they believe in it, when the current form of it taught is nothing but extremely selective and vague because of political correctness?

First of all, members of a species do not need to be alike at all. That is not what constitutes a species. What usually constitutes a species is the capability of interbreeding through a close common ancestry. That is the taxonomic definition of it. But just because a subspecies or a race can reproduce with one another doesn't mean that they were meant to or that they should. The wolf and the dog is of the same species. All the *Canis lupus*—the wolf species—which includes the dog, the dingo, and perhaps even the coyote, are capable of interbreeding. Should they? Of course not. They are adapted to their respective environments, and they diverged so long ago that their phenotype and genotype are no longer the same. *Homo sapiens sapiens* is the classification of humans today. This is called subspecies, which is the branching of the *Homo sapiens* species. Let us look at our closest cousins then: the Neanderthals and the Denisovans. These are called *Homo neanderthalensis* and *Homo denisova*, respectively. This is where the problem begins, because if one is to classify them as different species from *Homo sapiens*, then they would not fit with current taxonomical classification. This is because of the recent findings that Europeans and Asians have up to 5% of their genetic makeup from Neanderthals. And in South Asians it has also been found that up to 5% of their genetic makeup is Denisovan. None of these two genetic contributions were found in the sub-Saharan populations—namely, the negroids, which I will refer to as Africans or blacks from now on. Due to this fact, the geneticists and taxonomists had a problem on their hands. They had to reclassify Neanderthals and Denisovans as part of *Homo sapiens*—making them *Homo sapiens neanderthalensis* and *Homo sapiens denisova*—and group them as part of the same species as humans, because, as we know, taxonomically only those of the same species can interbreed. And this is the reason why we are called *Homo sapiens sapiens*, and not just *Homo sapiens* like earlier. Lastly, while on the subject of our cousins and ancestors, let us not forget Cro-Magnon, which is, in all likelihood, the predecessor of the European. A European race that has been here a long time, and recent genetic finds have shown that the Basque are direct descendants of them. Is the Cro-Magnon, Neanderthal, and Denisovan blood the reason why Europe and Asia did so well, and why Africa did so poorly?

Technically, even different species within the same genus can interbreed. Taxonomy and categorization is, after all, a human construct, and life is in reality very plastic and open to great difference, variation, randomness, and unknowns that are not always capable of being deconstructed into forms, rules, and classifications that fit all life with sweeping and encompassing generalizations for our convenience. Note, then, that I will be explaining through the use of normative taxonomy, and will not delve that much into the philosophical or empirical argumentations for or against current taxonomy. Where we get our human classification of *Homo sapiens sapiens* is due to this previously mentioned interbreeding, which is evidence for a greater closeness of not only these subspecies I have mentioned, but a number of others as well, and this warrants the classification of them all as one species. There is a further consequence of this too, however, because if one classifies the Neanderthal and Denisovan as different, and the European and Asian are partly of their blood, then there is no real reason to classify all current humans as the same. This is and was, of course, already pretty obvious to anyone with eyes and ears, and intelligent understanding. The differences are not just in phenotype, but in genotype as well—apart from what I have already mentioned. We have adapted for so long to our environments, and with such large geographical distances separating us, that all kinds of mutation, and even genetic drift alone, has made us very different.

The Arab (the Semite) is not as dark as the black man, or the Indian man, because he clothes himself to protect against the hot desert sun. His quite tall and slender figure makes him able to cool himself easier than a smaller, stockier body would. His large nose, and breathing through it, helps minimize water loss, but also to keep cooler. This may sound absurd, but such small physical differences are very important. One has to realize that such changes take tens of thousands of years to get. No, even more.

The black man who does not clothe himself has dark skin to protect him from the sun, and his need to hunt prey and gather food—having never evolved past the hunter-gatherer stage of the Stone Age—made him retain an animal physique. A different Achilles tendon, for instance, and a predominance of fast twitch muscles.

The Asian, much like the Mediterranean, is a mix of the northern and southern type—a cross between both. These live in that mild, gentle area of plenty, and as a consequence there are more of them. Because of this, they are more collective and therefore more dependent on structure and order, so that they can properly function and thrive. They are also smaller in stature, which is probably due to a lesser need for physical dominance, and them living and surviving on smaller amounts of food. Their civilizations, such as Rome, China, and Persia—all such middle kingdoms and empires—were great when they did what they were most naturally inclined to do: to organize their great numbers and structure their society. Which, incidentally, is the strongest and most effective of human traits when done right. In the animals one sees this, too. Like the lions, or wolves, that cooperate and hunt in packs with a strict hierarchy of leadership and order.

In the north of Europe, the Germanic and Celtic man would, in this very unique environment, clothe himself a great deal, and coupled with very little sun in this northern area, he would lose a lot of pigmentation, because lighter skin helps to produce more vitamin D from the sun. One has to remember that Northern Europe is the mildest northerly area in the world due to the Gulf Stream, and when people live that far north they receive very small amounts of sunlight in winter time. Less than in all those other places on Earth that were colonized by man up to that point. The fact that Europe was, and still is, so heavily forested is also another contributor to that lack of sun, and therefore the Celtic and Germanic man's lack of pigmentation was a necessity for survival.

There are a lot of such direct causes and complexities in nature. Like the different genes for resistance to disease in the human races, for instance. African populations have the genetic sickle cells, which helps protect against malaria and gives an evolutionary advantage in these areas, but they also cause the disease sickle-cell anaemia. The similar disease thalassaemia, prevalent in Mediterranean and Asian populations, is also a disease resulting from a malaria resistant gene advantage. In Northern Europe there is a prevalence of multiple sclerosis, which is caused by that lack of vitamin D, but this usually affects those most swarthy or the ones who see very little of the sun, and not generally the Celto-Germanic man who has adapted to this environment and gets enough vitamin D from a normal lifestyle. The Jew, specifically the Ashkenazi Jew, has all kinds of disease. The most likely explanation for this is their extreme bastardization and hybridization with any and all of the races, and also their life of comfort without having any mechanisms, or being part of the societal mechanisms, that weed out the weak and diseased. This has embedded the Jew with all types of genetic disorders and diseases throughout these last couple of millennia, leaving him a sickly human specimen. In fact, the most diseased specimen there is. And so, there is our warning sign against miscegenation and a completely broken selective process! This process that the Jew went through is very similar to the selective process we have in society today. Or better to say that there is no selective process at all anymore—non-existent as it is. In any case, we can see where we are headed.

The East Asians, and their close cousins the Native Americans, have a peculiar trait. They are very susceptible to alcohol, which makes them flushed and blotched reddish or white on their skin when drinking—called alcohol flush reaction. What causes this is their inability to process the acetaldehyde that comes from the metabolism of alcohol in the body. It also makes them drunk faster. This is genetic, and is because of the little interaction with alcohol that these people have had throughout the ages. They are also known for being much less resistant to alcohol on a mental level, but whether this is connected to the other I do not know. Corroboratively, the Inuit is well-known for his inability to control himself when it comes to drinking. We also saw this in the North American Natives when the European settlers met them. The European "got" them hooked on firewater, and it had a much more catastrophic effect than on the European. Which has been completely the opposite, really. One might even say that the European drank himself into mastery of the Earth. The British Empire almost ran on grog and rum, for one. The citrus (vitamin C) added had the great effect that it helped prevent scurvy, and it also kept it from going bad—alcohol is also a preservative in itself. The grog was thus a reliable source of drink on any voyage, and was used as a reward system for the crew. Back home here in Europe, the art of drinking has existed since ages past. The Roman drank, the Greek drank, and the Germanic man drank so much that it was the only thing the Roman found distasteful in him—having an enormous amount of respect and admiration for him otherwise. Alcohol has been with the European civilization since its birth. Available to any and all. That is why the European is so physiologically tolerant of alcohol consumption. And in this fact we see that not only does nature/environment change us, but we change ourselves through our habits and behaviours as well. Habits and behaviours that are from an intelligent origin; products of mind and technology, and not from an origin in nature itself. This clarifies the difference between a natural and an artificial/intelligent selection.

II. Adaptation and Hybridization

As long as men have had their widespread and common use of devices, tools, and machines, there has always been an influence by them. But that is not all. There are other mental constructs that have also had a profound impact. Society, religion, laws, and customs, for example. All these result from intelligence. Any intelligent selection directly affect our genes—as in the example of alcohol mentioned. To what degree and how they all affect us is harder to pinpoint. It is easier to explain the purely physical ones. For instance, if we were to make the drinking or eating of dairy products illegal, then it should affect us, over the course of generations, and reverse this process that began when we started drinking animal milk. I am, of course, referring to lactose intolerance and the likes. Lactose intolerance being more common in populations where drinking milk has been less common. There are other examples as well. Some speculate, and as I mentioned before, that the lack of vitamin D was the cause for the prevalence of depigmentation in northerly populations. Meaning that those who had less pigmentation had a better chance of survival, due to increased absorption of sunlight that contributed to vitamin D production in the body. But some have also been attributing vitamin D deficiency to a diet. And so, which is it? Environment or diet? It is not easy to determine. Perhaps it is a combination of both. What of language then? Would language affect us? I dare say that it does. Even the purely mental restrictions, or allowances, should have an effect. Let's assume that we had more phonetic sounds in our language. This would have us trim and use speech muscles differently as compared to those who did not pronounce the sounds we had, and therefore a use of different muscles, or in a different manner, may change the body and the genes. Or if we had a larger vocabulary in a language, then that would impel you to remember more words, and would help you think more clearly and explain yourself better. It directly affects, and helps, your internal dialogue with yourself and your external dialogue with others. When you sit and ponder and reach conclusions, you use your language, and by using a simple language that has few words and imprecise meanings, you are impeded by it. Or alternatively, you think in a more complex and clearer manner with a larger vocabulary, because it is the equivalent of greater understanding through being able to define and mentally picture something more exact and specific. We also see this when in a discussion with someone, in the way that you are being fully and clearly understood, and this in turn stimulates further conversation and understanding. Ultimately, a more advanced language will make those who are more capable of being understood, and more capable of understanding, rise higher in society. Being higher in society should, ideally and generally, make them better situated so that it increases their chances of having offspring. It also helps with securing the offspring's survival and their situation for continuing on the bloodline, which is the passing on of this capacity in remembering words and using language—directly related to intelligence. In this we see that intelligence itself allows for the survival of intelligence. Not as a strict rule unfortunately, and I venture to say that stupidity also flourish and survive when the situation allows for it. As seen today.

The use of our body hardens and strengthens it. We see this through a hardening of the skin, for instance, or the growth of muscles. And it is the same with food intake, in a way. We can eat or drink certain types of things, and the body will gradually adapt to it. For example, the body will work and adapt according to toxins and bacteria encountered. Lactose intolerance can be diminished through a slow and repeated use. And the body will also adapt to alcohol use and other types of toxins, and a tolerance for it will be built over time. Let me posit that even the brain will build and strengthen the synapses and neurons, i.e., the pathways of the brain, through repeated and heavy use. In any, and all, of these uses it is the body protecting and strengthening itself, which serves the purpose of enabling and preparing for a way of life. And when this happens, there is a chemical and physical change in the organism as well. What the organism is, and becomes, it will pass on to the offspring to a lesser or greater degree. The previously mentioned buildup of lactose tolerance or greater tolerance of alcohol is proof of that. We now also know that genes can switch on or off throughout life, and this is most likely the body adapting to our lifestyle, and to our environment and habitat. And that is why, if we are very diverse in our food and experiences by trying new things and pushing ourselves to our mental and physical limits, then we will eventually become stronger for it and thus master them. We do this all the time both intentionally and unintentionally. Our curiosity, this manifestation of the need to improve our situation and increase our comfort and happiness, is the main reason for this. All of these things comprise our evolutionary adaptation.

It is commonly thought that diversity and miscegeny, i.e., hybridization, will produce stronger offspring. It is known that incest leads to inbreeding depression, and thus biological fitness is reduced, and the common fallacy then occurs in thinking that the opposite is therefore true. This is not so, however. Instead, hybridization between different populations, i.e., races, can lead to outbreeding depression. This can be a number of things, but the easiest way to explain it is that a strong and important gene may be lost, or a weaker gene that is dominant is bred in. Or an introduced gene may completely alter the expression of others—called epistasis. In other words, you may be destroying good traits. Also, inbreeding depression may show signs in first generations, but outbreeding depression only very gradually show its dire faults. As such, it is a

Part One: Man

gamble to crossbreed large amounts of long lived strains that reproduce so slowly that results may not be properly seen in a long time. This expression of genes, that is seen after many generations and the time needed, is due to a hybrid needing time to stabilize itself between the different genes that are mixed in from different populations, and they will not properly show themselves until a stabilization occurs, which takes many generations. This means that hybridization between human races may be wholly detrimental, and may not be known until it is too late. Keep in mind that inbreeding depression only includes actual incest, and as such does not apply to the population (the race). Nature creates race for a reason, and this is because life sticks to their own for the purpose of building on what is there, and to strengthen and advance it. To illustrate with an example: you would not want to mix a German Shepherd with a Chihuahua, because this only serves to destroy the lineage of the Shepherd, and while it may be beneficial to the Chihuahua, it nevertheless leaves us with a crossbreed that is not nearly as useful and intelligent as the Shepherd is. It is breeding downwards and backwards, and it goes against what a breeder would do. Perhaps the best example of this, and warning against it, is the earlier mentioned hybridization in the Jew. While he has gained intelligence close to that of the Celto-Germanic man, he has also gained a number of genetic diseases along the way. Today, the Jew, the Ashkenazi Jew, is the sickliest of breeds on Earth. This is a well-known fact, and easily confirmed, if disbelieved. There are also reports of problems with human hybridization in regards to the need of finding donors. This is because the body will reject anything that isn't similar in its genetic mapping, which a hybrid will not have until it has a population of its own that has had the time to stabilize. This may take an enormous amount of time when mixing races in an extremely large group—the population of Earth today—as compared to mixing two races in a smaller group, and then building a large population out of those afterwards. We also know that there is a larger prevalence of disease in hybrid humans. Diseases not even found in the parents, or in the race of the parents, at all. This is what hybridization and outbreeding depression leads to. Conclusively, this also means that the concept of racial hygiene was right. As anyone would be able to intuit, and any breeder or geneticist could tell you. Still, the politically correct propaganda is incessant and widespread, and accepted as truth and reality—a testament to the ignorance and disinterest of the masses, and also to the power of stigmatization through the labelling of opponents.

III. Intelligence, Testosterone, and Miscegeny

The differences between the races may seem relatively small, especially when compared to individual differences, yet such small racial differences can have an enormous impact, nonetheless. You cannot cite individuals of non-European and -American descent and their achievements as an example against this, because there are always exceptions to the rule, and as such they are no more an example than showing two very different specimens of the same race. It is a fallacy and therefore not an argument. However, if a race scores higher in a field on average, then this will and must raise the ceiling of that race in general, and consequently raise the ceiling on how high the superior individuals of that race will get. Which we see in the fact that a preponderance of great individuals these last couple of thousand years have been European. Intelligence itself may not be the only factor in determining advancement. There must also be a drive; some have called it the creative spark.

One of the reasons for this creativity may be testosterone. As testosterone is what drives man, and as man is the gender that has driven mankind, then testosterone may be what drives civilization.

Part One: Man

But testosterone is only the fuel. What else is needed is a great machine that uses that fuel. This is the mind. Or more specifically, the intelligent mind. Intelligent men are more capable of learning the rights and wrong of society, because of their capacity to retain such information, which is the prerequisite for identifying it. Therefore, intelligence is what forms great idealism and ambition as well. Such men build good, and perfect, worlds and societies through the plans they create and weave in their minds. And how do these come to fruition? By drive, of course—testosterone. That is why man, and specifically the intelligent man, through it became the source of all advancement in mankind. This seems very in line with reality. The heavily populated areas usually devolve into a peaceful coexistence without much strife, because aggressiveness/drive, and therefore testosterone, loses its place in such societies. And then they stagnate. Like the Roman Empire did, and like China did, or India, Persia, and Egypt. Take your pick, really. Testosterone is merely an animalistic and uncontrollable hormone in general, but in the Germanic man in the north, when coupled with his intelligence needed to survive there, it came into full effect. Thus, with the means (intelligence) and the drive (testosterone), the Germanic man—half man and half beast some have said—would eventually rule Europe, then America, and then the world. And he is still master of this world, even though his infighting, such as the ideological conflict between his respective nations in the two world wars, severely weakened him as a whole.

Intelligence is a physical trait in itself because it comes from a larger or more complex brain. And with the brain being part of the body, which is expressed by the genes themselves, then this makes intelligence genetic. But just like the athlete, having the body and predisposition is not enough. You would actually have to train, practice, and work to get the full effect and use of it. Intelligence being gene-based is pretty obvious to a learned man, but to simple people it is quite difficult to grasp sometimes. Even when they see a difference of intelligence in animals, and those of the same breed to boot, it does not occur to them that this applies to them, too. This is much thanks to the Judeo-Christian socialist society of today, where we are completely brainwashed by the concept of human equality, which is also the reason why the differences in the human races are largely unknown today by the public. This dogmatic mantra that "we are all the same" is chanted to no end, it seems...

There is a conclusion to be found in the fact that intelligence derives from genes: if society is based on intelligent design with its rules, laws, practices, customs, etc., due to the complex creation and remembering of them—to which I consider intelligence and memory interlinked—then society is, very much so, a reflection of genes as well. Another conclusion from this would be that culture is then also based on intelligence, and ultimately also due to genes. To state that race doesn't matter is thus absurd and completely false. All those corrupt and backward nations and people are just that for a reason. And it is not a coincidence, or luck as some surmise, that the most advanced nations on Earth are, or were, Germanic, Celto-Germanic, or white in some way—all these European nations that rose to greatness before they voluntarily gave up their power, due to the propaganda about equality, individualism, and other types of nonsense. The fact that Germanic and European man is the foundation of modern civilization is a much loathed truth today. One that many vehemently try to explain away with fancy words such as *socioeconomic factors* or *discrimination*. They claim oppression, in other words. This has become standard practice in the U.S. ghettos and other such places where the minorities reside. Or the blacks, more precisely. They even go so far as to claim that they are just as oppressed as they were in the age of slavery. It is natural that this should happen, though, because there hasn't been a truthful view of this era as of yet. It has been buried under a ton of propaganda in order to justify the current status quo and to maintain order and cohesion—avoiding that chaos and civil war that would come about if someone exposed the truth. The same was done with the world wars, which is why they are so misperceived today. In fact, the propaganda about the Second World War only aggravated the view on the War of Northern Aggression (the U.S. Civil War) and slavery. This is because the minority and the non-whites now had another "proof" of their oppression—a fabricated proof that originated in propaganda. The real proof is right in front of us, however. Just see how the minorities—whether they are born citizens or immigrants, it doesn't matter—repeatedly fail in the Western world. But not all minorities. Not the Asians. They always manage to conform, and even do quite good, mostly. Which is yet another proof that there is not a repression of minorities. And it also shows us the very real differences of capability in the races. When we see the black communities fail in the U.S., it is because of themselves. They are the ones who have created a whole culture of their own there. A culture that is much reminiscent of African culture. And just as in Africa, they are more concerned about individual power and wealth than any solidarity, or societal structure and well-being. A truly primitive culture.

Let us return to this immigration briefly mentioned. This has been the largest and most devastating project that has ever been tried in human history. Throughout Europe and the Anglosphere we have had mass immigration from failed and broken down countries now for decades. And what is the point of this immigration? What has merited the import of such cultures, and such people? Truth is that nothing has. These people come from broken down, corrupt, and failed countries, and by importing these people, and their bloodlines, we are in fact importing and embedding their culture here in equal proportions. And given the premise that genetics and blood is the basis of higher culture, then mixing their bloodlines with ours will destroy our own culture and society. Or in the very least degenerate it. This policy of immigration is probably the greatest crime ever committed in history, and it is nothing but the genocide, or democide, of the native populations and ethnicities in the Western world.

The U.S., and a number of other countries, have had their minorities for a long time. Most of these countries have never really known a society of uniform ethnicity, and how important it is. But in Scandinavia we did, and we now have the comparison between a former nation that was pure of race, crime free, and happy because of it, contra the immigrant infested nation of today that is crime ridden with murder, rape, drugs, and all kinds of monstrosity. The thing that the U.S. and some—and I stress some—nations have succeeded in, and were aware of early on, was that patriotism, loyalty, and obedience to the nation and country must be demanded in the strictest way for society to work at all. It is, or at least was, a huge taboo, and extremely frowned upon, when newcomers came to countries such as the U.S. and didn't learn the respective language and customs—embracing the culture of their new homeland. Which is important, because this helps with building a kinship, respect, and responsibility for each other in a nation.

Multiculturalism and the current agenda is not a celebration of diversity, it is the destruction of it. It only leads to miscegenation, which serves to wipe out all previous adaptations and specializations. To ignore the way nature formed and shaped us, in order for us to survive and thrive in certain areas according to our genetics and race, is to spit in the face of nature and to mock evolution. We see that life on Earth has gained a foothold in the harshest and most diverse of climates. This produced some very tough and hardy creatures. And it is the same with man. We know the traits of Germanic and Nordic man, but there are many other examples: We have the Inuit, who conquered their part of the world in the icy landscapes around the Arctic. Their stocky and short build is adapted to such life. And to the diet obtained from such areas, too. And we have the Native Americans in the New World up in the Andean mountains, or various people in the Himalayas, that have adapted to the height and nature there. I have also mentioned the resistance of disease in the different races throughout parts of the globe. In any case, the elements and obstacles of our habitats are imprinted on our genes to a smaller or greater degree. To miscegenate is to squander and destroy the genes that are there. It is pointless and unnecessary. Just to fulfill some absurd fantasy of a completely mixed human species of great similarity in appearance and genetics. It is vile.

IV. Plus Ultra?

The evolution that brought mankind to where it is today is gone. The belief in it is gone and the practice of it is gone. Earlier we had competition, and a hierarchy for the successful. A natural order. The smartest and strongest benefited more than the weak and feebleminded. The class systems and feudal systems were based on such ideas. They were an attempt, and in some ways very successful, to make order and rules of the disparity in ability among individuals and groups. But as the nobles failed to further ascend, due to that comfort of position and decadence that caused a weakening of their blood, then that also resulted in them losing their superiority, and thus their power and control. This was not necessarily always such a great loss—at least not to all societies—but to start over in such a way is generally very inefficient if there is to be continued selection of the superior and thus a sharp rise, and not a rise in intervals. And so, this struggle of the great masses to move upwards socially was greatly helped by the complacency and fall of the upper classes. In earlier societies, the sheer need for the lower classes to improve their situation made them strive to become better. Which is far from the socialism of today that enables the fat and lazy to stay that way. Those that made it, and were on top, were rewarded by the collective of the state. In older times, the state was the keeper of the elite, and also the holder of power and money. The private was not dominant in the higher levels. Private affairs were thus state affairs. Those who wanted, or had, money and power would have had to involve themselves in governance and serve the state. Or be the state. At least if they wanted to keep their power and money—or their heads attached to their body. This persisted all the way up to the 20th century, but ultimately these ideas were lost or discarded, and actually discouraged after the Second World War. What we were left with was hyper-individualism and a separation of money from power and politics. And to what purpose? Only for individual gain, and this incessant pursuit of happiness. Such individualistic power and wealth is subject to, and part of, a great many political agendas. Agendas that may be in complete opposition to the state, and thus undermines, threatens, and conspires against it. Individual liberties and freedoms are no problem. Even freedom to buy and bear arms and such—because it is by the people, and for the people, the state exists, after all—but when such individualisms work against the state, i.e., the people, then their operations should be stopped and illegalized.

The purpose of man is the same as the purpose of life on Earth: To exist and continue to exist. Survival. And preferably also to become better, and not weaker, if we are to progress and evolve. Now that we have mastered nature, and eliminated and stopped war and other mechanisms that were earlier in place, we have found out that they were needed. And this is why we simulate mechanisms of nature. We eat in moderation, we exercise, and we stimulate our mind and do mental gymnastics. What else can we do when all needs and wants are met, and the means to select worth and value are suppressed and illegalized? The intelligent do not rule, and the strong do not control. The superior have no place or function in government and society anymore, and competition and struggle is effectively eliminated, because want and need has been greatly diminished. So, we set personal limits, or limits according to others, to compensate for this. Such intelligent behaviour is indicative of a living creature having reached that threshold when he is intelligent and knowledgeable enough to understand the importance to do so, and he will therefore continue the practice of struggle and evolution so that he can better himself and ascend further. However, this is only true for a very small part of the global population. For the majority, a degeneration will continue or stay suspended and will not approach this threshold, and probably never will. Not unless massive changes are made. The lesson learned from life in general, and the human races, is that if we are to become stronger and better, then we have to be challenged, and we have to overcome. We should emulate what nature has done to us, could do to us, and would force us to do, in a situation or habitat: A physical adaptation to harsh and hostile environments, and to diseases. A demanding life and society that require large amounts of knowledge and higher intelligence, which will in turn foster better ideas and great inventions. Anything and everything, really. We should push ourselves to the extreme. Always, so that every generation surpasses.

A basic and simple explanation of evolution: life is one of constant change and variation, and evolution is the process of eliminating these varieties of life by competition, dominance, and survival. In a hypothetical scenario where competition and strife between different life-forms has stopped, or has been removed, then they may yet live on and thrive, but it is arguable that life suffers for it and becomes weaker and frail. A soft living makes for a soft being, and a very hard and tough life makes for a hard and durable being.

"In soft regions are born soft men." – Herodotus

Part One: Man

The Genders

I. Base Differences

The mystery of woman. She is an enigma they say. A riddle that will never be solved. Why is that so? Why is that a belief? Could it not be that no one has ever truly bothered with discovering the inner workings of woman? Or maybe it is because the actual truth is too lacking in idealism and romantic thought—a truth too hard to swallow perhaps. They also call woman the romantic sex. The mystery of romance locked within woman; or is it actually man instead?

The difference between men and women are surely noticeable in both their behaviour and physiology. And we certainly do expect different behaviours and values in men and women. Or at least we did throughout much of history until more recent times. Why are men and women different? Simply because nature has made it so. It is a matter of survival in the species that we have these behaviours. Where men are promiscuous and have the near constant urge to procreate with females of his liking, then women are almost the complete opposite. This is because when women chose men to breed with earlier, it mattered. It was important. If she was to bear and rear the resultant offspring of an encounter with a man, and the offspring would be feeble, weak, and unable to survive due to her selection of a poor male specimen, then she would have wasted her precious time and energy for nothing. And therefore the act of sex does matter more to a woman, because there is always a feeling of consequence and importance ingrained in a woman's choice from that evolutionary and biological standpoint. She has to be picky. She has to care. The survival of her offspring depend on it. That is why she rightly feels that she must mate with men of quality, or that she at least "knows the man", as is commonly said. And by knowing she means that she has to find some or other quality in him, in order to find comfort in the knowledge that her young will be stronger or better for it. Or at least not weaker.

A woman is by nature the one who has to raise the young. This is the case almost everywhere in nature. And so, this caring nature is a trait of women. And there is much evidence for it. Even in the completely gender equal society of today—equal in the civilized parts of the Western world at least—women overwhelmingly choose occupations with a more social environment, or with care and nurture as job prerequisites. This is natural. Care and nurture by women are, and always have been, necessary for our survival as a species. With the time spent carrying her young in the womb, a bond has developed, and she is less likely to abandon it after birth. Although, this happens, and quite often, in nature, because if there is a defect with the young, an aberration that is seen or sensed, then a mother may reject and kill her young. She asks herself: Is this worth the time and energy? Will it be better to spend that time and energy on bearing the seed of a better male specimen? If, however, she finds that her offspring is healthy and strong, then she will nurture and care for it, obviously. Her effort in finding a proper mate and carrying his seed has not been for nothing. All of this embody a great deal of her view on her young—they are the sum of all the time and work that has transpired.

A woman's sexual need is different then. It is one of selection and direct consequence. Which is why we label a woman who is loose and promiscuous, and why it is such a bad notion, because a woman's role in nature is to be picky and to bear life. And so, if she fails to discern among men, and sleeps with many and any, and if she also does this for other reasons than procreation, then she has failed in the assignment that nature has given her. Proper judgement and good choices are expected of her. She need not explain it, but she should sense and feel what these rights and wrongs are. Or female intuition, as some have called this behaviour and action that they cannot explain by words or intelligently understand—this animal instinct. And more animal than man she surely is. This irrationality—being so completely lacking in sensibility and devoid of intelligent thought in such moments—sometimes utterly cloud the judgement of women. Or at least it appears so. This is also why a woman is so often likened to a creature or an animal by poets and scholars. An unexplainable, yet very worldly and natural character a woman possesses. And it is therefore not strange that the otherworldly and spiritual religions, in particular the Abrahamic religions, find her so offensive. These same religions that consistently not only call the world evil, but nature evil as well. Disdain they have for the cruelty of nature. And cruel a woman may also be. A slight, or certain, cruelty in a woman is quite often a trait most wanted. And for good reason. After all, the arrogant woman, or the woman who rejects you, shows that she is very particular—certainly the trait of a discerning female. And a coldness and harshness in a woman also make her seem more intelligent and calculating, and thus more likely to be a good teacher for the young—one that prepares her young pupils to the harsh realities of the world.

A woman not only feels the sexual urge in a different manner than man then—not counting pure sexual stimulation—but she also has to do much of the work in making sure that the continuation of life is ensured. She is directly responsible for the propagation of life. She selects it, carries it, nurtures it, and teaches it. This process is what we call the greatest love—the love of survival and continuation of the self. A certain word is attached to this type of love: romance. This is also why other events in life that involve survival of some sort, and conjures up great passion, importance, and urgency, is called romanticism. Like nationalism, for instance. Which is the survival of your kindred on the highest of levels—what great emotion it stirs up, and for good reason. The notion of romance for women, however, is really just to have men doing what they want. In other words, they want men to pay as much attention to them as they do, and to cater to their every whim. They want men to have and share the interests they have, such as to provide and care for women and children. The word romance thus means womanly interests and behaviours—putting the woman first. When we think of romance toward women, we think of someone who serves and caters to someone, and mostly in a non-sexual way. What a man wants, however, is a woman who shows a willingness to have sex with him. And most importantly, exclusively to him. That is the highest value to him. Men want eroticism, and women want romanticism. This is why women are called the romantic sex, or at least according to that definition of romance that women speak of, and the way it is generally thought of when it concerns the interplay between the genders. But man is very much a romantic, because he falls in love and values certain things in life so highly that he is willing to go to death for them. Like his people and his country, or the girl that he loves. It is always man who is the performer of romance, and it is he who determines romantic notions. Women only demand it according to the standards set. Just like a nation, or art, would demand certain things according to its romantic notions and criteria. Which are really just the perceived values in a point of time that nature or our surroundings demand and place on us, if we are to compete and survive. Meaning that these are the traits needed or already there to survive, and therefore noticed and appreciated by us—our ideals. And as man has conquered and replaced nature—having become the sculptor and creator of his own way of life; the god of his own existence—then he is now the one who consciously or subconsciously set the criteria for survival.

A woman being too willing to engage in sex is not attractive, because it is too much of a male trait. And if she were to behave too much as a male and have a willingness to have sex with many and any, then that would be even less appreciated. Although, men uncommitted to this woman, and who would not have any other opportunities available to them, would appreciate it for the sexual release. When a man is being too romantic with a woman, we view it negatively in the same manner. A male's willing submissiveness to a woman shows his affection, but if he is submissive all the time to this woman, and to people in general, it would be very unattractive and sexually unappealing. Thus, the worst thing for a woman is to be loose and engage in debauchery, and the worst thing for a man is to be a coward, and not to have sex. Or in harsh terms, the worst thing for a woman is to be a slut, and for man it is to be a sissy. This is because they are opposites to the nature of the genders. A woman is to be selective, and therefore not promiscuous. A man is to be brave so that he competes against other men. And a man who has a lot of sex, or an availability of it, indicates his worth, and his success in competition.

II. Man in Relation to Woman

Men are not necessarily that bound to their offspring as strongly as women are. This is because men do not spend as much time and energy on them as women do. After all, they escape the physiological and chronological burdens of pregnancy. And because of this, they are physically free of it. Free to continue to follow their sex drive; moving them onwards to spread their seed further. And because they are not present, they will not establish this emotional attachment that females have for their offspring, either. But the burdens of men are quite different, and perhaps heavier and far more fatal. Women only have to choose between the numerous willing partners that come her way. She is only free to select and choose partners between pregnancies, which usually includes the time spent rearing her young. Only after they have "flown the nest" is she free again. A stretch of time from start to finish that may be quite long. I am not counting the scenario where she stays pregnant almost constantly with new partners, because that would leave her too burdened physiologically. And physically as well by having too many children to care for and feed. No good would come of it. It would impact herself and her children for the worse in most cases. Unless helped or enabled in some way, that is. This means that she is not left with much spare time throughout life then, and as a result, not that many partners. But men are physically free to get back into the struggle of sexual competition. And this struggle against other men manifests itself in every way possible. But most markedly through war. War being the greatest and most advanced expression of survival that there is. By taking land and resources, you increase the chances for your survival and the ability to spread more of your seed and that of your own kind. And through the outcome and emergence of a victor, the survival of the fittest is ensured. But war has been corrupted in our time, as everything else is. War today involves atomic weaponry—or it at least it looms over us as a constant threat of annihilation—and there are a number of other extremely cowardly and destructive devices as well. The obliteration of your opponent has been taken to such an extreme today that it involves the obliteration of yourself and your own survival. Even when victorious. Mutually assured destruction they call it. And with that they have dissolved the natural processes to a large extent.

Men then. They live hazardous lives and they fight to the death for power whenever they can. Men are more violent than women because they have to. Still in modern times men fight over women to show who is more dominant; women always prefer the more dominant males. Men who sleep around is natural, because they maximize their potential that way. Women maximize their potential by selecting superior men. Both of these behaviours constitute the collective potential for survival in our species. These men who have outwitted and won over other males have proven their worth as better specimens, and therefore also their seed. These victories, or proofs, are their justification for coupling. The justification for coupling in women is the selection of these few superior male specimens, and how she proves herself is by giving birth and raising not only acceptable, but worthy and successful, children. And it is through this that she gets confirmation of her value as a breeder and the worth of her blood. By nature, all males will mate with any fertile female they can find. Nature does this to maximize the potential survival of species and life. And then natural selection weeds out the weaker specimens of these that are born. Well, ideally at least. And if you take away all these mechanisms, you may end up with weaker and dumber specimens over just a short amount of time. And if these use up all the resources and destroy the habitat for the rest, you have your cataclysm.

Where does the (traditional) romantic notion in men come in, if men are only interested in sex? Truth is that it does not. Men are seen as romantic when it eases the burdens of the female, and taking on her duties and roles. Women who are romantic toward men are of a different kind. Women are by default romantic, because being romantic is the want of survival. Her children, in other words. With her womb, her pregnancy, and therefore herself as a priority. But by this criterion, the want of survival in man is instead to continue in competition and procreation. Which is his children, but he can have many at the same time—provided he has the female partners for it. This is why the romantic notion between the genders is not the same. Although, men do seek out, and notice, better specimens among females. And when they find the best or most ideal possible, then they, too, will stick with these women. But this is for the convenience of themselves, usually. Man is able to take advantage of woman, because of her need for help and assistance with the children, and woman is able to take advantage of man, because of his need for coupling. A woman needs children, or to take care of life and nurture it, and man needs sex. Both are extensions of the same thing, and serve the same purpose and function in the eyes of nature, which is that of survival. In these circumstances, the woman plays on man's natural function and behaviour, which is eroticism—she is erotic. Man plays on the natural function and behaviour of woman, which is the romantic—to nurture, care for, socialize, etc.

The love in woman for a man may still be the same as romance in man towards woman. That is to say, the man who settles down with a woman to help her, and behaves romantically, is thus a selfless man that gives up on his erotic nature—his natural behaviour of needing to spread his seed. This need to spread his seed is the same need as that of a woman's need to find the best male specimen to impregnate her. Therefore, when a woman stays with a man throughout life, she is limiting herself and restricting herself to him. Meaning that if she finds a superior male specimen, then she would show great sacrifice to stay true and faithful to her husband and father of her previous children. Women, though, usually stick with men for the benefit of themselves and their offspring. Men, however, stick with women for the benefit of themselves and their sexual urges. Men are by nature egoists. If they take on a selfless act such as caring for children, abstaining from sex, or staying in monogamy, then they are going against all their natural drives. But are they womanly for taking on the female role of caregiver? Not necessarily, because intelligence and necessity may find this type of behaviour that protects and takes care of offspring beneficial. If it increases the chance of having successful offspring, it maximizes potential survival.

Take note that a man's need to accomplish, achieve, build, and create can very easily substitute his need for sex to a great degree, because they are both intrinsically rooted in his sense of worth. Meaning that his successes, all successes, give him that same feeling of his value. Man takes pride in his achievements—pride being the remembrance of success—because it is a list of his worth, in a sense. That is why man feels the urge to be useful and productive, and to do something, and anything. If a man can be useful to others, as in being of service to a woman, then he fills that gap of sexual desire. Men can very easily become subservient this way. Which is not necessarily a bad thing, as long as it's for a good ideal or cause.

Women are by nature caring, but only caring of those that they perceive as helpless, or in some sense weaker than themselves. And because men are the stronger sex, and should be more capable or independent, then women see men, all men, in that regard. Therefore, women have no sympathy for men, and especially not for the weak and inferior ones. And as this is their inclination in sexual selection, then this also blurs and paints womanly perspective on all matters. And the fact that women despise men to such a degree—seen today with free flow of information and opinion—makes that quite evident.

Thus, both genders are selfish. Selfish of their own natural needs. Woman in the need for offspring, and caring for them. Man in the need of seeking superiority and power. I.e., the improvement of himself and his own situation. And by extension those of him: Those that belong to him, those that he rules over, and those he ranks above and control. His lands, his people, etc. Both of these gender behaviours serve the same purpose, which is the survival of their kind.

A survival through man's willingness, and women's selectiveness according to what is available. Man engages in competition so the differences are clear between them, which makes that selective process possible, or at least easier, for women. And with man always being willing—and capable of taking it by force if need be, or if the possibility is there—you have the multiplicity and proliferation needed for survival through numbers.

III. Woman in Relation to Man

When women treat men bad, or with indifference and ignores them, it is a sign of superiority, higher worth, or being otherwise unavailable. If this was not so, then that woman would have noticed the man of equal or superior worth. This gives men the incentive to try harder—to conquer her. If he can show her his qualities, any quality, so that she relents, then this gives a man a feeling of worth and success in being with such a woman of high worth and great taste. As such, man is a shallow being, and nature intends him to be. If the man is rejected and he finds her irresistible, he may take her by force. And some men do not bother with female opinion at all and take them regardless. By taking her, he rises to her level of worth. Or put differently, he has taken something that would have been out of his reach, or otherwise unavailable, in regular circumstances. The things that are forbidden to us always tempt us. If it is kept away from us, then someone must want it for themselves and for their own benefit. And thus we want what we cannot have, because we think we will benefit from it. And this is why a male will absolutely want to mate with a female of high worth. It is the same with women. They want to be taken by worthy and superior men. It all serves the function of nature: to produce the best offspring one can get, and the most of them.

Part One: Man

The reason why unfaithfulness hurts is first and foremost the feeling of having lost some worth or value. In a man this is almost always felt. And even if the woman only did it for sexual pleasure, it is still taken as an offense, because it goes against the nature and function of the sexes. But when a man is unfaithful to a woman, it is not necessarily such a great hurt, because a woman knows that a man just goes by his natural drive if he does. However, if he does this while losing interest and withholds his seed, then she will become jealous. The reason for women being more lenient to a polygamous male—or unfaithful male, if you will—is because it is not a detriment to her, as she would still have access to his superior seed. This includes any of these females. They allow it because they at least still have access to it—man can be shared. This is not the case for a man being with a polygamous woman, because a woman cannot be shared. If she has sex but once she can be fertilized and so her use is "spent". It will be nine months until the next opportunity.

Men seek younger, and the youngest, women they can find, because it secures the success of fertilization in some way. Younger women are more likely to be virgins, which increases the chance of fertility because of less wear and tear, in a sense, and if childless she will pay more attention to man and children; she is unencumbered with prior offspring or engagements with other men. Younger females are more fertile as well, as it is with age, and they tend to be more beautiful, and their attractiveness will be an indicator of the value in the man who has her. Therefore, male sexuality, and the success of survival through fertility and exclusivity in the female, is the reason for the preference of young women.

There is almost always a lower value in a woman who has been with many men, because it shows a lack of discerning attitude. It is perceived as a sign of having low standards, and a man thus lowers himself, his worth, if he is to be with such a woman. Another reason is the threat of possible future competition and complication. She may sleep around later on, seeing as she has done it in the past, and then beget a child from those encounters. A child which you may have to care for. And you may not even know that it is not yours. There is also the thought of the "easy" woman. That is, if a man finds himself having persuaded a woman too easily into bed, he might lose interest in her. And may even feel slightly disgusted or ill. "If it was that easy, then she probably sleeps with anyone", he concludes. That which is easy to get may not be worth having, after all. If it is easy, it may not be worth much, as a lack of standards or restraint shows a desperation, or a need that is otherwise unfulfilled or unsatisfied. Or just a lack of value or worth, in general. Promiscuity is thus viewed negatively in both men and women, but less by women in men, because access is more important to them. An access to a much sought after male specimen that increases the chances of begetting strong and capable offspring. Women, on the other hand, have an exclusivity to men, because of the nature of impregnation. Men are therefore either selected, or excluded. And so, if a woman fails to be selective, then she has failed in the worst possible way. For instance, if a woman has slept with a man, due to being intoxicated or having fallen for his charms and persuasions, and then realizing afterwards how unworthy he was, she will get the feeling that some wrong was done. And she may be right to feel this way, because a violation of natural law has occurred: an inferior male has mated with a superior female. The same end result as when a man rapes a woman. The similarity stops there, however, because it is the woman who has failed and done a wrong. She let the violation happen. She failed in what is one of the most important duties of women: Being selective. To pick out and choose among the best. But with such great harm done, she rationalizes and then blames the man instead. "He took advantage of me" and other such statements are extremely potent today with the haywire female empowerment, and it is ruining male lives every day.

When females reach puberty, it is given much attention, and is seen as something beautiful—a thing of celebration. They talk much about it, and women are given comfort and understanding of their sexuality. It is also a bit more noticeable due to the monthly bleeding. However, when a male reaches puberty, it is not so noticeable, and it is not talked about. It is treated as something dirty and shameful. This is because a man wants and needs to have sex, and will in any case. A women does not. Female sexuality is viewed as something more functional and sacred due to her position as life-giver. The male as a fertilizer is seen as something minor and rather trivial, and of pleasure. As opposed to that of womanhood, which leads to birthing and pain. Female sexuality is thus one of hardship, while male sexuality is something frivolous and easy. These notions have gone completely awry today, however, and man has just become a pervert and pig, while a woman is an innocent and pure flower. But anyone who sees the world for what it is knows that both genders are quite capable of the most despicable, or the most saintly, of acts. It is all a matter of individuals, and what morals and values they have.

IV. Masculinity and Femininity

The attraction of a woman is her beauty and grace. A woman is like a beast—something to be tamed. She should be animalistic, yet dignified. She should be caring, yet self-confident. She should not be self-conscious; she should behave in the manner of a wild creature. This we call the feminine.

The attraction of a male is his strength, his power, or his worth. The visual signifier of this is usually a muscular body—commonly seen as male beauty. But this is a poor man masculinity. One that is easy to get, and not much power in anymore within the herd of the modern world. The peak of masculinity today is money, power through leadership, authority, or some other form of control over the masses. Just as it has been in most cultured civilizations, where power is in the mob and not in the individual or the few. This is masculinity.

This is not to say that beauty in a man has no value to a woman, because a woman, like a man, does not want ugly offspring. They do not want children who differ from ideals, such as phenotype. Like begets like, after all. This is the prevalent order of nature. A woman may go for a feminine beauty in a man—and by feminine I mean superficial looks like fine hair and skin, or other pleasing features—and not masculine beauty. Her sexual attraction is, like it is in men, responsive to a man's beauty, but this sexual attraction to a man of feminine beauty is one of superficiality. It is purely a selfish one. Like that of man towards woman. It is the masculine beauty that is important in a man, because this signifies what the offspring may get, and certainly what it needs: the strength and power to survive in the world. This is not found through male selection of females as much, because man will spread his seed whenever he can in order to ensure maximum population at all times. This prolific nature in men is there to maximize chances for survival, and it has been ingrained in man since he ascended from the animal. That is not to say that the population in the modern, intelligent world should not be moderated, however.

There is no selection of females by men, really. There is only feminine beauty that helps to encourage him and nature to select and prefer beauty. Or the aesthetically pleasing it is better to say. A man will prefer beauty or other qualities in a woman, certainly, but not enough to stop, and cannot stop, his need for offspring. And that is why selection is left in the hands of women—which men are worthy to fertilize her womb? A beauty is only a plus, and not a major factor or goal in a woman's choosing. It cannot be, otherwise she will degenerate her offspring. She must choose the men who dominate and control. The intelligent, brave, cunning, strong-willed, and forceful. Sometimes a woman may recognize a corrupt system and see that unworthy men are in positions of power and wealth, and so she may not care for the structure and finds a better male specimen to impregnate her. All the while keeping the encounter clandestine, of course. She does this not out of selfishness, but out of rationality. She does something noble. She reinvigorates the blood, or raises deserving blood to the heights that it belong. But, as I said, she must not do this out of a sexual need or superficial attraction.

When a man falls in love, it can easily be due to a woman's beauty, and not the thought of offspring, because a man is first and foremost interested in his own self-gratification. Which means that he enjoys her sexually and her sex appeal. He falls in love with the image of himself when with a beautiful woman, because it raises his status and worth. He flaunts it to other men like that of a jewel or some other item of worth—yet another symbol of his power. This is because the most worthy of women, the most beautiful women, will always choose the most worthy of men: those with power and wealth. If men of power compete and measure each other, and they have difficulty tallying the score, then they can compare mates to settle such doubt. And even if the men were equal in wealth and power, then the prettiest of women would have chosen among these equal contenders out of beauty. Either masculine or feminine, it doesn't matter, because a greater feminine beauty in one man, compared to a smaller proportion of masculine beauty in another, is overall better when the other mechanisms of male selection have been followed. That is, such men have already proven their worth, and their remaining masculine qualities are slightly trivial at this point. However, I mention greater feminine beauty over smaller proportions of masculine beauty, because if there is greater masculine beauty in a man, then a woman should, and I dare say that she would, prefer him. But a man, however, will always choose the most beautiful of women, as it is a measure of his worth. And as beauty is the highest value in a woman to a man, then that is the greatest compliment one can give her. Or actually it is the second highest value and compliment after faithfulness, but this is not something that can be truly known or seen as beauty is. Yes, unfaithfulness can be seen and known, but how prove faithfulness without access to a person's mind and thoughts?

The sexual organs themselves are very symbolic of masculinity and femininity. The male organ is one of activation, force, and strength. The female organ is passive, caressing, and soft. Thus, they complement the gender qualities very fittingly, and they most certainly developed in tandem with that. By which I mean that the genders developed in thread with their organs and their respective function.

A woman falls in love with a man that will produce offspring of his calibre. Or so she hopes. She looks for a man's internal or external qualities. Qualities that are likely to be passed on. It can therefore be said that a woman falls in love with the idea of their offspring—that combination and outcome of them together. Women love their offspring more than man and even herself, because of her limit in getting offspring. Men do not have a limit. They can reproduce daily if they had the chance, which is why both offspring and womb is somewhat secondary to him. He can continue on and seek out new women to fertilize, and that is why he is most important. Or at least in his own eyes he is, and he has to be so that it drives him on. To women he is easily replaceable, though. A woman usually lives in a group for protection, and only needs a man for fertilization. She is thus a social beast by nature. Man, however, competes and struggles on in the hopes of planting his seed, as he must have someone to carry it for him. He is thus a solitary beast. A female being social, and the male being solitary, is seen throughout nature as the norm. Man is meant to endure and overcome, and it is therefore natural for him to go his own way; and by himself, if he cannot find kinship or brotherhood.

Have faith and courage then, brother. You shall endure, and if you continue to improve yourself mentally and physically, you will rise to the heights you strive for. A body and mind is capable of growth, advancement, and becoming stronger and more agile throughout a lifetime. Therefore, read and learn to grow intellectually, and train and push your body to grow physically. Nature only limited you a little. Whatever shackles and restraints there are, they are mostly placed there by the self. Break free of these and go forth and shape the world in your image. Never relent, and never give in. Destiny is in your hands.

V. Realities

The reason for the perceived stereotyping of homosexual men and women is because of the gender attraction regime I have explained. In the lesbian we see a more masculine woman because it attracts females. By mimicking a male she will appeal to the innate sense of sexual desire in women. Yes, even in a woman who is interested in other women, because evolution has retained this sexual role with the survival of predominantly heterosexual people through procreation. A homosexual nature, in itself, cannot survive, after all. And therefore the sexual attraction between the genders are there latently. It is the same with homosexual men. They act more feminine and submissive, because it appeals to men, in general. Homosexual couples each have a feminine and masculine role, because they, these two, have found their counterpart. A masculine lesbian will look for a feminine lesbian, and vice versa. This is because they are attracted to their opposites, and it also makes it easier for defining the gender roles in a relationship. Homosexuality, and indeed all types of sexuality, will to some degree never disappear, and it must be accepted as natural. But it should never take the place of what is normal, however.

Today, there is much celebration of any type of minority in society, and it has gone so far that there is no celebration left for what is regular and normal. Such a society does indeed make people want to be part of any of these minorities, if it enables them to celebrate themselves more freely, and be happy. This is insanity. We need to stop celebrating minorities and start celebrating normalcy instead. A normal family and a normal life is the best and most important part of society. These are the values best pursued. If they are not celebrated, then they are not deemed important. If not important, then they're not sacred. And if they're not sacred, then these values, these family values, will not be taken seriously. Families then dissolve, and divorces take place, without any consideration for the children. This is selfish behaviour, and this incessant individual pursuit of happiness is to blame for much of it. Women get pregnant without marriage or commitment to a man, or even an ideal, and children grow up as bastard children. This is also the fault of men, because they, too, only care about themselves—these useless men of today. What all this does is to create a society that breeds worse and worse people. Immoral people, with no sense of grounding or belonging. This is not even a society anymore. It has become a state of individuals. Like animals in the wild.

There is a lowered sense of masculinity and femininity in daily life between men and women today. Gender ambiguity, in other words. Women are taking on male roles by having more education, and having more important jobs and positions in society. And they are less feminine in appearance by wearing pants and suits, and having short hair. Proportionally, men's roles have diminished, and in doing so they have lost masculinity. We have all heard the term metrosexual, for instance, which is used for these soft men who live in the city. Men are taking on roles that are, or at least were, considered more feminine in nature. Such as staying at home, doing housework, and taking care of the kids, and that is why there is also a greater prevalence of men being more feminine—overly sensitive, weak, and crying. Men are losing their pride somewhat. Their pride stemming from their sense of worth. But even with the continued pressure from the now outdated women's rights groups—outdated in the Western world at least—this agenda of total, mindless equality that was rammed down our throats has not taken hold. There are not equal numbers of men and women as directors, engineers, and construction workers. It is shown today that women would rather be in their old position of care worker—dealing with children, interacting with other people, and talking about such things—instead of being interested in, and finding importance in, the financial market or the military budget of next year. There just are certain occupations that do not interest and excite men and women. People do not want to spend their life doing something that they don't like or enjoy, obviously. Men like to build and develop new systems and ways. Women like to care for other people, to nurture, and to be social. This communist thinking that the mind can be shaped into whatever the state wants is nonsense. It is the body, the whole body, that shapes a mind. The mind consists of chemical reactions, too, after all. And with these chemicals in the body—these chemicals that make, and are, the difference between men and women—they impact the mind.

The Third Position

Why are women given the role of housewife and cook? Because it is natural and convenient to do so. In pregnancy a woman is left more stationary and needs a more careful mode of living than man. And then with the birthing and raising of the children, she is also bound more to the location of said children than men. When a woman has found a man of worth, she will try to hold on to him. She needs him for future fertilization, and this is also why she will care for him. She will let him indulge and be in accordance with his selfish, or self-important, nature. I will illustrate with the behaviour of lions: In a lion pack where the male lion is one, or very few, then the females are dependent on him. Even if he serves as a burden on them through taking his share of the meal in the kills the lionesses make. This is because this male lion has shown himself through battle with other males that he is currently the best specimen. And this the females know and respect. They recognize his superiority, and his right to breed and feed. This is not to say they will accept any behaviour from him, but they will accept a great deal before it comes to chucking him out. And that seldom happens. Furthermore, a strong, and the strongest, male specimen is useful for protection against other animals. He will also join in on the hunt when need be, such as if the prey is too large, or if some of the females are not capable or present, or in times of hunger. Or simply if the opportunity is there for taking down a good prey. And so, animal behaviour is not equally comparable to that of humans, but there is great similarity, and the pattern of thought is not far off. A good male specimen is thus a precious thing to a female. And that is why she will cater to him. To a certain point.

VI. Capability

There is little indication that women are of lower mental capacity or ability than men. It rather seems that it is simply the case of a difference in priority with them. Men are driven by their primal urge to explore and find new things, and they are therefore more prone to solitude and wild ideas, and building and creating. They have to find something of their own, or to take it and hold it, in order to get their sense of worth. This sense of worth to a man is quite essential. Which is also is why he is so concerned with respect, honour, and dignity. These are all expressions of a man's worth, and a lack of value or worth results in having no honour or respect. The male concern about these things is there because it is the mechanism of how and why a woman chooses a man—according to his worth. Man will therefore compete, or make something of his own. As a prime example, the highly divided and competitive Europe of old, where the land was taken and at times an almost suicidal gambit to take by force, drove European man to explore the world. This circumvented the current order by establishing or gaining that which stood outside of what was already known and taken. Much like nature does when higher evolved life enters a fresh, unspoiled area of opportunity—decimating weakness and purging it anew. It is man's natural drive to prove his worth that has enabled him to spread across the globe. And this, too, is why it was primarily man who invented and discovered things. Also, man had the time to do this because he escaped the burdens of childbearing and rearing. Does this make women unable or unwilling in in these matters then? No, but they are not driven to it by their nature. Yes, some are, but there are always exceptions to the rule. In almost everything. And these exceptions, or should I say exceptional women, are comparable to men in achievement and ability when they appear. No need to illustrate with exceptions, though, because we can easily see this through the fact that women are just as capable of learning as men are, or how she can join in on any conversation and offer clear insight when on the same competency level.

So, I would say that women are just as mentally capable as men are. But this different nature of hers may not drive her to it, or in the same manner and way as it does to men. And this may also leave her blinded to, or unable to recognize or see, a point. Or even unwilling. Although, the latter may also be true for men. In other words, I stand by the viewpoint of Plato in regards to women. Which is basically meritocracy, with a smudge of recognition in the reality of the differences between the genders. A woman should thus be able to want and achieve anything a man is allowed to, and the sexes should compete in the mental areas freely and ranked according to their merit without differentiating between them. As for the physical areas, one must take account for women being weaker, and therefore given lighter loads and work. Women should also be able to be in the military, but they must compete on the same physical level as men if they wish to be their equal there in job and rank. Women that do not fulfil this criterion should be allocated to working in areas that have lower physical requirements, or in designated female sections. Or in purely intellectual areas. This also goes for men. Men who fail miserably to be on par with the rest of the men, or those who have some physical injury or flaw, should be placed with the women, or in these intellectual areas. I say intellectual areas, but for this discussion the word may be conflated with any work of lighter physical requirement, because not all who are physically unable to work has a worth in doing intellectually important work, since their mind may not be so bright. Also, some work that requires a sharp and even brilliant mind may involve physical work. In conclusion, men and women should be chosen on individual basis according to ability and merit. With men setting the standard in physical requirements. And this should not only apply to the military, but also to society, in general.

One might think that there are only two ways to see women today: you either believe in gender equality, or you hate women—the commonly used false dilemma. What is gender equality then? Even those who speak of it are unable to answer that. The feminists would even have you believe that women could outdo, on average, any man in physical strength. Such irrational beliefs make me think that much of this seems like it is rather due to a hate of men—misandry. And I have never seen this misogyny these feminists are talking about, either—in this very Western world of mine that I have lived in all my life. The reason why these feminists have turned their movement into one of hate is because it coincides with the zeitgeist of the modern world. Today, none are more hated on this Earth than white man. He who once ruled over the world, and who is now viewed with envy and scorn; they all despise him for his superiority and success. This is why the man in the Western world—that is mostly white—is hated. Even by himself. And the feminists have also fallen for this propaganda. Propaganda that spouts the notion that white man has oppressed everyone, and then they ascribe this to the case of women as well. When they see the failure of women in having the historical importance that men had, they blame man for it, and in particular the white man, who is accused of "holding back" everyone else. Have women really been suppressed in the West? Perhaps. But it is more likely that women in the Western world, and in general, have been quite content with the positions they have been in. Like females usually are. It is natural that male domination happens, though, because what is stronger will dominate and assert itself over the weak. This is not only a natural fact, but a Universal truth, as certain as that of the gravity of a sun that pulls in smaller matter and absorbs it, fuelling it further. In any case, such is the time we live in today. Did deliberate propaganda cause this, or was it a natural reaction that spun out of control? It doesn't really matter. The only thing that does matter is that we eliminate this hateful sentiment of Western man. It can do no good. It only causes divide in society, and in the world.

Part Two: Mind

"Ignorance, the root and stem of all evil." – *Plato*

Part Two: Mind

Free will

Free will is the cornerstone of civilization. We need to have the belief that we are all not only responsible for our actions, but also free to live our lives the way we want to. Even if a totally free will cannot be proven, then that is no hinder to us becoming what any other man becomes. It is only a hinder insofar that we are not able to become the things we do not know of, or the things that are otherwise out of our reach. This is not to say that a man can eliminate everything as being out of his reach until it only boils down to one outcome, in order to justify himself in choosing it, because any situation of personal choice and action is always one of many potential outcomes. For every single choice there is either a do or don't. The nuance comes from the great many of these for every intended action, and we can intelligently identify which of these to perform so that it gets us to where we want.

As man becomes aware of the things he can and cannot become, and the way to do it, his options widen. He is then free to act on this and to take the choices that lead him down each road. It is intelligence, and knowledge of outcome, that enable us to do this. And even though we are only free to do whatever our knowledge gives us the option to take, it is nevertheless one out of many possible ones. As opposed to that of an animal, which lives in nature according to its drives and instincts, and not in accordance with goals and aims. Man may not be totally free, no. He is only free to do that which he is capable of, and that which he has knowledge of. But this is enough for the purpose of acquiring responsibility for yourself. Responsibility, which is the mark of a man and of the citizen.

A man who is knowledgeable about society, and its values and morals, is therefore aware of right and wrong. So, he is given a choice.

Knowing the potential consequences, or rewards—which is why crime is committed—makes man truly free. Many excuse their criminal behaviour, saying they were hungry or cold, or only defending themselves; that they had no other choice, and that it was a matter of survival. This has even gained such sympathy, and has become such a sick attitude in society today, that people actually accept these excuses. Another play on sympathy strings is the Christian conversion in prison: They have found God or Jesus, and this somehow absolves them of their crimes. They are claiming that they have changed, in other words. This comes easily to criminals, because most of them are liars by nature, anyway. They lie to themselves and to others. Which is why they are criminals to begin with. If they actually were repentant, however, then they would do their time quietly, and then live honestly if they get out. Also, with having such a sympathetic and charitable society as today, that has so many wealthy people and an abundance of food available, then that alone allows for an even greater responsibility in not doing crime, because one can so easily and unhindered beg for any of these means needed for survival. And it is readily given out—even in the most unsympathetic of places. There isn't much starvation or some other fear for your life in the Western world, and so any crimes committed are inexcusable.

This deterministic view—that being poor, uneducated, etc., somehow absolves criminal behaviour—is therefore bunkum. Just because you have had it harder or worse than other people, and that the situations and circumstances in your life drove you down a certain path, is no excuse. After all, you are not a wild and cornered animal that lashes out on instinct; you are human and intelligent, with a massive amount of information available. And in modern society you are bombarded with it every day—this should or should not. If you claim determinism as an excuse, then you are assuming the mantle of an animal and you will be treated as such. But even in nature you tread lightly and learn from your equals, your betters, and your enemies. There are rules there as well, just as in society, but the consequences of breaking them there are much more fatal.

Intelligence

I. Measure and Comparison

Our senses can betray us in circumstances where our knowledge and intelligence would not. We may endure a pain, because not to suffer it may end our life altogether. Or we can suffer through a pain, misery, and suffering in the hope for, or expectation of, something better in the future, or as a result of it. Humans can deliberately work toward something and then reap the rewards afterward. Animals will not do this on their own, and only when pushed or trained by humans to do so. Animals may learn, but only in accordance with their intelligence. They are not intelligent enough to toil the earth for planting and harvest, or able to consciously plan for the seasons. This is the reason why intelligence gets ever higher in evolution, and why it did in man, because when intelligence is able to produce results that improve the conditions of life, or just survival at all, then that individual with a mutational/evolutionary high intelligence lives on. And when he begets offspring, then they will further those genes so that they live on, and another mutation of even higher intelligence may occur and do better as well. And so on.

This is why we may determine how advanced an organism is through the complexity of their behavioral understanding. We do this all the time, in fact. By animal intelligence, and their social interaction in between themselves, we order and categorize. Dolphins and chimps we classify as smarter than a snake or a cow due to their more complex behaviors, or their understanding of intricate and difficult tasks and assignments. We used to do this with man as well, but some took offense at their poorer results and so they cried about being discriminated and other absurdities. And that was why political correctness, and political power, took a hold of such measuring methods. Manipulation started, and even on state levels for propaganda purposes. The Chinese and Jews only measured their smartest, while the West had to take everybody into account—including people not of the respective national ethnicities, and even non-citizens. It undermined the whole process, and people no longer take it seriously. A prevailing sentiment among the masses is that IQ tests and the likes are just made up, inaccurate, or otherwise worthless. It has been thrown into the bin, and people were partly right to do so, but there is nothing wrong with it as long as it is truthful, and correctly used. It should be taken out, dusted off, and implemented fully in schools and society, in general. After all, intelligence is the basis of all progress and the indication of higher evolution.

The difference in the intelligence of men can be enormous. How the person with an IQ of 125 sees a person with an average IQ of 100 or lower, then so does the person with an average IQ of 100 see a person with an IQ of 80 or lower. The differences are always noticeable. So great are these differences that it is comparable to that of men and primates. When people below average see themselves as more capable to understand and learn than chimpanzees, they see that difference of their own IQ and that of an IQ of 50 or lower in the average chimpanzee: 30 points is this divide between a chimp and that of a below average human of 80. So, imagine how great the unseen differences are between those who are averagely intelligent in the 125 IQ range compared with the average IQ range of 100: 25 points, which is almost that mentioned in regards to primates. Or when comparing the averagely intelligent and those of a below average IQ of 80, then the difference is 45 points! And this is only the comparison of the ones who are averagely intelligent. So, when you go above the IQ range of 125, the differences are staggering.

II. Empathy and Fallacy

Naturally, humans are able to overlook these differences in intelligence to a great degree, due to our common physiological and physical traits and behaviours, such as speech and laughter, and facial and emotional display and recognition—the body language. This we are able to in the way that in and by ourselves we recognize others. Just as animals do. They know the sounds and manners of themselves, and consequently that of similar life-forms. And with similarity comes empathy. We can, for instance, detect hostility or even sadness in other animals. And they can in us. It is seen in the eyes, or of a particular sound. This is how we are able to connect with our pets, or other living creatures, and some people take it to such an extent that they equalize these animals through an emotional attachment that is usually reserved for other humans. So powerful is this bonding that can occur through this common understanding between types of life—this empathy. And so strong is it that it deludes us very often, such as that excessive attachment to animals. But the strongest way this empathy displays itself is toward other humans. People see too much of themselves in others. A love of themselves gone mad. And so stupid at times, that they see themselves in anything and everything, and they turn maniacal if anything should do harm to this reflection of themselves. There are three main factors in why this is so prevalent today:

In a society where individualism is the pinnacle of human goals, with this worshipping of oneself, then you have the first piece of the puzzle.

The second one is the socialistic aspect, where they teach you that everyone should pitch in and help each other. Socialism, in itself, is not a bad thing. This thought of giving everyone the same opportunity to show their skills and abilities, and to rise in society according to their worth. Or helping those who have met sudden misfortune. Why not, this person may be of great value. And besides, in a properly run society, the individual, on average, should be able to produce or contribute more than what the expenses of his life are. It is hard to set a value on intellectual work and ability, but should it be important or needed, then (the Good) society will recognize and fund it somehow. And if not, the individual is forced back into an industrious capacity. But when socialism takes that most extreme form which involves equalizing all persons in society, you get a number of effects. In communism this equalizing leads to the thinking that individual life is worthless or expendable, because equal lives means that no one is worth more than others. The next logical step to them is that if no one is worth more than others, then individual life is worthless compared to all others. And with this principle that the collective of these equal people is more important than the individual, and this collective is represented by the state, then it follows that the state is more important than any individual. And from there on it is only a matter of time until this turns into a great many individuals. So many individuals that it comprises entire cultures, people, and races. Such thinking enabled Communist Russia to murder tens of millions of her own inhabitants, and in peacetime at that. This cleansing of "individuals", and the labelling of it as such, also enabled them to avoid getting a label of genocide. Somehow. With the exception of Holodomor perhaps. And I say perhaps, because it is not widely recognized, even though that incident alone probably took more lives than the Holocaust. Another form of socialism is called altruism. Or perhaps it is better to call it an extreme form and outgrowth of humanism. This altruism aims to help all people everywhere. And not only your own kind; no, everybody. This socialism and altruism is ingrained in us today: "Everyone matters." Or "all individuals matter", when coupled with individualism.

The third point is that humans are now more detached from the "cruelties" of nature than ever before. Such as not knowing how meat is produced, or even where. And then there is the absence of war, hunger, and any kind of suffering. The self-serving and hedonistic, fluffy lives of people have made them as soft as babies. Or more correctly, as children, because just like children they are blissfully unaware of the suffering in the world, and in nature. They are also unaware of the consequences of their actions, any actions, most of the time, and they cry for the littlest of things, and whine when they don't get what they want. The smallest of occurrences during their day are of the highest importance, and as such they prattle on and on about the new and fascinating. How trivial and ordinary these things are, they do not notice. And how solipsistic and narrow their mind span is, they obviously do not know. To be child-like is one thing. To be exactly like a child is another. The difference is that a child grows up. He learns. You can be inquisitive and find fascination in things, but it should be appropriate to your age. Meaning that when you have grown older and learnt more, then your interests should have grown to a higher level as well. There is a reason for why people today are so uninformed and less aware of what goes on in the world, and having a lowered level of education and knowledge, in general. And I know that education may be at the same level of completion as before, but education in turn has become weaker and less useful. In any case, it is individualism and free speech that is to blame for all this. Individualism has turned into self-importance. Free speech, or being allowed to utter your opinion on matters—originally meant in regards to political issues, voting, and general democracy—has been interpreted that they should have any opinion, and that their opinions matter despite their ignorance. An ignorance they are not even aware of possessing. And with free speech being guaranteed by law, they take it as the right to have their own opinion. Any opinion.

Therefore, the right or wrong, information or misinformation, and anything between heaven and earth, is subjugated to the opinion of the individual this way. These things, such as right or wrong, do not matter to them, and this enables them to pursue the ridiculousness of the past—that of pure fiction and imagination. This is why these myths of aliens, cryptids, ghosts, and other types of pseudoscience flourish today. Lies become prevalent and commonplace with the allowance and embrace of stupidity and the utterance of it, which is caused by this perception that they have a right to believe and promulgate anything they want to. And we now have to let them do this, because if we were to stop it, and then expose these lies and fantasies, and inform and tell them the truth, it would be seen as hateful. Hate and hater being words and labels used rhetorically in conjunction with political correctness. Another reason for all of this is the freedom of religion, and having made it a guarantee by law. In the same manner as freedom of speech, it enables and protects any statements and beliefs, and as such it stifles truth. Both freedom of speech and freedom of religion in themselves are not, and were not earlier, a threat to society. But transformed into these abhorrent variants of today—by abusing laws and manipulating public opinion through rhetoric, propaganda, etc.—they are no longer a private right. They have become public nuisances, nay, societal sores that fester and putrefy, and cause great harm to the nation and the people: It disrupts unity and uniformity, and social cohesion, in general. It warps people's view on the laws and the rights of the citizen, and subsequently it weakens the authority of the state and law. It harms and lowers the education and intelligence of the people and their general knowledge. The list is long, and the damage is pervasive.

Therefore, due to these three factors summed up, this prevalence of uneducated, ignorant, and narrow-minded people—which have no conception of the needs of nation or race, or what is natural—leave us with a population that is overly sympathetic to anything, everything, and everyone in the entire world. If only one individual should suffer, just a single living thing or cause, they would stop the whole world from turning. In their mind, it would be better if the world did not exist at all than to let an injustice occur. This is not sheer hyperbole. Many organizations such as PETA or Greenpeace, and their members, would rather injure and kill humans than let a single animal or tree be harmed. Their oversensitivity has transgressed into psychopathy, and this oversensitivity is due to a mentality that is instilled in people by modern society. The living of a sheltered life away from nature, and from not seeing or having any suffering in general, and the view that one should seek happiness and be happy all the time, has made people that way. And the concurring ignorance allows them to be easily manipulated by empathy and propaganda. As opposed to becoming hardened and realistic. As age and nature does, or should do, to you. Modern society is breeding mentally weak individuals that are not aware of, and not capable of, handling the realities of life. The elimination of suffering, and this incessant search and obsession with happiness today, is a belief with no foundation in nature or truth. Life is suffering. If life did not suffer, it would not bother doing anything to alleviate it. Which entails absorbing nutrients, competing, and struggling on. It would not bother with continuing, in other words. Life would then cease to be.

Empathy only helps us to relate to each other by identifying emotions, and therefore needs. The identification of intelligence, or more precisely someone with higher intelligence than yourself, is of another character. The problem is intrinsic to itself, really. To be able to understand and see the difference of IQ in people, you would have to have a higher IQ as a rule, and that is why the problem is always an unresolved one when assessed or dealt with from below, or when treated lightly and unsystematic. Just as the ape would not be able to fully understand the complexities of average human life, the average human does not understand the complexities of life in a more intelligent human. Yes, we show them glimpses of it, but the chimp can also catch a glimpse of actual human life. And even though we humans do have the possibility of proper communication through our language—some of which are very advanced, and enable very detailed understanding—it still does not help much at all if the minds are not on the same level.

All humans have a lot in common, though. Our physiological similarities for one: we have the same bodies and bodily needs. We are all "human, all too human", as Nietzsche says. By which he means that the noblest of men have the same needs, urges, and drives that the lowest of men have; all men are at the mercy of, and driven by, the needs and necessities of the human body. Hence, we are all flawed, with different weaknesses and faults. Even those that are better and superior. It is a faulty logic that the more intelligent, the genius, cannot be wrong. They associate the intelligent and the genius with being right, and the following chain of thought is that they are always right, and from there into being perfect. But we know that any man and his character, or his knowledge, can and will be flawed in some way. Therefore, you do not need to be perfect just because you are better and superior. If a work is done or a good idea is had by a man, then his actions, character, or even hypocrisy will still not render his work or idea worthless. To think otherwise is a fallacy. Ad hominems like these are committed repeatedly throughout history, and even today it is still a favourite. This is the power of association, which is the primary tool of the fallacy. To fully understand this, read the chapter *Association*.

III. Consequence

The animal will indulge in any sex, food, drink, drug, etc., that it can. It will continue to do all the things that makes it feel good, and while it may feel poorly afterwards, it is unable to connect it to the previous actions taken. It will continue to drug itself or eat until it dies, because it does not know the folly of its actions, and it does not realize that there is more information to get, and it has no means of getting it. Man with his intelligence does, however. We can identify and connect the things that made us feel this or that, and then we learn from it and pass this knowledge on by telling it to others. That is why we can go hungry out of choice, and deliberate on which action to take, and thereby ration and plan ahead.

To learn you have to remember. How much we remember is contingent upon how good our memory is. All animals have memory, but learning does not necessitate an understanding of how that thing learned actually works. Only that it does this or that, or the function of it; you remember what it did and how it was used. Learning, then, is not the same as understanding. To understand you have to be able to connect together previous experiences and memories, and by induction you can predict or anticipate a certain outcome. This type of connecting is what we call intelligence. It is being able to see patterns, interconnections, and the bigger picture. It seems that this is also due to memory, because memory allows for the creation of even more scenarios and pictures that are abstracted in the mind by induction. Higher intelligence is therefore due to a higher memory capacity and complexity then. A greater learning is thus allowed by higher intelligence, even if there is no understanding.

Those with higher intelligence learn and understand quicker and easier due to a greater room for information. And this greater capacity allows for more connections and therefore a complexity, which is the basis for the associations and patterns that are the measure used in IQ. The intelligent man absorbs more information, which we call being open-minded, but this also leaves him more susceptible to associations made—both faulty and true ones. However, his capacity, his open-mindedness, will allow for a continual flow of information so that a correction can easily be made. This is also why he is easier to persuade, and willing to embrace newer and higher truths, because of his capacity to learn and understand them easily and fully. Open-mindedness is usually seen in in the form of naivety. The intelligent man has a beautiful mind with a vibrant fantasy, due to his capacity and complexity of thought, and this makes him a noble creature that always dreams in terms of rules and the Good—he is a proper idealist. However, in a bad and cold world and society, the intelligent man can quickly find himself at odds with it. So much more easily he sees and recognizes the bad elements in society than the less intelligent, and he can become hardened and cold himself, due to this unravelling of truth and reality. This makes him unable to live in ignorance and childish optimism. This they call prejudice today, but it is simply having learnt and understood. Prejudice is commonly seen as the opposite of open-mindedness, but the truth is that the open-mindedness that they speak of is actually just blissful ignorance—being so oblivious to the world that you accept anything. Such men are characterized by their lack of values, and the consequence of that is the failure to take anything serious. This lack of values make you like and love less; you simply do not care, and you are less likely to be moved or interested by something—also known as indifference. Stupidity directly causes this, as it is the incapacity of the brain to understand issues, and especially complex issues, and this is why there is a failure to assign a value and worth to them.

Democracy, in its present form, is doomed to fail because of people's failure to recognize or understand the intelligent. They will therefore not empathize with intelligent men, and this will keep them from getting elected. And those of them who already lead will be ousted from government altogether. In other words, democracy ensures that the government is exactly as stupid as the average citizen—which is quite a scary thought. With stupidity comes this failure to understand, and even simple definitions then become problematic and difficult. People may get hung up on a word and may start associating it with other things that use that same word, but in a different setting or meaning. And as simple as that they have strayed from the topic or subject at hand. This type of rhetorical failure or trickery is also very often committed and used in politics, where politicians will attack an opponent for a word he has used, or start goading words out of him, or they may start placing words in each other's mouth, in order for them to twist it around through straw men and other fallacies.

The animal is passionate—yes, passionate in the same sense as they call Latin men passionate—and will act out more readily on the limited knowledge and information it has. Once it has learned something, it will be extremely difficult for it to let it go. This is because it doesn't have the capacity to relearn, or learn more, which is why we tame an animal from birth, and why a wild and full grown animal is extremely difficult to tame or train. The wild animal acts quickly without thought, is driven by instinct, and behaves cautiously and warily, because that is how it survives in nature. A domestication of an animal therefore usually takes a long time over many, many generations. But this is not so for all animals. The more intelligent animals are readily available for us to train very easily. Like the crow or raven. Or the dolphin. And it is their intelligence that enables this—they learn much easier and faster. A social and fearless way of life in these species may also be a reason. Furthermore, we breed and domesticate the animal into a calmer and less aggressive nature, for sure, but it may also be that the domestication process is one of getting higher intelligence out of an animal.

There are human groups and races that still live as the wild animals do. Nay, they do not even manage that. While these human groups may be able to ascend to the heights of the beaver in their ability to make a dirt hut, they still fail in a number of other areas that animals, and even insects, can handle. The ant, for instance, organizes his colony and institutes order. And the wolf and hyena packs are capable of hierarchy, with the rules and leadership that this entails. So, when we find human societies that are, and always have been, completely lawless and without any system or order—just a total chaos without any leadership—then what failures of life they are. The only reason why these "societies" are still able to exist is because of the food and medicine that is brought in from the Western world profusely and continuously. What utter pointlessness that is: sustaining a population that cannot sustain itself and was doomed to die out. And what sheer stupidity it is to actually import these specimens to the West through immigration.

IV. Decadence

The interest in wearing jewellery and brightly coloured, fancy clothing is one of a primitive nature. The animal is fascinated with the shiny and bright, and all that is strange and unusual. This fascination is particularly seen in animals with higher intelligence. The magpie, for instance, is known to collect shiny objects. And the feathered splendour of the peacock came about because of such sense of aesthetics—these bright colours and patterns that captivate the mind. Not that the peacock is particularly intelligent, though. Fascination is a very shallow type of curiousness that seeks no answer, and which only "wants" to be awed by incomprehension—a nonproductive curiosity. It is primitive fascination, and this is why we observe in the cat or dog an interest in things that humans find quite ordinary. We see, then, that there is a threshold of intelligence or knowledge required for this dumbfoundedness of fascination to happen. Fascination is the recognition of a rarity or unusualness of some kind, but it only has to be strange and rare to the mind that finds it so. Meaning that if you have seen and experienced it before, or if you can understand it and account for it, then it may not affect you as much, or at all. And that is why aesthetics, or at least aesthetic sense, increases as intelligence increases. And as it does, it moves away from its primitive nature and into understanding.

We see this primitive nature of fascination with the shiny and pretty throughout some particular places, and in some people, on Earth today. Particularly the Indian, the Persian, the Arab, and the sub-Saharan Africans. These have a culture and need to adorn themselves with gold, silver, and gems, and they will dress in the most eye-catching of colours. This is particularly seen in the African, both in Africa and America, and they do this in the most absurd of ways by wearing extremely over-sized jewellery and vividly coloured clothing—and whatever else of gaudy things that can be found. Truly a bird-brained behaviour if there ever was one. All of these places, cultures, and people are incidentally the worst nations and places on Earth: From the slums of India to the barbarity of Africa, and all the way to the African-American ghettos in the United States. Or the Africanized ghettos on both American continents for that matter. These places have a huge amount of riches and fertile lands, and there is no lack of rich people either, but nevertheless their societies are in shambles. And this is because of the failure to prioritize, due to their primitiveness and such primitive fascination. And as these twisted priorities leave their society dysfunctional, then consequently there is no progress, order, or anything. And therefore no opportunity for jobs, which means no money or income. And that is why people in these societies, who seek to attain this decadence—a motivation, ambition, and drive that caused the ruin of their society in the first place—resort to crime and corruption. In other words, the unintelligent are driven to crime by their lack of intelligence.

Intelligence increases to the point where it is able to gain a comprehensive and near complete knowledge of the function and nature of things, and in doing so it sheds the primitive notions it had earlier. The intelligent or knowledgeable man knows of the pointlessness of primitive fascination and decadent behaviour, and he is therefore not moved by it. He would use the metal and wealth to build and do something productive, and also knows the consequences of maldistribution of wealth and the crimes committed to attain it. As such, the civilized man finds the whole decadent behaviour vulgar and stupid. Instead, his intelligence and clarity leaves him fascinated by a different type of curiousness that is more functional and will lead to answers—a productive kind. Such a man is moved by the more intricate and complex things in nature, and he finds beauty not merely in the existence of himself, but in his people, life, the Earth, etc. This intelligent man builds beautiful cities and societies; his concern is of something else than just himself, because of the amount of knowledge and greater understanding he has.

We see the many variations of both ways throughout history. The behaviour of incorruptibility and a lack of decadence was exemplified by the Spartan, which is the reason why the characterization of such behaviour and living came to be called spartan. And we see the opposite peacock behaviour and such decadent ways in some of the leaders of WW2, for instance. Mussolini and Stalin repeatedly dressed themselves up in all manner of nice and fanciful clothes, or wore uniforms with an excessive array of medals and adornments, and their lives were filled with debauchery and every kind of indulgence and decadence. Contrasting this was Hitler, which usually wore the simplest of clothing: a plain suit, or his NSDAP party uniform with only one medal, which was his First Class Iron Cross. By performing an act of great bravery you would get the Second Class, but the First Class Iron Cross was reserved for a repeated and consistent show of extreme bravery and soldiering. It was, and probably still is, the highest distinction one can get. And so, that single medal not only spoke of his lacking need to show off, but also of his contribution to his country and of his character. It is also worth to note that these three mentioned had very different backgrounds before their rise to power. Mussolini was a deserter and traitor; Stalin was a hard criminal and convict of robbery and murder; Hitler, on the other hand, was an honest worker and had volunteered as a soldier when the First World War started. Another show of Hitler's dedication to his cause and country was that he didn't touch his salary from the state after becoming Chancellor, and he never would. Although, he wasn't a poor man either, having become a millionaire after the massive success of *Mein Kampf*. Through his participation in the war he had shown himself very brave and dedicated, and through his writings it was seen that he was extremely well-read and intellectual. This is probably the reason why he didn't suffer these issues of insecurity, and other faults, that are found in the examples I mentioned. Or in other men.

V. Ignorance and Evil

When we are children, we are constantly taught what is right and what is wrong. And why. We are born with no shame, and no guilt or bad conscience. But as we grow older, this is instilled in us throughout our childhood, and as our learning increases, then so does our understanding. I limit moral notions to the intellectual, because the animals, even though they are ignorant, are still largely unintelligent and fail to understand even that which children do. I am not saying that they do not, or cannot, understand right or wrong. Even animals have rules and boundaries, after all. They, too, teach their young, and those who stray out of line. They also base their good on information, and their bad on the ignorance of, and not following, the rules. A domesticated animal or pet may be taught our human rights and wrongs, and feel shame or guilt, when doing things that go against its training. But it is a shallow feeling. It knows that it was not allowed to do a thing, but it does not know why. The animal does not understand, and it will never understand. If we had a way to communicate in words to an animal that they'd fully grasp, then perhaps. But if they would be able to perform such complex mental actions as understanding definitive words, then they would also be able to deduce why they were forbidden to do such a thing in the first place. Children can do this deduction. If they unwittingly do a wrong, and then are lambasted for it, they can still come to a conclusion as to why, even though they did not think it wrong at the time. This is because they can base it on some information regarding their action. For instance, if you had not been taught that it was wrong to steal apples, and you went into the neighbour's yard and picked some, then you may still have doubts as to whether it was right or wrong. If you had been caught and scolded for it, you would then have to ponder your actions. If someone asked you what you did wrong, you would most likely answer that it was probably not right to go into someone else's yard, and that it was probably also not right taking something from his yard. We are taught about the wrongs of stealing, and respecting other people's private things, early on in life. We know that children are aware of the concept of ownership by them saying "this is mine" and such. Even animals think in these terms. But what animals do not understand is that we live by a social contract, and we expect others to abide by it. We do no harm, and we trust others not to either, so that no harm will befall us. An animal, even a trained one, will not understand this. They will take the apple as long as they think they can get away with it—the behaviour of animals. It is possible to prevent such behaviour, but behavioural reinforcement has to be very strict and professional to get the proper results. In any case, suffice to say, children are much smarter than even the most intelligent of beasts. As children grow, we see their behaviour become more and more aware of their surroundings, and more empathetic. What we deem as cruel behaviour is quite common in all children. They are prone to torturing animals, and violent or verbal attacks on other people. Mostly other children, though, as they are not physically intimidated by them, and they will be on par with them mentally. Their ignorance and curiosity are the main instigators of such behaviour. They have a need to learn and know. Ripping off the feet of insects, they get no negative response, and so they will not deem it bad. Or beating a dog, or abusing a cat: if they do not get a directly bad and negative response, then they may continue their behaviour. The less they empathize, the less they will reflect on their actions. The toying and playing that predators do with their prey, and other creatures, is also done out of curiosity. And of boredom. Their lack of empathy is what makes them behave this way. And children—closest as they are to that of an animal, due to their young age—will behave in similar ways. However, they will grow out of this quite quickly, and with good parentage the child will learn to behave properly. Even at a very young age.

Let us entertain the notion that there is such a thing as evil. Not in a spiritual way, but as one that is opposed to the Good, or does absolute harm to the Good. If you have to know, or be taught, what is good in society and how to behave accordingly, then ignorance could qualify as evil. With ignorance as evil, and that you are born ignorant, then you are as such born evil. This, I speculate, is the philosophical origin of the concept of original sin in the Catholic faith. This is also the basis of the religious thinking in that knowing God and scripture can save them from their sinful ways: that by learning the respective rights and wrongs will redeem the sinner and absolve him of his former sins; making the sinner aware through repentance and learning, and that this will change his ways. And just like that they are forgiven for their former ignorance—I am not sure that I would forgive sin so readily. By forgiving the sinner, one also forgives the circumstances that made him a sinner. Just like the vicious dog, the sinner has also caused much harm and will be near impossible to readjust. You put down the dog, and you put down the maladjusted man. And not just for his crimes, but to serve as an example to other would-be criminals as well. The death penalty was a very efficient deterrent, obviously—reserved for murderers and the worst of crimes. But without the threat of punishment, there is no incentive for a man to change or do right. It is an evil caused by evil. And it should therefore come as no surprise why men turn bad in droves today.

Where there was moderation and duty before, there is now hedonism and egoism. Marriage and family used to be a sacred institution. Today, however, the norm is to get married several times, and only for pleasure seeking—this constant happiness. So, what lesson does this teach young impressionable minds? Simply that they should always feel good. At all times. And that it is not worth it to work together and listen to each other—just move on and seek your own fulfilment. Another commonly used excuse, in their neglect of the children, is the harping on the age old mantra that "in my days we had it so much worse". All these things exacerbate the problems of the modern world. What poor idols children grow up with today.

Even in their homes! No wonder the world is what it is, when ignorance breeds ignorance.

The old concept of evil was defined by Christianity and the *ressentiment* of the slave, and it is still the same today. This evil is the inversion of the old values and the Good of the masters. The master did what he pleased through his dominance and power. He held the weak as slaves and he had no remorse or sympathy, and he did not curse the world for what it presented to him. With his lack of sympathy, he also lacked the virile hate that is so pervasive in man today. This hate stems from slave morality, which instil notions of equality. And through this unnatural mind-set that all men are equal, and therefore should be equal in all respects, comparisons are made and those lacking are found. If some are found without some of these things, then this is where we start pitying. Which is the same as our perception of injustice, really, but without that rooting in law. Or any apparent or obvious illegality at least. And with the delusion that equality is the normal state of things, then someone must have made it unequal. And then the blaming game starts, and those who find themselves lacking and pitied will start to look for the "culprits". Most of them fail to see that nature itself is to blame, but some do and they deem nature and the world to be evil and cruel. Those who are the first to be blamed will be those who not only have what others have, but have more. The excessive will be interpreted as the cause of the deficient, and the holders of excess are therefore held responsible. Hate then occurs and is directed toward them, because these have broken the perceived right and correct in this society. Slave society.

The master was more in touch with nature, and more like a beast, really. Taking what he wanted and without the shackles of sentiment. To him it was natural that the strong should rule over the weak, and that the weak would have to suffer their lot in life because of it. Such notions as pity or humility were a weakness to the master, and something bad—as any weak or foolish element would be to him, and as it is in nature. When the slaves revolted, they inverted these values of the master. They made the bad things the master had defined, and which was attributed to the slave and the weak man, the new good. They even took it one step further and called it holy. And with that they also turned the master's previously good things, this which now stood in opposition to the new holy, into evil. Slavery, greed, gluttony, and lust—all turned into bad, or just evil, notions. The traits of the slave, which had now transformed into something good and holy, became something sought after and wanted, because of their new status as virtues. And the traits of weakness and timidity were now called meekness, which by definition indicates virtuous choice. This total reversal of (natural) value is seen in the Christian virtues, such as chastity and general temperance, charity, brotherly love, and care for fellow man. These were seen as weaknesses, and even bad sometimes, in the eyes of the previous masters. The master had derived his Good from what was natural and naturally occurring, so when the slave and his *ressentiment* inverted the morals, it resulted in having made nature itself evil. And by making nature evil, he had turned the world into a hell for himself. A new, wonderful place would have to be invented that would fill the slave with hope and make him righteous and rewarded: heaven. The consequence of all this is clearly seen in our time, with suffering as something evil. In particular when suffering is imposed upon someone or something by man.

A proper definition and understanding of this terminology, that followed the new agenda and which we take for granted today, is as follows: the bad is something that does not work toward or benefit the good, and an evil is something that actively works against the good.

The Third Position

I will not go much further into details than this, and if one needs further enlightenment, then Nietzsche is the place to go. His works mostly revolve around the unravelling of these concepts and notions. He was the one who gave us the definition and duality of master-slave morality, and the origins of good and evil. It is highly recommended that you read his books if you have an interest and need to understand this in full detail. In which *Genealogy of Morals* and *Beyond Good and Evil* would probably offer the greatest insights.

Part Two: Mind

Valuation

I. Causal Value

Valuing is at the heart of life. We do this from the moment we enter this world. From our very first experiences we get imprinted on what good or bad was derived from the outcome. It is our senses that help us determine and differentiate, and the results set the values for us. A person having a bad experience, and another having a good, from the very same type of situation, will determine a great deal in how we respond to future events that are similar. We are always curious and willing to try new things. We always want to test the limits. And the bravery of our past experiences, and the results, set the pacing and dare for future endeavours. Bravery is hard to define as something that you are either born with or not, but if you continue to push your limits, you will find either reward or punishment. You will find your limit, in other words. And so, one man's bravery can be another man's folly. Or undoing. Our calculation of risk contra reward, and our past experiences, set the bar. And as mentioned, when we push this bar, we find out how far it can be pushed until it is no longer beneficial. This is an ingrained part of evolution. We always try to surpass earlier accomplishments. And in man we see the need to try to surpass the accomplishments of others—being competitive. Now, nature and evolution is surely in a sort of competition, and all the time. But it is not aware. It does it merely as a means to survival—competing to survive. This survival instinct always seeks to maximize how well it can thrive to ensure the most effortless or rewarding way of life. That is to say, life values according to its feeling of well-being. When one expends the least amount of energy, and gets the most for it, well-being increases. However, that is not to say that sloth and idleness is necessarily rewarding. And in any case, nature would not know. But intelligent life can. Man does. We predict and know the consequences of our actions. We take preliminary measures and plan for something. We know the effects of eating too much, and that is why we restrain ourselves, even though it tastes good, and makes us feel good—this feeling of well-being. And not only do we try to surpass ourselves, but through intelligence we set up competition against other humans, and in it we aim to surpass each other. Essentially the same principle as in nature, but intelligence has set it to play out in different forms, and not just by mere natural instinct of well-being and survival. Valuing is key part of this.

Valuing also teaches us what not to do then. It tells us what to beware, what we should not want, and what is destructive or negative. We may learn this through experience, but there is also another way to learn value, an intelligent way: learning from others. Through verbal or written forms people tell us of their past experiences. Some to warn and some to encourage. Some argument for their opinions, and others base it on very shallow, or non-existent, reasons. These tellers of stories may even base their opinion on that of other storytellers. And the less cogent it all sounds, the less reason there is for us to heed the message. This learning of others also exists in nature. But it is not in the form of explanation, it is in the form of demonstration. When lions hunt or monkeys crack nuts, there is demonstration. However, even if deemed somewhat intelligent, they have no language and speech for exact communication, and no written forms or drawings to either show or understand. Perhaps this is the definition of what a truly intelligent and advanced being is.

So, we know that valuing is done in both a physiological and intelligent manner. We enjoy certain types of food or drink, because we get a bodily stimulus. But eating or drinking too much of something can make us sick. Or consuming a substance, because of the intoxication and feeling of temporary well-being, may cause harm. As a rule, anything that is not in moderation or properly used will be detrimental. When our bodily urges drive us toward harm, then our intelligence recognizes that harm and from where it stems. Thereby, we learn and remember, and even educate others about it, as said before. But what is a good or bad experience? If the first time I ate apples, I ate too many of them and I became sick to my stomach, then I would not value the apple highly, and I might avoid it or dislike it for fear of something like that happening again. I may also conclude, quite ignorantly, that one would always become sick by eating them. This example I have given could be of many things, but it is in essence the reason why, or the scheme of how, we value even the most mundane and ordinary of things so very differently. The impact of this can be quite profound and long-reaching, too. If, let's say, a king or a priest of old would have such a good or bad experience, then his decree in mandating or outlawing it might resonate across the lands and throughout the ages. This kind of valuing is known as having an opinion. It is shallow and not well-founded—in contrast to the informed opinion. This personal opinion, which is so faulty at times, is the reason why we rely on the consensus, because in numbers, and in averages, we can find the truth of the matter. And through the study of a great many sources and experiments, and the testing and verification of them, truth and fact emerges. And it is on this the informed opinion is based. Science, in other words.

Something can always be determined as better than the other. At least in specific use and function with given criteria. A gun is better than a club, even though it is more complicated and requires higher intelligence. The monkey, or the man without knowledge, finds the gun to be nothing but a chunk of metal, and will instead use the club for its reach and weight. The gun, however, when one knows how to operate it, will outmatch the club in most situations. We always judge items this way. When you know how to operate a car, you will find it faster and more convenient than the bicycle. Know, then, that we always fail to consider and appreciate the sophisticated and complex things that more intelligent people use, because we do not see much, or any, value in them. This is our cognitive bias playing tricks on us again, and this is either due to a lack of information and know-how, or a lack of understanding (intelligence). Most, but not all, of the things that are more intelligent in their use or composition are considered comparably better than simpler and more primitive ones. This is natural and understandable, since intelligence and knowledge is what separate man and civilization from beast. And by the by, this is also why we grade animals in hierarchy and life-value according to their intelligence. Intelligence is knowledge, and knowledge is the path to understanding, and with understanding we can overcome the forces of nature and become masters of this Universe. Instead of mere ignorant pawns and spectators.

II. Subjectivity and the Situational

A newborn animal finds its image of familiarity and comfort right after coming into the world, or early on in life. And this image and imprint of comfort, security, etc., stays with them. Valuation is dependent upon the difference of experience according to each life and each circumstance, and also of the different behaviors and ways of living. It is something ad hoc then, because of the blank slate of experience we start with. The memories and associations formed later on—which is still important and of greatest importance to intelligent life—will only be contributory to that method of valuation. Learning and experience is therefore subjective. Such subjectivity happens because we have had different outcomes of similar experiences, and that is why we want and expect different rewards from any given scenario. There are a great many reasons for why we have different preferences, and some may be extremely hard to pinpoint. As said, these results and experiences are the largest determinant, but a like and dislike of certain foods may be caused by a difference of taste due to different genes. The cockroach, for instance, can be propagated into disliking sugar by weeding out the ones who like sugar with sugar traps. There are many differences in our bodies, and between the different groups and races—some of which are very small, and even undetectable or simply unknown to us—but they may have a profound effect in total. Like how some food products are preferred and liked in some parts of the world, and not in others. In addition, a predetermined mind-set on a physiological basis—the structure of the brain from genes, before birth, and throughout life—may also be a determinant. That is slight conjecture on my part, however. It is not unreasonable, though, because there is always variation and randomness. Even in siblings a brain pattern may be completely different. Also, if by the thought that intelligence and physical attributes are inherited from the parents, then these attributes, and others which we may not know of, may also be present in the kids. If a runner does well, and has parents that were also good runners, then "it is good genes" we say. It is noticing them and choosing to continue and build on these patterns that make us breed selectively. And it is the emergence of these patterns that cause competition in nature and enable evolution, and why nature specializes. And even sometimes to an extent that may be ultimately harmful to the life-form. It may even spell its doom. Is intelligence in humans such a specialization, and will it ultimately bring about our own end?

As man sees the world through his values, and every action he does is in accordance with them, then whatever said or done reveals something in him. This is why people are so prone to exposing themselves. Even when they try to hide it. Our values are ingrained in us and paint all our actions, and they therefore tend to blind us to them. Meaning that we do not see where our values are wrong or different, because we do not know a higher truth, or a better way. When I say this, I primarily think of things that can be done better and where higher truths are found. As in and through science, for instance. And not as some sort of right and wrong through morals. And not even with the moral standards of our age in mind—flawed as I think they are. To illustrate: Throughout time the chair has evolved, and it has become more and more ergonomic and comfortable. As our knowledge and intelligence grows, the construction of a chair will, or at least should, become better. A right way of building a chair in older times may be a wrong way today. The newer and better knowledge, or higher intelligence, changed our values in regards to the chair. To get true values, one needs true(r) knowledge—a truth. And therefore our values have to change according to the knowledge we gain; when we make new findings we adapt accordingly. A truth is not eternal, so to speak. Some are, though, and this we call fact. It is something that is undeniable and never changes. Or at least it shouldn't, ideally and by definition.

In regards to morals, values are not necessarily dependent upon knowledge and intelligence in the same manner as things of material and concrete uses. Indeed, morals have changed for the worse today. For example, family life has withered away and promiscuity has flourished. And this is not due to a higher truth and knowledge gained, or even intelligence, but only as a consequence of hyper-individualism, which is contingent upon a number of other values that may, or may not, be seen as more advanced and intelligent. In other words, a value and moral may be a side-effect of another. To remove or change these side-effects you would have to remove this root cause, and this will not happen when the root cause is something of high or ultimate value. Therefore, any of these minor or smaller side-effects are permitted. Even when in opposition to the current morals and values.

Valuing is an intrinsic part of life, and it is in harmony with the way of life. But the way of life is different everywhere, and the largest, to the smallest, of things may have a profound impact or change. Especially in the world of men. A lack of resources or materials may inhibit people, or they may rise to the challenge and overcome that obstacle by devising new methods and technologies to circumvent that lack of something. For instance, the harshness of the steppes formed the Mongolian and his customs and ways, and also necessitated a dependence on the steppe ponies, which was perhaps their greatest strength. This hardship on the steppes and their symbiotic relationship with the ponies—both as a source of food and weapon of war—enabled them to travel large distances with everything they needed at hand. The ponies themselves were very hardy and could survive in meagre conditions. The mobility through horsemanship and the mastery of the bow—that was utilized best in their famous hit-and-run tactics—made for a deadly combination that was hard to counter. Thus, what was at first a necessity and value, because of the sheer need for it to survive in a tough environment, became an unstoppable force when it pushed into soft and weak areas. Which ultimately turned into one of the greatest events in human history. The irony is that what made them they so successful—their pragmatism and lack of sympathy—is being thought of today, and even then, as a very uncivilized and barbaric thing. A difference of values and morals, to be sure.

With the hydrogen bombs of today, war is not a large scope event anymore. It just cannot be, as the risk of nuclear annihilation is not an option. And the natural conclusion and effect of this is that war is seen as an unnatural, unwanted thing in modern times. And much of our values, and valuing, is because of this. Today as it was before. A reaction to an action. An assessment in accordance with what is known, and expected.

III. Failure to Value

As our values set our morals, and make us like or dislike, love or hate, then this is why we have an opinion. If we do not have an opinion, then this stems from a lack of values, or not having done a valuation. This is what we call indifference. But not all lack of value and valuing can be called that. There are some things we do not know, and are not expected to know, and therefore cannot have an opinion of. A true indifference is towards something that others normally will have valued, and that they care about. Such indifference towards important and much talked about issues is the worst type of indifference. Valuation is probably the most important thing we do in and throughout life, and if someone have failed or otherwise escaped a need to valuate when all others have, then it is a sign of something wrong. If one has lived a life that has been privileged or spoiled by eating few varieties of food, then one would not have had the opportunity to form an opinion about other types of food, because they have not been experienced. This is the same with other failures of valuation, such as an indifference to politics, due to having had a snug and secure life without any of the problems that the common man may have had. A lack of intelligence is also a reason for this failure to valuate in society when all others do, or the more intelligent do, because if one cannot understand the problem or implication of a thing, then one would not be able to have an opinion. As an example: I have no knowledge of quantum physics, and if someone were to ask about my opinion on string theory or loop quantum gravity, then I would have no answer. In other words, I have no opinion, and this is also why I am completely indifferent to the matter. This illustrates the problem of a lack of knowledge, or a lack of intelligence. However, advanced physics are fairly complex, and that cannot be said for the things I am referring to, which is general political issues, or simple life choices. If you were to be asked a question whether to raise or lower taxes, then that is a simple question. It may not be simple as a whole, because the effects of either choice implemented would be potentially uncertain—even to the greatest economist or politician—but we can make simple judgements in accordance with the arguments for or against it, though. Ignorance is not really an excuse, since as a democracy we should be informed and involved. To participate and be up to date is the duty of the citizen, actually, as that is what a good and functional democracy relies on. Therefore, we cannot compare an indifference to advanced physics, if one could call such indifference that, with indifference to simple politics. Additionally, a lack of passion that can cause indifference to things may be due to a lack of appreciation. This is especially true in the modern world, where we get everything we need, and we never want for or suffer a lack of anything. This diminishes the value and worth of a thing, and we get less thankful and appreciative as a result. This has nothing to do with intelligence, but it is still one of information. Information through the experience of life. In conclusion, in order to value you must have knowledge and understanding—information and intelligence. Then everything follows from that valuation: morals, ambition, ideals, hope, dreams, wants, lust, etc. A base and low society, therefore, would have to be one that lacks knowledge or intelligence, in general.

The population in primitive areas look up to the rich and the selfish, and this is because they are selfish and want to be rich themselves. They accept and perpetuate this behaviour of decadence and selfishness, because it is of high value to them, and consequently do not see it as a problem. And as they do not see it as a problem, and are not able to, then they will not be able to rid themselves of it, or change. Instead, they blame other cultures and people who have different values that actually work and make society better. And because they do not share or understand such values, they identify them as wrong. And as it feels wrong to them, they equate it with being wrong altogether. They will then take this "wrong" and use it as an explanation and reason for their problems, and what is wrong in their society. With this magic trick, this utter stupidity, they have shifted the blame away from themselves. This is much helped and reinforced by the anti-white propaganda, and this brings it into a perpetual loop of avoiding responsibility, and shifting blame, for such people and societies. "The white man holds me down", they say. It feels good to rationalize and to have excuses, for sure, but it will not make you deal with the real issue or solve the actual problem. And by having such a mind-set you can never engage in proper democratic politics and principles, or any politics at all for that matter, because it always derails into the absurd by never taking any blame or responsibility. Agreements and compromises will therefore never be reached. It seems as though this mind-set of rationalization and blaming is quite common in the helpless and witless, i.e., those of low intelligence, and it should be quite clear to us now why this latter is so detrimental to social cohesion, order, government, and politics. And take heed, when morally low people and their behaviour are not only tolerated by society, but even accepted and embraced, they set a standard for the rest. Everyone will then start thinking "if he can do that, then I can as well". Any preventive measure or deterrence in having proper values or higher morals has therefore been lost. The general populace will follow suit, and moral decay—and consequently social decay—has begun.

Part Two: Mind

"Pardon one offence and you encourage the commission of many."
— Publilius Syrus

* * *

The want to be valued or appreciated in some way is common in all of us. Even in the most advanced of societies. But as values are different between societies, then this display is also quite different. We see that bird-brained, peacockish, strutting-around behaviour—this wearing of fancy clothes and jewellery to display their value, which is nothing but vanity—in primitive societies. But in societies where community, people, order, and progress is valued, then we see it in the form of how much one contributes, or what place or position one has. In the modern militaries that evolved in Europe there was a great number of distinctions and medals, but also a number of ranks, which would indicate the merits and abilities of the individual. Even honorary ranks were given out. Such practices were, naturally, used in the civilian sphere as well. A leftover of this are the honorary degrees that are given out to those who show outstanding insight and knowledge in a field that they have no degree or formal education in. In Norway, medals are given out to civilians and military alike for a wide range of achievements and accomplishments. For instance, being in employment long and faithfully for 40 years could earn you the *King's Medal of Merit in Silver*. Sadly, much of the criteria for a number of these medals have been changed or removed to make them harder to accomplish. Or the medals have been discontinued altogether. This is a sad progression in society. We then lose honour and distinction to differentiate and identify, and any incentive for the population is lost. Nobility of man—nobility that is not inherited but earned—is then taken away from him, or actually not given at all. In a good and functional society, where the people work together and progress, and where we elevate and appreciate the superior and the worthy, there must be a system of reward in some way or other. Things like *Employee of the Month* in the U.S. are such kind of initiatives, but it is much too trivial, and people laugh at it and do not take it seriously. It is too short-sighted, and too little of a reward, or of consequence on your status and life. And as a result, it is not revered or important. And with no respect or value comes no seriousness, either.

IV. Morals, Ethics, and Law

Morals are the extensions of our values. As such, they are very different from people to people, place to place, and even between individuals. Laws, ethics, and morals are therefore nothing more than artificial creations suited to each set and setting of factors that are purely conditional themselves. Their distinguishing features and differences can be illustrated in an example: The jailor will think it unethical to free a man that he knows to be innocent from his custody. But he will find it immoral not to. Where ethics compel duty, morals compel the conscience. The jailor puts his trust in the judiciary system to set the innocent man free, and thus does not intervene. But the jailor who has seen the system fail, and many wrongs committed over and over again, may be compelled to take justice into his own hands. The law says that he needs to follow a procedure, or else he, too, will find himself judged by the law. But he may take advantage of this. If the law states that he has to hold a prisoner for an amount of time, and the law is followed, then he can release the innocent man. But when others find out, they may think it unethical and wrong that he did not bring the prisoner to trial. Even though the jailor acted in accordance with his own perception of right, or even society's perception of right. We now see clearly what differentiates the three concepts. We see morals as the view of *what is good*—right and wrong; ethics as the view of *how to be good*—conduct and duty; and law as *what you can do*—what you are allowed to do, with impunity. A law may be immoral or even unethical, just as something immoral may be ethical and lawful. The three are separate notions and not dependent on each other.

Both consciously and subconsciously we set moral standards. When subconsciously, it entails that all the impulses and instincts that drive us to live well, or survive at all, will set these values whether we are aware or not, and whether we want to or not. Consciously, it means that when one is intelligent enough to realize one's existence, then one is also intelligent enough to understand what can cause, or lead to, a loss of that existence, or how to better that existence, and therefore morals that serve this purpose will arise. By arise I mean that they will be created, accepted, embraced, or implemented because of the benefit seen in them to a way of living. The problem of setting these moral standards and ingraining them in people is that it puts everything in black and white, and moral condemnation is then sure to follow.

People find themselves questioning the world more than ever. In this day and age, where we have never had more answers, we still stumble around in the dark. The answer to why this is so dangles right in front of our eyes, really. The telling of what you should and should not do, and therefore what you should and should not want, is as prevalent and strong as ever. We are so indoctrinated today, or dare I say brainwashed through the media from early age, that most do not even stop and consider what the moral codes, or even laws, cause and do. You shall respect religion? Why? The least of things one should respect is religion. There is no positive proof of gods and such figments; the principles of science and the modern completely oppose the notion of the supernatural. Still, freedom of religion is guaranteed by law. A bundle of laws now also benefit the minorities, which they systematically exploit to no end. And even women's rights today is an issue. In the Western world, where woman is equal, she still wants more. The problem of having these laws is that they privilege these groups beyond the common citizen. In a society that is supposedly built on equality, there is no longer actual equality, and that is a recipe for disaster. Even free speech is curtailed or tailored according to certain dos and don'ts. Known as political correctness. The much used term "hate" or "hate crime" rules here. Anything that gets that label is a guaranteed taboo, or even a punishable offense to just talk about—what good is free speech anymore when it is not actually free? And anything can be this "hating". All it takes is for someone to be offended and the label is immediately used. Which are usually the religious, minorities, or women. The white man is miraculously never a victim. Ever. Instead, the white man is always the one to blame for everything. How did such thinking start? It is simple: the vilifying of the German after the Second World War, and consequently all Germanics and whites, has completely backfired. Even the Ashkenazi Jews, who have been the main instigators of this propaganda, have been feeling the effects of this. The "racist" fascist white man has boiled down to a simple association of just being white man. Racism is not what is attacked, either. It is only racism from whites that is a problem for them, because their deductive processes always end up with conjuring up the image of a—now completely fictionalized—National Socialist or fascist. So absurd and detached from reality is the view of these two political groups that they are not even a proper stereotype. What other human groups could garner such movie and book titles like "zombie Nazis from outer space" and other nonsense? A political group being compared to, and conflated with, the undead and extraterrestrials. This underscores where the extreme propaganda from post-WW2 has taken it, and how far from reality it really is. Why do I mention this? Because it is the staple of the moral landscape of today.

Through this thinking that evil exists, and consequently that there is something or someone that is evil, you have created a very powerful label. A label that can entail any number of things that follow logically from the principles set by Christianity and slave morality. If everything Christians or the Bible say is a good, then the opposite is therefore called evil. If I do not give to charity or I do not share my house or my food, then I am selfish and that is evil. If I do not embrace and love every human on Earth, then that is evil. If I do not forgive like Jesus did and what the Bible says with "turn the other cheek", then I am evil. Everything that goes against the Bible, Christianity, and their morals are then bad or evil. When a moral agenda has been set and ingrained into the public, you do not even need to label something evil or bad, really. You only need to point out what is good, and what you should do, and everything else follows. There are a number of such fallacies drawn from the democratic principles, for instance. Like free speech, and therefore you are not allowed to tell someone to be quiet, when they are completely ignorant on the topic of discussion. Or equality—if I value someone lesser or higher, then I break that notion and I am seen as bad. With the advent of socialism and social democracy came the notions of social rights, such as free healthcare and education, and here we also see this mindless attitude: If you have smoked for your entire life, you still feel entitled to healthcare. And you even think you should be prioritized. Or you are the dumbest person in the Western

Hemisphere, and you still think you should go to school. And if you get bad grades, you will blame the teacher, the school, or even the curriculum. Conclusively, most notions are seen as either good or bad, right or wrong, and therefore those who do not adhere to them, and accept them, will gain the opposite label. The classic false dilemma.

The change in morality of master into slave came about as a result of moving away from nature. From the massively populated world—now dominated by the masses whose primary enemy were other men—came the first revolt with the rise of Christianity. The second revolt came with moving one step further away from nature through industrialization, urbanization, and globalization, which resulted in the rise of socialism. Both of these were the result of values changing in society. And as values change, then so does everything else that hinges on them.

V. Love, Hate, and Envy

The strongest of your likes is love. These are the things that take priority in your life. The things you convince yourself that you cannot live without. They are the highest and strongest of your values. The notion of romantic love is so powerful and important, because it is intertwined with survival. The survival of life, which is the purpose and meaning of all living things. Reproduction is the greatest expression of survival that there is, and therefore the coming together of man and woman, which we tend to call romantic love, warrants the importance we place on it. If your blood lives on forever, you may also live on forever, in a sense, and that is why, when love manifests itself in a person, it is seen as the greatest of all loves.

What about the love of non-sexuality then? This love of your parents, your siblings, or other people of importance. It may not be seen as the greatest of loves—not these days anyhow—but through

Part Two: Mind

the thought that your family and bloodline also constitute a part of your survival, it is understandable why it evokes such great passion and emotion in us. This blood bond of your kinsmen, or some familiarity and expression of yourself thereof—like an authority figure or an idol of yours, or even a thing, a cause, or a movement—is, in essence, the same as the great love. The values that you share with this person, or thing, is why you show such love. The importance of it, and its survival, coincide with your own survival, in a way. You live on through that someone or something by a commonality that is felt as that of a blood-bound survival.

We may therefore conclude that the greatest love of all is simply that of yourself. If you sacrifice yourself for a romantic love or an idol, then it is that part of yourself you see in them that you react to save. It is a psychological reaction. A delusion of the mind, and not found commonly in nature at all. Animals do not sacrifice themselves for anyone; we see offspring readily abandoned all the time. They understand with basic instinct that they have to survive first and foremost. They sense that as they are capable of rearing offspring, and that they have survived thus far, then they are the better option for survival than new and fresh life. Life yet to be tested and proven. Or perhaps it is merely the egoism of the will to always prioritize itself and ensure its own survival. In any case, that is not to say that all self-sacrifice is nonsensical. To face death in war for the protection of your people—your race and kin—or to gamble your life when your children are in danger, is an act of risk assessment. And when you see that a loss, or a consequence of not taking action, spells certain doom to you and your kin's bloodline, then you are left with nothing to lose. Not much of a choice then: survive or die trying. Love conjures up such strong and extreme emotion because it is linked with that most important thing in life, which is the continuation and survival of life itself. And since we creatures of higher intelligence are able to foresee future threats and consequences, we therefore plan ahead and do things pre-emptively to secure our survival and to improve our well-being. The animal does not contemplate such things, and only deals with that which confronts it at each and every moment. To actively go out with a clear vision in mind and see it accomplished is therefore quite sophisticated thinking.

Positive emotion—your loves and likes—are always the default. They are the bases. This is because they are rooted in life and living, and as your love for your life and survival comes first, then this follows. One may argue that some only seek death, and this happens when hate of one's life is projected outward due to rationalization, and death then takes default position of value. Such men are only destructive, though, and as such they will not be accepted by any majorities, because life-affirmation is the pinnacle of society and civilization. Or life itself, actually. This destruction I speak of is not the one of other people and groups that oppose you, but the destruction of the self and all expressions of that instead. Which means your family, friends, society, your people, and your culture. Know that the need for the destruction of other people and nations can indeed be life-affirming if those are threats to that and those of your own.

Hate is never unfounded or ungrounded. Hate never springs to life and exists on its own. It always has some origin in positive emotion through value. Let's say that I came to hate blueberries because it made me sick, or I didn't like the taste and that made me strongly dislike it. I see that sickness then as a threat to my life and survival, or an awful taste as a threat to well-being—that good and pleasant survival in life. Hate and dislike always find some root in life itself. Life, which is the positive default of value and valuation. Love necessitates a diminished value of other things compared to it, or that which opposes it. If you do not value or love, then you will just end up being indifferent. One simply cannot accept and love everything, because most things are polar opposites. Therefore, by having a great love, then a great hate can follow. This also means that when you have few things you love, then you also hate less, and if you see yourself as very accepting or tolerant, then it may just be that you are very indifferent. To go around whimsically and say that you "love" this or that and whatnot makes you look like a dimwit then. Truth is that you do no truly love these things. And because of your ignorance of them—which is the reason why it can be said that you do not and cannot truly love them—then that is why you do not hate what stands in opposition to them—you are unaware of what they are, or unable to identify them.

We see, therefore, that the negative emotions of dislike are the equal countering emotional responses to when your positive emotions, and the things that constitute them, are threatened and in danger. So, when someone hates, you know that his loves are attacked. Or if these loves have been annihilated, then this hate can turn blind. This can result in the need for revenge, which is the equilibrium of loss. Or more precisely, revenge is the need to correct a previous injustice, or equalize because of it. And, as the words indicate, these wrongdoings stem from notions of equality and justice. As men see difference, and therefore haves and haves not, then this is why we seek to either appropriate for ourselves what others have—what we call equality or socialism—or we seek to take away from others when we do not have it, or they do not deserve it—what we call envy, justice, revenge, etc. They are the giving and taking away of the things that we see in terms of should and should not be. Right, and wrong.

From justice and equality, or what is correct and fair, envy arises. Envy is seeing something that someone else has, and then wanting it for yourself. Or the feeling that the ones who have it are not worthy of it. Which is why we generally do not feel envious of people who we feel have worked for it, or earned it in some way. Envy can arise swiftly, though, because it is hard to determine who has earned what, and how much physical and mental labour has gone into it. However, we do not go around envious of everyone and everything. Envy is mostly of the things that are very common and ordinary, and which we see ourselves lacking. Or if someone have gotten something, but are undeserving of it because of their bad personality, or a lack of effort and skill. Jealousy is something similar to envy, but what is envied here is affection. And as humans and living beings are the source of affection, then the possessor of affection is also one. Meaning that there always has to be a giver of affection and a receiver of affection, and the one which envies the receiver of affection, and consequently therefore cares about the one giving affection, stands outside. Always three parts or more. It seems that these two concepts are hard to differentiate and grasp by some people today—thanks to the perpetuated dumbing down of society—and they have started using the word jealousy, instead of envy, altogether.

VI. Moral Polarity

When one loves something that is opposite of what is politically correct today, then the diminished value one places in these things is interpreted as hate. Yes, it is hate to them, but understand, then, that what is politically correct and liked and loved by you is also deemed as hate and hateful by the opponents of these views. As I love my land, my people, and my culture, I therefore hate this unrestricted immigration, because I see the consequences of it as a direct threat, and in opposition, to what I love. Or I hate immigration and immigrants, as the politically correct would have it, but they never truly ask themselves the reason why. They will just shrug it off saying that one must be filled with hate to say such things, and then they resort to labels such as evil and hater. Moreover, they will say that it is something psychological, and that it is a mental disease. Anything, really, to make themselves feel better, which is nothing but blatant rationalization. The mind has to find a cause, and the simplest explanation to these ignoramuses is that there is something wrong, in one way or another, with that which confronts them. Why do they not seek truth? Because the truth is potentially a threat to their values, and if they found this truth, then they may have to change a lot of their values, or even their whole mind and mind-set. Which is a long and painful process, and sometimes causes real mental disease. In any case, this is the reason why it is seen as hateful if there is disagreement of opinion.

We can, however, become blinded by the things we love and hate through focusing on, and valuing, individual parts too much. If we find one very important thing, or opposing thing, then that may colour our entire view of the larger picture. When we see a high value placed, or a strong rejection, in disregard of other qualities, then this is what we call romanticizing or having blind hate, respectively. This mechanism is also why first impressions are important, because they take precedence and form the principal, strongest, and clearest view. This may fade over time, or it may linger on forever. This is also why people who fall in love with someone, that later on treats them badly and rejects them repeatedly, may continue to be in love. Although, rejection or being treated badly may serve to indicate higher value in the rejecter, and foster a sense of lower value in the rejectee, and therefore perpetuates it. Making the argument slightly moot. In any case, this falling in love with someone or something is that instant recognition of some great value. This is why it can be so hard to let it go, and the mind may rationalize away many great faults in order to hold on to something. We can also—through familiarity and the acceptance of later revelations—see faults as acceptable, useful, or simply rationalized into a good, or of a use, in the things we love and hate. This is the same as when the individual rationalizes with itself. It seeks to make it as easy, and least problematic, as it can for itself. We do know, however, that too much rationalization may build up to an intolerable amount, which may then break the mind from this pressure—this cognitive dissonance.

As there is only life or death, these two choices of either or, then it is this that causes the polarization of our valuation. Good, like, love, and holy on one side. Bad, dislike, hate, and evil on the other. And with love and Good stemming from life—life, which is the basis and default of life itself—then this is why love is seen as a greater force. By which I mean that love and Good comes from the valuation of what is good in, and for, life and its survival. This complex notion is very susceptible to fallacy and rhetorical trickery, however, and people commit them, and fall for them, very easily. This is because the love of life for one can be hate for another. To serve as an example: What is good for the panther is hunting and killing its prey. And as he loves himself and his survival, he therefore loves the death of the prey. The prey calls this evil because it loses its existence. And because the panther does not love the life of the prey, but his own instead, he is called hateful. Know that what is love and good for the panther is at the cost of what is love and good for the prey—they both value and want their survival. If the prey got it his way, and left the panther starving, the panther would see it in the same manner. This is what I mean when I say that Good and love is life-affirming, and bad and evil is life-denying, and that this is purely seen from the stance of life which beholds it, and not as some universal measure or truth.

That was exactly what happened, though. Christianity took this natural feeling of life-affirmation found in all individual life and universalized it, and then associated it with God, the Church, and scripture. This way it created a monopoly and joker card on what is right and wrong, and it could appeal to the sense of life-affirmation in the individual for support. Which was achieved through the fact that people constantly take this very subjective sense of worth and importance of one's own life—this will to live and survive—and then project it outward onto the world. It's not quite true that the Church has a monopoly, but it can be said that it is the originator of the moral agenda of today. Liberals have mastered this slave rhetoric in our time, and they persistently use the notions of charity, the embrace of all cultures and races, or being against war or any kind of killing, to their benefit. This they have taken from these Christian views on what is good and evil, which is indoctrinated into us at early age. Socialism, and communism, also use a number of notions from Christianity. Such as the needs of the group, and the large masses being more important than the few, or the individual. Which is much of the basis in the rest of their thinking in regards to everything. It should be said that communism embraced atheism for the sole purpose of removing the competition of another slave power—thereby having monopoly, as the communist state has in all things—in order to build a blindly fanatic religion of their own.

The moral notions of today may be conflated into what I would call utilitarian life-affirmation: a moral agenda that seeks to maximize the greatest number of life-affirming actions. In other words, it seeks to deny any restrictions on life, and is therefore completely at odds, and out of touch, with nature.

VII. Shame, Fear, and Laughter

You get the feeling of shame and embarrassment from a perceived attack or threat to your character. This is usually due to a lowering of your value and worth, and could be through a loss of control in a situation, or through a revelation and failure to conceal something. Specifically, embarrassment is a superficial, circumstantial lowering of worth that leaves no deep imprint of failure and lowered value in your person and character—what was done was merely a common mishap. Shame, however, is something deeply rooted that gnaws on you, because the thing of shame is seen as something expected of you by standards set by yourself or society. And if you fail to do what is expected of you, it diminishes your worth according to others or yourself, because what is expected is normal, and what is normal sets a standard, and if you cannot live up to that standard, then your worth, on average, is lower than that of others. Or, similarly, a discrepancy between expected or intended outcome and actual outcome; to fail to match action with result. And so, if you err in such things, you show that you are inexperienced or ignorant in what you are doing. And as there is embarrassment in this inexperience or ignorance—when it is in things that one is otherwise expected to have an experience or knowledge of—there comes a diminution or loss of value and worth because of that failure. Value or worth is in direct connection with ability, and being able to deal with threats—or should I say life?—is basically survival. Embarrassment also has the tendency to trigger further embarrassment, because with it comes the unavoidable bodily act of blushing, which indicates doubt, and doubt is a sign of insecurity, ignorance, and any number of negative traits. The reason why shame may not always trigger blushing is because it is expected by the person in question, or he has become used to people knowing. It may still bother the person, but he has experienced it so many times, and he has thought of it so much without having found any solutions, that it has become rooted in him. It has become a given.

A shamelessness in a person, apart from this desensitization or that of a difference of values such as other cultural norms, tells us of an absence of standards or values, and thus there are no expectations. Shameless we call such behaviour that is outrageous to us; we are condemning their values and ways, because we would feel ashamed if we were in their situation. And many people do in fact have such a response—called vicarious shame. More colloquially we call it cringe-inducing, cringeworthy, and we say that "it is hard to watch", or that it left us with a feeling of, or that there were, awkwardness. Shame is from a threat and danger to the mental image of something, or yourself—what one should and should not do is a big part of that image—and shame is therefore something that is bound to intelligence in some manner. An animal has no true shame, and so we see that this is attributed to intelligent behaviour. But it is also a sign of being civilized, or being learned and well-behaved as we say, which boils down to being knowledge. Complex knowledge is reliant upon certain levels of intelligence, and some animals therefore pick up on our societal rules. Such as dogs who can also feel shame of some sort, when they are caught doing something that they know they are not allowed to. The feeling of what is right and wrong is a powerful thing, and this is why law and crime prevention can be so successful through the proper use of it. One should also know, then, that it is normal to be embarrassed, even if an action was purely accidental and not something of great concern or consequence. Such as tripping, dropping something, or accidentally pushing something over. If a blushing and embarrassment occurs, it serves as an indicator to let us know that the person is aware that this out of the normal behaviour. But if a person were not to do this, then we can take it that he doesn't care, and as a consequence he does not have the values that we expect of him. Like a wild or untrained animal he is then, or even worse, because all civilized humans are taught what is right and wrong—these values and morals—throughout their lives. And so, if we meet one that is not aware of when his behaviour is wrong, we may conclude that he is a sociopath, or just extremely dumb. If it had been a domesticated animal having such aberrant behaviour, and showing such failure to conform, then that would also have been deemed damaged and not normal.

One of the most recognizable features of embarrassment and shame is becoming red in the face, and with a warmth that accompanies it. What we call blushing. This is due to a natural physiological response that is similar to fear, but because the threat is internal, and as such mental, the body rushes blood the head. This internally perceived threat is thus countered with the only way it can get out of it—namely, thinking. The flushing of bodily areas indicate increased activity, obviously, and the warmth experienced is because of this blood rush. It simply heats up in the same way as any body part would do when flushed with blood. A heating of the head is quite natural when the brain is overloaded or worked hard—as most should have experienced in their lives. The body responds with increased blood flow to prepare for this perceived necessity, which is to think and figure something out in order to find a way out of this threat and danger as fast as possible. This is quite similar to the way fear is shown in the body and its preparation for a threat. The external threat. Which it does by emptying itself to lighten the load, for instance. Or it prepares muscles for fight or flight by adrenaline and blood rush. The blood rush to the muscles and body is the opposite of that blood rush to the head of that internally perceived threat, and it therefore drains the head and all other parts into the muscles. This loss of blood that leaves the face pale is why we become white with fear—as is commonly said. And as the face is the most visible and empathetic of bodily features, and its numerous amount of muscles make it a large retainer of blood, then that is why it is so easily seen on the face when the body acts in accordance with these situations.

Another physiological feature I'd like to address is laughter. This evocation is a response to when the body or mind feels good. One of the most normal ways of feeling good is to experience new sensations, or sensations that are rare and not frequent. And that is why it is not uncommon to actually laugh in a state of physical relaxation or ecstasy, without any humour or perceived fun being involved at all. The way humour takes the mind away from stress and troubles is the same as how relaxation and comfort brings relief to the body. This feeling of lightness, and being carefree and unworried, in such moments, trigger this physiological response of laughter, which is a reaction to the strange and unusual sensation of being happy and comfortable in some way. This mental or physical relaxation will transmit itself throughout the body, and with it comes an increase in endorphin levels, among other things. The combination of these things, such as the endorphins lightening and easing up the body, the relaxation of muscles, etc., may cause laughter in the way that they might just be body spasms, or spasms in certain parts of the body, that come about as a resultant. And with man being as vocal as he is, it is not strange that he would voice himself of, and with, such sensations. As we tend to do in most things. With laughter, or the sensations that cause it, there comes a number of accompanying positive effects. When such spasms of the body happen, it may have beneficial effects that muscle spasms and the likes have: it stretches muscle and tissue, and uses muscle that may not be otherwise much utilized—it trims the body and awakens it. And there is also body and brain stimuli. Like endorphin release, increase in dopamine levels, and any number of effects, really. Most of which increase the feeling of well-being. This, then, is our body rewarding and encouraging us to engage in certain behaviours, such as physical exertion or relaxation in whatever form, be it leisure, entertainment, etc. Our body tends to drive us toward laziness and comfort so that we do not wear ourselves out. But too much of everything, or too little for that matter, is never a good. And that is why man has found the need for moderation, or to push himself and do the things he doesn't want to, even if it is tedious and hard. Too much laziness and idleness can do just as much harm to the body as too much work; but our intelligence recognizes our limits and needs, and any long term consequences and effects.

A final point on vocalization. Animals generally tend to vocalize and make sounds according to their moods and needs. As we hear sound, and feel vibration, we are aware of it in some manner. It is therefore natural that we not only send out responses to others, but also for ourselves as we take sensation in whatever action. This makes us feel alive because of that subconscious reminder of activity around us, even if only our own—no activity is like a lifelessness or death. That is why we sing to ourselves, and make all kind of noises, sounds, and notes—the need for greater variety of these different sounds led to the creation of musical instruments. And when we like these different sounds and put them in a certain order, we have made a tune or a melody. Which is the composing of mood and emotion.

VIII. Wisdom and Opinion

Everyone has an opinion. We have to, and ideally should, opine on most things, as it is how we valuate the world. They are the likes and dislikes of life, which is part of our reaction system and helps to keep us safe. We very often make subconscious decisions about things, and this is usually learned at very early age—indeed, an early start and good upbringing sets a good pace and path in life. As we learn, we get a better and better opinion through observing ourselves and others during a lifetime. This is wisdom. Wisdom is not necessarily synonymous with being intelligent or well-informed, however. It is merely the collection of a number of rights and wrongs seen in a lifetime. And as most people tend to improve themselves and their situation throughout life, then an accumulation of finding the right, and then doing right, is predominant over what is wrong. Being wise therefore means being right. Or at least relatively right, because being wise is still, to a great degree, dependent on oneself and others. Which means that an opinion is most of the time just an opinion, and thus not right. This is because situations tend to be too complex and relative for us to judge a clear right or wrong in them, and also because progress may stagnate, and people may conform to a more comfortable or convenient way of doing things. Therefore, an opinion may be hampered by the individual or the situation itself. Hampered by the individual because he may not be too clever or intelligent, or he may simply be doing something out of habit or tradition. Or a situation may cause us to do something a certain way for convenience or comfort. Wisdom, being a sum of this right opinion in a group or society, will therefore base itself on these opinions and ways. Even when they are faulty, or plain wrong. Meaning that it may not help being wise in a society that is primitive or very ill-informed. A wise man will thus only be of proper use in those respective societies and ways of life, and not always universally or generally. Wise men are still of great value, though, seeing as they are individuals who are usually very intelligent and thoughtful. And one has to be, if one is to learn so much more than others, and always being able to change and adapt to a better way of doing things. This means that not all can become wise. Old age itself is not a prerequisite for wisdom, nor is it a given that old people are wise. One may be wise at a young age through being quick to learn and intelligent to remember it all; and there are old people who are still as foolish as they were when they were young.

Opinion is based on what we know, and as knowledge is based on experience or education, there is a correlation. An informed opinion is made by one who has dealt with and studied the item or topic in question. Informed opinions are more specific than just a wise or clever way of doing things, meaning that they are not general or easily assessed. An informed opinion is formed from a very attentive, focused, and ultimately well-considered outcome and conclusion by comparison, correlation, and that of macroscopic concerns. We can only call an opinion informed when one has spent a great amount of time and effort considering it. An informed opinion is therefore an expert opinion. A quick and easy way of doing something or thinking about something may be completely right, but it is not informed, and it will not be until that same conclusion is based on a larger number of data, statistics, evidence, and the likes. Are all things worth, or do they merit, spending an enormous amount of dedicated time researching and studying? Not always. Sometimes a simple and easy answer, action, or value is enough. We do have a scientific studies on most things, though. Albeit, this is because of parallel uses and such, and not directly because one had to know for that specific reason. For instance, we do not need to study air for the purpose of finding out if we should breathe or not. We do, however, study the composition of air for a number of other reasons. Like the required composition of gases, such as oxygen, for the ignition of flammable compounds and materials, optimal mixture for efficient burning, etc. And so, much of the information and studies we have today, even about the most strange and useless of things, are mostly incidental—a by-product of some other or greater study.

"You are entitled to your opinion", they say. Yes, you can and certainly should have one, but to hold on to it no matter what, and also feel the need to tell it, as some sort of right afforded to you, is something else. We do not need or want to hear an opinion. Instead, we need something useful and truthful. Only when you can confidently show that you have an informed opinion should you be allowed to speak on important issues and expect to be heard. Otherwise, you are just another noisemaker that pines for attention. One that has no knowledge or insight into the discussion or topic at hand. You then only serve to occupy the space, or spend the time, of someone who may have had useful contributions. And may even have solved the issue itself.

Philosophizing and finding truth: To seek out the very factors that enable or drive conclusions, and to be so objective, and have such clarity, that one sees these factors. To start from a blank slate, and to behold a thing from above, and judge it without the bias of the vessel which perceives it. To look at a topic, and then ask: what could have caused it, what necessitated it, and what is the most reasonable explanation?

IV. The Good and Positionism

What is seen as "good" today is a mix of utilitarianism and protection of the individual. Almost opposites they are, but in general it is the thought that everyone should pursue their happiness and always have it the best as possible. A socialist capitalism, where everyone is taken care of, but some are taken care of better than others—almost like the ending to *Animal Farm*. And it has become a right not to struggle, strive, and become better today. Undoubtedly, competition is as shallow as can be. Only in economics and politics a leftover of nature is found. And what do they compete for in these areas? Just money. Which is, again, only a means to their pursuit of happiness. The way they achieve success in these fields is by manipulation, lies, and dancing around the laws, discarding ethics and morals as they go. And because of this it can hardly be called an intellectual competition, either. Only the promotion of the immoral and, dare I say, evil. Little does it indicate smarts or intellectual capacity to do what law-abiding citizens would not. It is only a competition of crime, and not a competition of who has a better product. And a poor ideal it sets for the population. It only begets more crime, because people will see no reason to be upstanding citizens at all when even the richest and most powerful of people are rotten to the core. These higher-ups are idols to the people, and supposed to be exemplary in conduct and behaviour, but instead they spit in the face of law and government. Yes, examples they set and the people follow. Unfailingly. How easily the weak willed and those lacking in self-respect are corrupted this way.

Out of one's values a number of beliefs and premises emerge. Those who only believe in living individual lives full of hedonism will only care about themselves and any and all politics, religions, etc., that will benefit them. Know that by your beliefs, and what you hold to be most important, your priorities will be exposed. A position will emerge clearer for every piece of information that is uncovered; in every given position of belief the stance can be explained by the values held. And even though an absolutely moral right or wrong, good or evil, is purely fictional, it can be said that there is a conclusively right or wrong in most situations. This can be said for something manufactured like a well-produced car versus a shabby made one, and it can be said for ambitions, goals, art, politics, etc., as well. You only need to examine intentions and values, and then compare between the many different ones, and you will then be able to find and distinguish between the noble and ignoble of values and goals.

What is a Good then? It must be something linked to nature and the natural. And what is more natural than the survival of life? And as the survival of one individual is not conducive to the survival of that specific life—the species, or that expression of life—then it must go beyond just the individual. The Good is the survival of the plural then. From the smallest to the greatest group. But does this involve all then? No, because only a few are worthy enough by their superior skill and ability to merit them having the right to procreate on behalf of the rest. The ants in the ant-colony: they are all needed, or at least wanted, for the function of the colony, but only a few are good enough to start and build a colony on. People of worth are found through competition in the form of physical and intellectual struggle and comparison. So, when they show throughout their lives that they are significantly better in some respects, and of course better on average than most, then they have merited their rise and their privilege to breed.

The current liberal agenda, or the neo-communist/communist one, and even most if not all of the religious ones, are destructive in regards to planet, flora, and fauna, and consequently and most importantly to us humans. They jeopardize the future of humanity and our evolutionary progress instead of building on and around it—that which nature did before, and still does out in the wild. This book's positionist stance is finding the best course of action for the survival of mankind and the highest and most evolved elements of our species and the different races thereof. Ever-ascending evolutionary progress and survival, in other words. This is the Good. Terming my philosophical stance positionism is quite fitting as well, since it is my conviction that all values, and the views that follow, are seen as right and true purely from the position from which they are seen. Meaning that whatever you want and value are therefore always the premises of the path then taken, or a path that is at least seen as right and proper, even if not adhered to. This path is what we call a belief or a system of beliefs.

Association

I. Memory Structure

The connections we form in our mind are made at very early age. From the pathways and assignments in the brain, they work in conjunction with each other, and it is these who assign value from the physiological response of sense stimuli. This is what forms memory. All the various patterns of imprint are different according to what physical action was taken, but also from what other patterns that are already there from prior imprints. The mind builds early on by simplicity, and from there it builds larger and more complex and conjoined patterns throughout for our mode of being and doing. We are shaped early in age on what we prefer or not, and what we connect to a thing. All images of these things are gained from our experiences, and these have an association with all the factors in the situation we got it from, and their dependent previous imprints on the mind. And also from value: Was it good or bad? Right or wrong? Association assign these positives and negatives for the reason of helping us to quickly identify and determine if there is a danger. A variety and difference of experience helps us at young age from getting too set in our ways, and to explore other possibilities and options more readily. Too often people narrow their focus and likes too much. Acquired taste, as it is called. And more often than not, it is the rich and spoiled who have this sort of privilege—this privilege of tastes. It does not foster bravery, that's for sure. It is natural that this should occur, however. Animals and nature also tend to narrow their focus, likes, and preferences. We see the consequence of this in evolutionary specialization. And how catastrophic it can be when their main tactic of survival, this specialization—which they had adapted to in such a degree that it neglected all other strengths, and has left them vulnerable or utterly incapable of surviving in other ways—is no longer viable due to a change in nature, because of extinction, introduction of various flora and fauna, or climate change. Still, life is driven to specialization, because if there is less to perfect, it conserves energy in the long run, and it leaves the body, and the species, able to adapt much easier and faster. Our intelligence can counter this, though. Through our intellect we are able to understand the need to push ourselves. To test out new, uncomfortable boundaries.

Let us return to the discussion of association—this powerful tool of the mind. The mind finds familiarity and ease in the things it has encountered earlier and grown used to, and this is why that what was learned, and the impressions had at young age, may stick for life. Like the hatchling who found someone, anyone, early on and developed a sense of belonging and kinship to this image and figure of familiarity, and to which he is unable to intelligently realize that he may be different to, or as to why he feels that bond. All he does know—having learnt—is that it is there and does no harm, and it gives nurture and comfort, and this is why he feels secure around it. This dependability which does not shake the senses, due to regularity, dulls him and habituates him; he is less alarmed and wary than he would be to anything new. Everything that is new makes the mind question and speculate what it is, what it does, etc. It is all a matter of expectations, really. Trust is gained through familiarity, and so when trust is broken, something unexpected happened and familiarity was lost.

All these mind connections—these associations—are not easily broken, because the mind is built in that gradual, interconnected, and dependent way. Similar to a building, or a spider's web, if you will. To illustrate:

Take out the blocks at the base, or pull at the anchored strings, and the structural integrity will falter, or even collapse. This is how it is with our mind, also. And if we were to do so, to start pulling on these strings, without strengthening or rebuilding the structure to prevent collapse, then the mind would experience unpleasant cognitive dissonance. This is where rationalization comes into play, which is the use of building blocks and web strings to act as temporary solutions and fixes. And they may do the job, for a while at least, but in the long run it is better to build a more proper structure of solid and durable material. Such a structure is much harder to build, and thus takes more time and effort, but it would be much stronger for it. The flimsy structures, however, we notice by their haphazard construction and their makeshift solutions, and they almost always collapse in strong winds. Yes, quite easily these ramshackle huts are damaged. And by simple tests we see how faulty they are, and just a huff can sometimes send them crashing down—should one wish to do so and destroy the living arrangements that these people have made for themselves. A truly solid structure is best built according to a proper plan and consideration early on. The earlier and better planned it is, the better one knows what materials to use, and how to weave it all together so that they fit and do their job properly. Or at least have a solid foundation to build on, because improvement and repair is likely to happen.

II. Involuntary Association

A thought is not easily removed or supplanted if put there. It weaves itself in whether one wants it to or not. Even when completely untrue and contradictory. It sits there like a monolith, taking up space and blocking the view, and seemingly too heavy to remove on your own. This is the force and potency of the word, and if uttered repeatedly, and over time, this monolith will become a monument of the ages. The power of association is such that if lies and half-truths are told over and over again through propaganda, or just through pure ignorance, then the mind will connect these notions together. Memory is not voluntary. And how could it be? After all, nature had us learn and remember from even the smallest impressions made on the mind, because this was what worked, and this therefore lived on. And so, by each mention of something, the mind will imprint and then remember. This is why propaganda and indoctrination is so powerful. As the communists have shown us, and a horrid but valuable lesson that was. Nowhere in history has brainwashing, and the attempts to perfect it, gone as far as with them. And their successor states, and still extant communist regimes, still continue this practice. With mixed results: a great effect on their own ignorant population, but a complete failure on a global level, and to which they only serve as a source of laughter and amusement. But even capitalism exploited the impressionable mind to fulfil their most important goal—the making of profits. And this they achieved with advertisement, which is really just propaganda and indoctrination of products: You can't stop thinking about it because of the repetitive message, and eventually you start believing in this message that tells you of a need for it. This perceived need soon turns into an effort to procure it, in order to alleviate this very natural urge for that which is assumed to be beneficial. Consciously or subconsciously, involuntary thoughts are that easily planted. Let's say that you are told throughout life that dogs are dangerous and vicious. Yet, you do not experience this, and you even read and watch a lot about dogs, which tells you that the opposite is probably true. And you may even meet and experience dogs—leaving you with nothing but a good impression. So one would think that the mind would disregard the faulty information that paints the dog as vicious. But it won't, because any information is still information. When an animal experiences, it gets information, and this always leaves an imprint on mind and behaviour. We humans, however, are not only able to get information through our own experiences, but also through other mediums, such as language, that tells us a story that we process in the same way as if it actually happened to us. This capacity of humans to imagine, fantasize, and speculate is quite remarkable. If someone told you some absurdity that you have never heard anyone dispute—like that there was a mouse with poison fangs and wings—then your mind would automatically create a mental image of such a thing. And if told over and over, this picture becomes more vivid. And then the fantasy may also be put in an environment, and the creature may even get a behaviour attributed to it. Imagination always runs wild, and if assisted it will sometimes run so wild that it borders on mental derangement. The lesson learned is that both false and true associations affect us, and will impact our personality and therefore our behaviour.

Words themselves can have a profound impact. If you have two words that sound the same phonetically, or look the same, then they may also start becoming associated with each other. Or a word that is commonly used in one situation, but stated in another—even though it is perfectly acceptable to use it there—may conjure up the image of that common usage. Or you can connect and associate two words or things by using them together. Like in the same sentence, for example. Even when it is a negative statement. If I said "the rabbit is not a maniacal serial killer with clown make-up, carrying an axe", you would still picture such a thing wouldn't you? This was a rather fantastical statement, though, and uttering it would not make it very believable. But you may still evoke such an image in your mind afterwards; or if you were to hear any of those words on their own. Especially if the statement and image had made a strong impression.

And if a statement could be believable, but still not true, then no proper barrier would stop you from doubting it—if you were not aware of, or capable of, seeing the truth, that is. The liberals tend to call the conservatives greedy and rich. And since privatization, for instance, is a very central pillar of conservatism, then the statement of them being greedy and money oriented will ring true, because they are analogous, even if not the same. So, if something merits a truth or is otherwise believable, it will be readily accepted. Yes, subtlety is, without a doubt, the master of persuasion. Easier it is to have a person come to a conclusion on his own, since the least opposed and firmest held ideas and opinions are always the ones you have arrived at by yourself (or so one thinks)—stubbornness we call it. A gentle push, or better yet, the carrot on the stick, is much better than something forced and imposed—the whip. You only want to do what your mind and will drives you to do, after all. Which tends to be something familiar, because it does not oppose your beliefs, or your natural self.

Rhetoric is the clever use of words, formulations, and associations to convince the listener of accepting a conclusion. As such, it shows its power and use again and again. This is the reason why Plato rebuked the sophists. And they are somewhat comparable to politics and politicians of today, where facts and dialectics still take the backseat to simplicity of just debating. Debate, which is nothing but personal opinion and rhetoric. And it works when the audience is stupid and ignorant. This audience, who has the power to place those who sway them into positions of government—or should I say trick them?

It is worth noting that the nature of words are such that they may only be tools to contrast and distinguish with, instead of actually being defining and specifying. If I state that something is green, then all that tells us is what it's not, which is any other colour. The word green therefore means not red, not blue, etc. Or a light green would tell us that it is not dark green, or viridian, teal, or perhaps even cyan. The word green thus came about because there was something to distinguish, and a need to distinguish it. Another good and much known example is the Inuit and his many words for snow and ice. There are many different states of ice and snow in colder areas, and so they have a much larger number of words to distinguish them. But in warmer areas, where there is little or no snow or ice at all, then there is no need or even a possibility to do so. People would not know or understand, because there is nothing for them to identify and therefore nothing to distinguish. Furthermore, this tells us that where there is higher complexity, then there has to be a larger vocabulary if there is to be understanding. Or at least when it comes to mutual understanding through communication and the transmittal of information. Hence, a complexity, and the need to understand and distinguish the things in this complexity, fosters growth of vocabulary, which then furthers and enables abstract thought, learning, and understanding, and a greater need or use of memory and intelligence follows.

The mechanism to prevent us from believing in nonsense is truth, basically. And if we are careful to analyse a situation thoroughly, then we are able to deduce what is true or not. A good technique to understand a viewpoint or action is to put yourself in their place—to take a side and go from there. This is especially important and useful if you utterly detest and despise the other point of view. Bear in mind that there is always a reason for something, and finding it is better than dismissing it in pure ignorance or by shallow emotional response and then labelling it as immoral, hateful, and whatever else. Only by having full knowledge of the problem, and all sides to it, can you fully tackle it. In any case, it doesn't hurt knowing the opposing side and their mentality. Or as Sun Tzu said: "Know your enemy."

III. Revisionism and Negationism

It is not easy to find objective information in the world. Obscurantism and half-truths are not only common, but the starting point and foundation of almost all knowledge these days. Indeed, the political agenda paints almost all fields of science. And where the Western world has its truths, then so, too, does Russia and China have theirs—they are all patriotic, nationalistic, and politically correct "truths". They are certainly not independently objective, these truths, and they are never properly questioned. The Western world has managed to have their political viewpoint of history become accepted in most parts of the world today. This they have done by creating a common history that is palatable for former colonial states and other underdogs of history. I am not saying that Western historiography is wrong, but only that it has become distorted, with some events and viewpoints being diminished, and others enhanced, to fit this political agenda. The Russians and Chinese do the same, yet they have garnered the label of conducting historical revisionism (what they are doing is negationism, more precisely)—a label for which it is hard to disagree with, in any case—but Western historians fail to see how this can also apply to themselves to a great extent. Even if, and when, they do not do it in such a lying and purely deceitful manner as these two previous and current cradles of communism. If one can even call the state capitalist run China that anymore. Revisionism is nothing but a label put on people who offer their study and opinion on history and events. Although, I do acknowledge that there is actual twisting and rewriting of history occurring, and as such the label may be true at times—even though the word itself is wrong by definition. This effort to peddle or fit selective truths or half-truths by the current political agenda is seen in many places and ways, and even in the West, which repeatedly likes to use such labelling. To make my accusations credible I will shed light on a few and very common ones:

We have all heard the story that Marie Antoinette said "Let them eat cake". This is done today to illustrate some kind of insensitivity and ignorance of the aristocracy and monarchy, and also to show a difference in resources and living standards. The only problem is that this saying is not true at all. It was never said by Marie Antoinette or any other aristocrat. It is loosely connected to Rousseau, and even that is dubious. The saying itself is also very imprecise and twisted compared to its original. Another such saying is the famous "Power tends to corrupt, absolute power corrupts absolutely" by Lord Acton. Which would have you believe that it refers to authoritarian governments and leaders being bad or corrupt in some way. In other words, it indirectly promotes democracy by denouncing authoritarianisms in any form, be it monarchy or communism. The quote is incomplete, though. The full quote is "Power tends to corrupt, absolute power corrupts absolutely. Great men are always bad men". This alters the meaning. This more complete quote tells us that being in power and control necessitate decisions that will always be scrutinized and questioned in some way or other; you are corrupted by the actions needed to be taken in that position. It is basically saying that if you want to be in control and get something done, then you have to get your hands dirty. When the right and proper action is taken, it may have negative side-effects, but these are not important or they may simply be a necessary evil, because the decision resulted in providing the right solution and fixed the problem. Hence, any man can be seen in a bad light by making the hard and tough, but right and proper, decisions. It is the implication of being in government by these necessary actions taken, or just the things that are beyond your control. Like that of war imposed upon you, or famines, floods, etc. Something always happens that can put you in a bad light. That is my interpretation at least. I am aware that in its original context Lord Acton was referring to the wrongful acquittal of men in power as compared to those in lower positions for equal or lesser crimes, and so it does not support my speculative analysis all that much. Most of this twisting of quotes and notions is due to political motives. Plato's Cave Allegory is repeatedly misunderstood and falsely represented today. This is probably because of the modern resentment and slander of Plato, which is itself rooted in his denouncement of democracy and having deemed it as the worst of governments. Another one is Hitler's Big Lie. Which is the explanation of why people usually dismiss a small lie—since most of us tell small lies, and they are everywhere, and quite trivial—but a big lie is readily accepted, because of the credibility in the scope of it, and the sheer audacity in telling it. That is to say, people are incapable or unwilling to believe that anyone would actually be so shameless as to tell such a huge lie—a lie that may be too complex and unfathomable for ordinary people to understand in the first place—and they therefore avoid a potentially painful confrontation with truth by just accepting it. What Hitler was referring to was the Jews and their fabrication of big lies. Today, however, it is being represented as some sort of formula for something he was going to use himself. This is reinforced by the extreme stupidity in that because we call it Hitler's Big Lie, they attribute it as a lie he made or planned on making, and not to the fact that it was named so after the one who discovered it and coined the phrase—as is conventional and normal practice. In any case, this is one of the easier ones to expose, because proof can be found in *Mein Kampf* itself that it is completely taken out of context. In there it is assigned to the Jews and their lies, and how they get away with it, and as such it would be more proper to call it the *Big Lie of the Jew* instead to avoid any further confusion regarding this term. But they have gotten away with it thus far—and ironically the Big Lie itself has become a big lie and an example of its original meaning—because most people do not read *Mein Kampf*, and in some countries it is actually illegal to have it and read it. Freedom of information?—even in National Socialist Germany you were not forbidden to have whatever books you wanted, and the book burnings that they had were merely symbolic as a show of dedication and belief in the cause. Book burnings and bans in the Allied and communist countries was of a different and much more evil and sinister sort: only intended to stifle the flow of information and truth. Lastly, exposing the lies about Plato is not as easy as these others, because even though you may read Plato, and freely at that, it is not certain you will understand and grasp what he is actually saying. And if you are given an incorrect explanation and interpretation, it may sound right because of some partial truth or fallacy. With that in mind, it may even be that the untruthful representation made by these people is perhaps not attributed to some agenda at all, but only to their sheer incompetence, and their failure to comprehend what they read.

There are history and events that the West do not want people to question, study, or debate at all. And in the case of the Holocaust it is even illegal to do so. Illegal to do scientific and historical studies! And if these occur, and results are found that contradict what is currently peddled, then this is when they use this label of revisionism. What the Russians and the West are doing is to leave information out, or enhancing some that serve their purpose. And not conducting new research at all, which is what actual revisionism means: to revise—the act of reconsidering or altering a thing in light of new information. The modification of history when new evidence is found, in other words. An example of proper, justified historical revisionism would be changing the name of Arabic numerals into Hindu numerals, because that is their actual origin. Or simply into European numerals, because this is where the transformation into the recognizable form we have today happened. The only thing the Arab did was to carry with him the practice from India.

And so, what the West, Russia, and other states are doing is negationism, and not revisionism, because if it was the latter, they would actually look at the new information found instead of just dismissing it, and then magnifying and diminishing whatever suits them best. Example being this distortion and twisting of quotes and terms that I spoke of. Such dismissal and distortion of information is the same thing as making information ineffectual, which is the very definition of negating. Revising, on the other hand, is science. After all, to research and find new information, and revisiting and reviewing the old, is the foundation for progress and advancement—finding higher truths. To say that some things are off-limits, and that they are eternal truths when they are not even facts, and that they are not even willing or interested in hearing or considering a thing, is horrendous, and is tantamount to religious dogma. Or it actually is dogma: they have made up their mind, and it is set in stone; this is how it is and that is final. Is that what freedom of thought and speech, and even truth, is? Some truth!—that you have to be told what it is, and not allowed to discover for yourself. Or even question or study. And this is by the same leftist political agenda accusing the Roman Catholic Church of intolerance and dogmatism, but even they had more leniency than this.

IV. Presentism

This historical arrogance is another problem of today, because what is the condemnation of the actions of the Christian Church if nothing but presentism? We do this relentlessly and thoughtlessly today, and it is quite common: thinking that we are better than people of the past. Almost everyone does this. Even our intelligentsia and elite. They definitely take advantage of it, that's for sure. I doubt most people are aware of the concept, though. It is, after all, not wanted that the people should be aware of the mechanisms that control them. And presentism does help the current agenda, because if they can distance themselves from any and all past events, and always paint themselves as better and more advanced than that of older times, then they can maintain an impression of superiority in the eyes of common man—that we live in continually "better times". For who does not believe that we are better today? We think we are morally better, certainly; but what is that but moral absolutism? We think we run a better state: "Surely, those outdated dinosaur states were corrupt and incompetent", we say with great confidence, whilst the Western world is more plagued with crime and corruption than ever before. We also think we are smarter and more knowledgeable, and this is reinforced by constantly impressing ourselves, and fascinating our minds, with newer and newer technological gadgets and our "mastery" of them—technological marvels so easy to use that even monkeys can handle them. But the truth is that we are dumber in terms of knowing history and politics than ever before, and our mathematical skills are dubious at best. Most people don't even read books anymore. Not counting sappy romance and fiction novels, that is. We also generally think ourselves more physically fit than those of earlier ages, but we know that this is not true. Even our grandparents lived longer lives than we do today. Attributively, they worked hard, and ate moderately due to a necessity of thrifty budgeting. And consider the Romans, marching all over the world, and working the soil as farmers. Or the Vikings, sailing and rowing throughout and beyond the known world—from the shores of the North American continent to the busy ports of the Eastern Mediterranean. But the average couch potato thinks himself pretty active if he should do anything at all, or if he can just stay slim. People are plainly and simply too ignorant to know any better. And by only seeing very average people in their lives, from the politician to the celebrity—these poor excuses for idols—to compare themselves with, then how could they possibly know?

This comparing, and the prevailing general ignorance, is why presentism takes such a hold of us. The information we are fed today through books, TV, news, etc., are all presentismic, and as a result this will continue to propagate these views in people. If, for example, you saw a documentary on Vikings, and all you were told was murder, plunder, and mayhem, then you would not know anything else about them, and attribute only those things to them. But if you were told the whole truth about them, such as their popular assemblies, their laws and their respect for them, and their hierarchical society, you would start to empathize and understand. This hierarchy and societal structure merits a bit of enunciation:

In Viking society, and in Germanic society throughout history, there was a clear line of distinction between the legislative, the judicial, and the executive. The same model as the separation of power, the tripartite principle, in government which we have today. In the popular assemblies, a legislative and elective power was vested. These assemblies were called *things* (ting) and were held a certain number of times, and on certain dates, during the course of a year—or convened if needed otherwise. All free men and women were able to attend and speak there. They spoke and debated on laws and prospective laws, and they voted on implementing those they felt were needed. They also elected officials to magisterial posts, which were usually older and trusted members of society: the elders—also called lawspeakers. These elders constituted the judiciary, and they had power in their district to interpret law, and to judge people and cases as they saw fit. The popular assemblies also elected leaders: the kings and chieftains, and their lawmen—the executive branch. And yes, they, too, were bound by law. They had powers of state, and their first and foremost duty was to protect the people, and to uphold the law and bring criminals before the elders. They also executed the laws according to the judgement of the elders. So, if a ruling was fines, banishment, execution, or whatever else, then the leaders would make sure it was carried out. Kings were usually only elected in wartime. However, in areas of constant warfare it was often deemed necessary for efficiency and convenience to make kingship a permanent position. A holmgang, a duel in Viking society, was a trial by blood. In cases where both parts demanded blood, or where there had been committed a grievous injury, then such a trial was permitted, or even demanded. It was not always to the death, and if you showed bravery through the act of actually showing up and being willing to fight and bleed in combat, and competent enough not to be killed during it, then the elders may have deemed it sufficient. It was a great shame in these warrior societies not to show up, obviously, and in some cases, where a great offence had been committed, you could be declared a *niding* (coward), and even be declared an outlaw, for not showing up for the duel. Being a niding was not unlawful in itself, but you would be a social outcast for it. If you were greatly outmatched by the opponent you were pitted against in the holmgang, or old and otherwise incapable, you would be allowed a substitute. If one was willing, that is. Holmgang had the habit of being abused by great warriors and berserkers that claimed insult and injury wherever they could profit, and it became such a public nuisance, and outright threat to society, that it was finally abolished and made illegal.

And now the picture of the Viking is very different. We see law and structure. Not that different from today, really. And one then realizes that this label of barbarian is one that is placed there by detractors. The only difference between the Vikings and those of the mainland was that their homes were far enough away, and in such secluded and inhospitable places, to not be at any risk for reprisal, unlike those of the mainland and the various isles there. But when these mainlanders found themselves not fearing any reprisals—in the many forms it could take: invasion from the offended, neighbours taking sides, or threat of excommunication by the papacy—then they also used the same tactics that they would condemn the Vikings for, and are still condemning them for. Such condemnation is usually because of that difference in values, circumstances, and consequences. For instance, pacifists today fail to see that the situation was not such back in the Middle Ages that they could avoid war and bloodshed. In medieval life there was too much to gain, and too little of a consequence in losing an existence that was as hard as it was, and therefore everyone did go to war—even the papacy. Another very common fallacy today is the *appeal to emotion*. If someone says that the Vikings killed and stole, then through the moral attitudes of today, and a number of other factors, such as the near complete absence of war and suffering (which makes for soft minds), people will judge them. Such projecting of morals, laws, standards, and norms into the past, and then judging them thereby, is nothing but pure presentism.

V. Cognitive Bias

'One should not utter a word about his own inadequacies. In the Oxo it says: 'When a man lets out a single word, the long and short of him will be known.'" – Takeda Nobushige

As the mind perceives the world, the mind-set will influence how the world is perceived. Likewise, man will always project himself onto the world, and his values will therefore colour his every interaction. An honest man will assume that the men he encounters will also be honest. He will continue to do so until circumstances tell him otherwise. And when he meets nothing but thieves, and finds his valuables missing time and time again, he may change his expectations and may even change his own values as a result. Another man may think only himself to be honest, and may start avoiding others altogether. A third may set out to right the wrongs and rid the world of thieves. There is also the one who will turn dishonest and a thief himself. Such a man mutters: "If I am the only honest man there is, and only lose while others profit, then I must change my ways so that I can profit as well." Whatever forces that push and work upon us will shape us one way or the other. A man that changes drastically in character is not common, though, and it takes big events and much turmoil in a man's life for him to do so. We see, then, the paths and circumstances in our life that made us who we are. Not counting that basis of body—different in each individual organism—such as a man's intelligence, or a talent due to a physicality, that will always interpret and handle the world differently. In sum total, experience through and of our body make us who and what we are, and how we perceive and value the world.

Since we attribute and judge others from our own, we therefore very easily and swiftly judge without consideration and deliberation. A man who speeds his car we instantly condemn as an outlaw—this kind soul that was speeding in order to get a wounded person to the hospital. We always make quick judgements and decisions based on the information we have, and usually neglect to speculate on the information we don't have. To consider what it may be, and not what it appears to be. In most situations it is the failure to identify and assign proper cause to the effect, and instead you assume that most likely or easiest of explanations.

By this same ignorance we also attribute more, or less, to ourselves most of the time. Like how we take for granted the things that we or others excel in. Our power to estimate a skill is always hampered if we do not have a comparison, or any sort of indication of proficiency. To learn to ride a bike or swim—who has not misjudged the skill it took? And those who learnt by themselves, and continued to do so on their own, and learnt quickly: how easily they took for granted the ease of it, and how they failed to see how much their expertise had grown. And so, even when you have a lot of information and expertise about a thing, you may still lack the information to know that you possess it. Meaning that you are not aware of what information you have, because you take it for granted. This is until you are reminded or informed in some way, of course. If you possess something that others generally do not have, then you would be reminded of it very often. If it comes up frequently, or ever, that is. For example, if you're an astrophysicist, and you only socialize with other astrophysicists, then this may leave you unaware that what you and your colleagues talk about and do is not commonly realized or known at all. In short, when we are not reminded, we usually forget, and when we are not compared, we usually take it for granted.

Another such case of failure in the objectivity of the mind is the historian's fallacy. When one reads history, and learns each and every detail, then one may start to falsely attribute knowledge to the person that one reads about: why did he do this and that, when we know this or that? The problem is that he did not know, or may not have known. Or he may have known, but also known some other thing that factored in on him taking a different course of action. This is very similar to the presentism I spoke of, but different because the historian's fallacy is one where the reader assumes that something is known by those he reads about. Presentism, however, is the projecting of values into the past, or in other words, a person assumes that those in the past have the same values as he has. They are both prime examples of biases, though, because they are judgements taken by the individual based on his information and stance, and then projected back into the past or onto a situation. When it is not into the past that morals and values are projected, but onto different cultures and values that people have today, we have the cultural bias. In simple terms, a bias happens when we observe an action taken by someone without knowing their motives and what they know, and then judging it with our own knowledge and rationale.

As our information and values make us who we are, then they are also the source of our feelings. Be aware, then, that a feeling or emotion experienced may not be felt or understood by others at all. Emotions, such as anger, have a general tendency to cloud the mind. They also have a contagion effect on the self: if you are in a good mood, you have a tendency to do stuff that accompany good moods, such as laugh more and uncontrollably, and you may have increased energy, appetite, etc., and these things themselves reinforce that mood. This type of emotional bias is not wholly an intellectual one then, as it is very dependent on the chemical state of the body—its own intoxication.

We should and must be aware of the many biases of the mind. It happens to all of us and it is not easy to avoid—and probably impossible actually—but by being aware of it we can analyse ourselves, our thoughts, and our actions a lot easier and more clearly. It also helps us to question and dig deeper in things, and makes us more wary about making false assumptions, and of committing mistakes, in general.

Age, experience, and knowledge tempers us in our cognitive faults: we learn that things are not always that easy to learn or master. Cockiness, therefore, is a symptom of childishness and inexperience. Not always, but usually. However, labels such as cockiness and arrogance are much misused today. The ruling mob always tag the superior with such labels in order to invalidate their qualities. Where the wise and learned man, or the strong and brave warrior, is competent and proficient, the ignorant and weak masses feel their inferiority to a proportionate degree. And they are often seen firing off a few verbal shots, and then excusing themselves and their own faults, before they slink off back into their crevasses where they feel snug and secure. Rationalization—what a splendid tool that is for the mind to avoid pain and suffering. To be able to tell yourself "I am just as good as others", without any justification for it. And if you were to err, and be repeatedly proven inferior, you would continue to make these excuses. One by one they lift you out of negative emotion—trivial and fictional as they may be. And when you make awful decisions that go against your own principles, you will make even bigger excuses and even more preposterous claims, and quite readily blame others if need be. And by lying to yourself, you will find it easier to lie to others as well. Yes, avoiding these conflicting thoughts, this cognitive dissonance, is vital and natural. But to make a habit of it—to constantly abandon yourself, as it were—is surely going down the wrong path. Instead, do as you think is most important, and follow your greater ideals and goals, and your heart will be light and unburdened. You cannot rationalize endlessly, after all. Too many excuses will bury the mind, and this will only result in self-hatred, which is only steps away from your own demise. Self-loathing—excessively at least—is a terrible thing. But it can also be helpful. It may help you to focus on your problems, and to learn and adapt, so that you may improve yourself.

VI. Dissociation and Ideal

When we gain an imprint on the mind a number times in a variety of situations, we eventually lose specific connections and similarities from the setting of these experiences. A loss of memory, sort of. Memory is always lost to some degree, as we all know. The mind does this to avoid overloading and to clear room, in a way, for new information gained throughout life. Distressing experiences leave a greater impression, due to a greater biochemical reaction in the moment when it occurred. And because of this distress felt—that shocked you so in the first place—it will recur and maintain, and therefore not fade as easily. This is natural, as it is important to remember and recognize danger, and this physiological mechanism thus developed because it survived. But when there is little or no impression through an experience, then the body obviously does not make a big physiological imprint, and it therefore doesn't revisit to maintain such an impression, either. Memory will then fade, because of a lack of use in that specific imprinted pattern. This mechanism is the cause for the loss of association—this dissociation. When an experience is repeated in a variety of ways, a specific association is lost. If I play football ten times on ten different football fields, I will lose the association of football with one specific field. Given that there are no other special factors that would make one of these stand out, that is. And so, if you play on many enough fields, then there will only be the commonality left, which is football. Unless an extraordinary experience were had, as said. If one were to be asked about football, or football fields, then a very generic image that is a sum of commonalities would appear in the mind. This is the Ideal of Plato. The Ideal is the sum of the commonalities in a definite thing, and that which is similar. For example, there are many chairs in different shapes and sizes, but they all have a specific value, which is why we call them all chairs—the value of a chair is that we sit in it—and this is the similarity of them all. The image we conjure up when we hear the word chair is a generic one, which is the dissociated one, or it can be a particular one, which is the associated familiar one. For instance, I think of a common type of wooden kitchen chair—one that I cannot clearly visualize, apart from its specifications. Dissociation happens due a loss of non-important, unrelated, or irrelevant memory by dissipation, due to a lack of use and imprinting, or because of the absence of it in conjunction with the thing, and therefore it is less and less associated. As such, an Ideal will emerge that gets more and more specific in regards to its commonalities, and that person's Ideal can then be clearly recognized by others if described. They may perhaps never have the same exact Ideal, though, because they will always have either old or fresh experiences with imprints that differ widely. Or their minds may have been built differently, or they may have different values derived from a thing altogether, because of a difference in valuing overall. As an example: A laid back and carefree person may only see the fun and play in football, while a health focused person may primarily see it as exercise and beneficial to health. Or the competitive person only as a means to win. Their difference of valuation therefore, quite obviously, result in a difference of association. Variables in the mind such as these are great, and seemingly endless, and this is why it is so difficult to pinpoint this or that.

This is also why we do not call psychology an exact science, and its complexity is why it took so long to gain some understanding in it. There is still a huge lack of knowledge in how the mind works, and few other fields have sported such failures in making definitions and classifications. With ignorance and failure to understand a field of study come a lot of assumptions and claims in seeing patterns. Disorders are then carelessly made up, and faulty diagnosing according to criteria and symptoms that are nonspecific follow. And then medication starts, and chemical imbalance is induced. I am not attacking medication per se, but I am attacking the amateurish work and sloppy practice in the field. Such as diagnosing ADHD in small children, because they are a bit restless and full of energy—as if this was not normal—and then doping them up with Ritalin, which may have extremely adverse effects. The malpractices are so numerous and well-known that there is no need for particulars, really. No, this will not do. We must be more cautious and certain when it comes to drugging people up.

Suffering and Happiness

I. The Pursuit of Happiness

Happiness—the great goal of the modern era. As the main purpose of human life today, nothing is more important. And it is idolized and worshipped everywhere. A hunt for the Holy Grail it is, and their quest to find this happiness seems to be just as sacred—as if on the hunt for an actual relic. Seemingly divine this act has become today. So holy that none must stand in the way of this pursuit. Not the fate of race, nation, mankind, or even Earth itself. Whatever it takes, and whatever may perish in the process. Yea, this zealotry evokes great similarity with church and religion. But instead of angels and prophets, we have mockers and purveyors of lofty promises. And where there is promised and hoped to find a great deal, there are only meagre findings and portions, few and far between—if at all. However, the meekness and humility seen in the religion of Christ is nowhere to be seen in this church of hedonism and pleasure, and the people who find some holy substance are eager to flaunt it with great passion and no inhibition. As if happiness—the act of deluding yourself—was something to boast about. Or indicated some importance of your life, at that. And yes, it is a delusion. It is certainly not an objective thing, this happiness. One man may find it in others, and another may find it only in himself. Being made a king may satisfy one, or the bottom of a bottle to another. So very subjective are these valuations made by individual men, which makes for just as great a difference in expectations and wants. And when some of them reach these great or not so great goals that would or should have achieved happiness, they usually find themselves still wanting and unsatisfied. Was it just a delusion, after all? They thought they would attain happiness, but then what? They thought it would last as well?

Or that it would be complete and utter happiness? The state of bliss they mistook it for. And it isn't strange that they would have made such a mistake, given how permanent and dedicated the pursuit and praise has been for this happiness. In truth, they were on a mission to eliminate its opposite: suffering. And this is quite an impossible task in life. They played a silly trick on themselves, and this without having seen any proof that this happiness truly exists, or having met a truly blessed creature possessing such a gift. They think they may have seen such people, and surely there must be: after all, "happiness exists, else no one would dedicate such time to it".

The truth is that happiness is fleeting and almost always short-lived. Just like pleasure. In fact, most if not all of happiness stems from the memory of pleasure and pleasurable activities, or a mental satisfaction, which may or may not have root in experience, or even reality. It is usually through the pleasure of the body, though—even the simplest of pleasures. That which makes the body feel good and elated is food and exercise, and when the energy and strength built from either one gets drained, the vigour will fade. Repetition is needed to sustain such well-being. And so it is with mental joy and elation. The mind forgets as memories fade, and while a strong and distant memory may still do its effect, it is a numb feeling. And not like that which is fresh in memory, such as eventful days that produced extraordinary dreams in the following nights. The effects of freshness, and exercise of body and mind, always do good. Stagnation and lack of stimuli surely do not. Stagnation is akin to small and numerous deaths; avoid this and fill your life with as many bursts of life as you can. Do not rest on laurels—nothing lasts forever, after all.

II. Suffering

Verily, life is suffering. This is what drives all life to better its situation. It must, obviously, since it's the sole factor in this drive. When we alleviate suffering momentarily, we are rewarded and given new incentive to do it again—to repeat the action. This all works in nature, but for man having become cleverer than nature, and having found new ways of living and surviving, then such a change may cause a great many problems. And we see the symptoms clearly today. These very visible ones, which are linked to either a sedentary lifestyle or one of overeating. The initiators responsible for this are laziness and idleness. These are things that nature use as a drive towards recuperation and saving energy, among other things, and to which life is unfamiliar with except in small doses, because of the struggle that is always there in some way. Even the most sedentary of animals have to spend a lot of energy, and continually move about, in order to feed themselves. Hunger drives us to eat, and as a result, a physical exertion in finding food is imposed upon us as well. These are sufferings, in a sense. They pain us more than what the opposite would, which is being full and content, and not having to move around. The intelligent and knowing mind knows otherwise, though. But it is a problem nonetheless, because the young, and society as a whole, is not encouraged, and not given the information, incentive, and motivation to be healthy and active. There is not too much of a stigma in being fat or lazy, either. There is suffering in being fat and unhealthy, though. And this is usually realized, but sometimes the damage is already done, and in some cases it is already too late.

Man must embrace suffering in the same way as he embraces most experiences. Or at least the great and spectacular of men should, because they would surely not want to be without these factors that have shaped them, and all the lessons and experiences they have learned from. Those who do not suffer will have no force, will, or incentive of any kind to reflect, find out, or do something. And so, if you have not suffered—as it is part of life, and the largest part thereof—then you have not truly lived and experienced life.

Life is suffering. In this Schopenhauer was right. And it is true that asceticism suspends suffering, but in doing so you actually suspend living itself. This was what Schopenhauer failed to see—or do, actually. He failed to embrace life for what it was. But perhaps we should be thankful for that, because his glorious mind and intellect would not have been of much use, or properly utilized, without that unique position from which he viewed the world and the Universe. And then we would not have had his self-appointed successor Nietzsche develop his life-affirming philosophy, either.

What is disappointment, heartbreak, and feelings of hurt and betrayal but the collision of reality or outcome with that of expectations, a dream, a vision, or ideal? The man who is very intelligent has proportionally greater dreams, hopes, and ambitions, and with the clash of reality, the fall is thus ever larger. This is seen and understood by contrasting the man who has great plans and is thwarted, with the man who has no plans and is oblivious and largely ignorant of the world, and for the most part only lives life in the moment like an animal. In this, then, we also see why depression is largely a modern disease, because of the dreams and fantasies that are all around us, and the many restrictions that make us unable to achieve them. And it not only afflicts those with higher intelligence more in the way of positive notions, as in having big plans, but also when it comes to negative notions and external influences, such as loss or betrayal, because they retain more memory of said losses and are therefore affected much more by them. Thus, a sensitivity is bound up with intelligence, because of this greater capacity and understanding. And with greater sensitivity comes greater capability of suffering. A devastating impact on the brilliant mind, and from the mind, can come from quite ordinary happenings, and it can then become a very serious issue that leads to an unhappy life; and ultimately a self-termination. It also affects lifestyle and living, and thereby directly affects physical well-being. Let me make a comparison: A content man who is plagued with a physical suffering in the form of a bad knee, or back, or any aches and pains all over his body, can live a very good and long life with just having a positive outlook on life. His mental happiness will have him be physically active, and that alone may be enough for a long life. A physical pain may also result in a greater appreciation of health and life. But a mental suffering is intolerable, because it is a damage in the very instrument that values life and living. Therefore, a mental suffering is always greater, or has a much stronger impact, than a physical suffering. Only a very torturous physical existence would welcome death, after all. If otherwise happy, that is.

Man can push himself physically. Even beyond that of animals. This is because man can have water and nourishment on him, and he can pace himself. Man also trains purposefully. Meaning that he can train and notice the difference in doing so. An animal does not train. It merely conforms to the needs of life, and this is why it only stays as fit as it needs to be, and not as fit as it can be. However, as most animals have tough and demanding lives in nature, they will be exceptionally fit. And for man to outperform the animal, he has to live under such harsh demands that nature set. Or he can simulate such living. Which many do. And so, even this excellence in man over animal, in the purely physical, is still attributed to intelligence, or to knowledge. Such knowledge is also why a man can willingly do harm to himself in order to do a good. Which an animal would not do, and would not know why it would want to. Armed with knowledge you can find the limits in life and in yourself, and then make adjustments and calculations, pushing yourself further and further. That is why Amundsen succeeded, and why Scott only found the South Pole a very icy grave. The mental can overcome the physical, and the greatest enemy of the mind is the mind itself.

Part Three: A Recollection of Events

"They assembled from all sides, one after another, with arms and horses and all the panoply of war…"
— Anna Comnena

Part Three: A Recollection of Events

The Sculpting of Man

I. Civilization and the Aryan

From the earliest of times, man settled and thrived in the warm and fertile areas. Areas in which life was not too hard in those days when technological advancements were still small and insignificant, and did not alleviate much in the struggle against nature. From there on it took quite a while, but with the slow and steady advance of simple farming techniques, animal husbandry, and better tools, they greatly improved on their lifestyle. This effectivity made the farm work easier to handle, and in general freed up more people to take up other trades, apart from that of farming. Craftsmanship was born, which stirred on the advancements. And with different advancements and resources in different regions, the trader, along with his domesticated pack animals, was able to go between these areas to trade and barter superfluous goods with wanted goods found elsewhere. Already we have a man that had conquered nature, and grew weaker. He had much too much, and he had no reason to work hard with his body, or even bother much with the strenuousness of thought, either. And there were now a great many people in these climates and areas where food and wine flow in abundance, and the population then continues to grow and grow. And with such numbers it also multiplies the chances of genius and invention. Even among these masses of inferior people. All this until the resources become sparse, due to the great quantity of people and their consumption. And then the wars begin, when the people and their leaders see opportunity for gaining resources and land. And if no land and resources are to be found in the areas around them, they wither out or disperse. Or they turn inwards, in this same pursuit, and make enemies there. In the case of internalizing, the civilization will decay, die, and may even vanish without a trace, or they may suddenly be found and conquered by a people still in advancement. In most cases, however, there are external enemies in sight, and then wars ignite, and competition and struggle is allowed to sift the blood of man once again—separating the gold dust from that of sand and ash. Civilizations start competing, and those nations where the most brilliant and crafty of people reside—those that device advantages to secure victory—will grow ever larger. But in the end they run out of enemies, or run into nations, people, groups, and climates they are unable to conquer—climates that may be too harsh or imposing to them, or too challenging to what they are used to. And when they generate these problems and run out of the mechanisms that forced them to always grow better, stronger, or smarter, then their process of advancement stops. The inferior lower classes will start to grow out of proportion, due to the lack of these wars that earlier thinned their numbers, and society then degenerates. And without external enemies, they turn inward again, and eventually start destroying themselves. With a lack of food and resources, and a hard life in general, the great masses of the lower class will start to blame the ones in charge for the problem they themselves have caused with their incessant and unrestricted breeding. Lastly, the final nail in the coffin for that once great empire is hammered in as the nobility and upper classes are eliminated. The slave revolt, as Nietzsche calls it, and with it, most values and virtues of old are inverted.

The nobility that was overthrown in Europe and Asia down into India were usually of Aryan blood. We call this Aryan the Indo-European today, in particular when speaking of the origin of our European and Indian branches of language and culture. This is due to the propaganda made after the Second World War, in order to avoid its association with National Socialism and Germanic man.

Part Three: A Recollection of Events

The Aryan came from and migrated out of the Urheimat somewhere in the steppes of Central Asia, and then they spread their dominant culture to Europe and India. We know that he was the ruler and aristocrat of the lands he invaded and conquered, and with him came culture and advancements that revolutionized the world. Note that the word aristocrat come from, and has the root in, the word Aryan in Greek. Throughout Asia and Europe we find such evidence of him. In the Middle East and India he found large populations already there, and he ruled over them and made some of the greatest civilizations in existence. In India he created the Sanskrit language and writing, and the Vedas were made—some of the oldest extant writings in history. However, over time the Aryan man would eventually degenerate and mix with those that were already there, as almost always happens, especially in these middle lands of fertile soil and mild weather. But Aryan man also migrated to Europe, and penetrated deep into the forests there. He would eventually push down from the north of the forests into Greece and Italy, and was most likely the source of Ancient Greece and perhaps even the older Bronze Age Greece, and also that of Ancient Rome. He was the source of the great civilizations and empires in Europe, just as in Asia.

In these deep forests, which were largely uninhabited—apart from a few minor people, such as the marsh-dwelling Slavs in the east—he attained complete mastery over the rest of Europe, and he avoided the miscegenation that usually happen in those other very populated areas. The Aryan man in Europe diverged into two branches due to a difference in geographic location, which then developed into two unique cultures, languages, and ethnicities. The Germanic and Celtic man came into being. The Germanic man was master over the north and northeast, and the Celtic man throughout the northwest, west, south, and even the southeast. In these dark forests, and their mild weather, the Celtic man emerged, and he is easily recognized by his red hair and dark blue eyes. He spread throughout the forests of Spain, France, and into the British Isles from there, and east into the Alps, the Balkans, and Eastern Europe, in general. From the Jutland Peninsula the Germanic man emerged, spreading outwards in all directions, and he is recognized by his blonde hair and greyish blue eyes. Because of their isolation and the lack of miscegenation, these branches of the Aryan man were the most pure of his descendants, which is still true for the Celts and Germanics, or the Celto-Germanics, left today. The commonality of the Germanic, Celtic, Roman, and Greek is seen in their pantheon of gods and their similarity. Even myths and legends are similar. The physical description of people and gods in these tales are very much alike as well—they all have the Aryan ethnic characteristics. This also goes for the famous Greek and Roman people in their time. Kings, emperors, poets, and warriors all have the light features of the Aryan. There are also the other obvious commonalities, such as similarity in language, being branches of the same Aryan (Indo-European) language family—so familiar at times that anyone can recognize the similarity of words and pronunciation about a given thing.

Nietzsche designates the Germanic as the *blond beast*, and he sees him as the successor to the Aryan. But unlike Nietzsche I contend that the Aryan is a bearer of culture, and not a destroyer, as he repeatedly states. The Aryan, and later on the Celtic and Germanic man, has throughout history birthed culture and civilization wherever he has set his foot. If Nietzsche only meant to label the Germanic man, or the contemporary German which he despises, and not the Aryan, as a destroyer of culture, then I cannot see how he would come to such a conclusion, and I believe that world history has proven him wrong. The Germanic man could only be called barbarian due to his lack of refinement in the north—where progress came slowly, due to a late arrival of people and its harsh and meagre landscape. When progress did come, however, it exploded onto, and throughout, the world. In any case, anyone would call an outsider who is not used to their customs, or having a different culture, a barbarian. This we see repeatedly throughout history: The Egyptian would call the Roman barbarian, and vice versa. And even the Roman of the Greek. The Roman did look up to the Greek most of the time, but he nevertheless thought the Greek had stagnated. And the Greek most certainly saw the Roman as barbarian, as compared to himself. It is all a matter of cultural bias and pride.

II. Death and Rise of Empires

Let us return to the matter of internal and external strife. Not all civil wars and revolutions are suicidal or self-destructive. Some borrow from other cultures to sustain their own vigour for a little while longer, and some implement successful reformations, and some come out of it even stronger than they ever were. However, without a real return to, or implementation of, the better values of old, and without any enemies or new mechanisms in place—for this important and most primary task of ensuring the survival of the fittest—then this civilization in question will eventually die out as well. And it seems as if some death throes never cease. As in the case of France, where they nearly reformed completely for the better under Napoleon, but biting over too much at a time with excessive warmongering, and the unrelenting will of its enemies to destroy this risen phoenix, was too much in the end. The death throes of France has continued ever since. Just in the last few hundred years they have had several kingdoms, two empires, and five republics—a slow death indeed. One of the reasons for this is their strong culture, and their national feeling and pride. A strong vigour, so to speak. It takes time for such vitality and strength to drain from a dying body. For some civilizations, however, internal wars are a natural way of life and they absolutely thrive on it, and learn. Japan had a number of civil wars, in which groups fought for dominance, and in that way they also continued on the survival of the fittest. But it never really splintered, due to a great many reasons. Their national feeling and cohesion for one. And also their feudal system, the intricate court system, and the imperial family and the emperor. The high value and place that war and battle had in their culture also played its part. A culture of understanding war, and the realities of life, nature, and struggle. Same as it has been with the Germanic tribes and people. Japan put restraints on the inferior throughout time by thinning them in war, and also by their complex and refined culture, which meant that only intelligent people could hold a position, or at least be learned, and thus they had to better themselves. Japan propelled very quickly onto the world scene when new technology and industry found its way there from Europe—advancements that were, comparatively, nowhere to be found on the Chinese mainland. This adaptation and adoption the Japanese were able to do due to having maintained their intelligence, creative spark, and drive. The mainland of East Asia, and especially that large part of it which is China, had, on the other hand, stagnated and slowed down the progress of the entire region with it; as that of a dying Roman or Byzantine Empire, but without any invigorating forces left to take over it, or reignite it. Europe had wars, plagues, and every imaginable thing to force and continue natural selection and evolutionary rise and advancement. When war and strife is constant and a part of life, such as in Germanic society, it does not lead to a downfall; the people only become stronger for it. And when there was no ongoing war, and the population became too large, then the ones without any prospects—those not first-born and thus without any hope for land and inheritance, including the poor and landless—grouped together and left their homelands peacefully.

Part Three: A Recollection of Events

And as word travelled, these groups were joined by other groups from friendly and even unfriendly tribes. And so the groups became bands, and bands became hordes. Thus, a great migration begins. The Germanic tribes left in droves when they heard of the opportunities for conquest, due to the stagnation, and ever weakening state, the Roman Empire was in. The lands and riches were there for the taking. The Romans had grown fat and stupid, as is a trait commonly seen, and heard of, when an empire starts dying.

The power vacuum did not originate with the Germanic tribes leaving. They were only responding to the great power vacuum in the farthest west of the known world: this crumbling Roman Empire. The Germanic tribes, however, in taking their whole tribes with them, probably left a near total vacuum and not just a power vacuum. With the empty space left in Eastern Europe after Germanic departure, the Slavic tribes moved westward, and they thrived and multiplied on their new, ill-gotten lands. The luckiest people in the history of the world? Perhaps. There has been some speculation that a push from the back of the steppes caused the steppe tribes and hordes to move westwards—or a push from further in to the centre, with the movement of Huns and other steppe people—but it seems just as plausible that the total vacuum left by the Germanic tribes was what started the continual move west by tribes in the east and the steppes. And therefore when these tribes left, the old power structure in the east crumbled. Tribe by tribe. In the momentum some snow balls rolled over smaller ones and packed them on. And the snow ball grew to great proportions at times, which led to the formation of the various steppe hordes. This theory of vacuum seems just as likely to be the case as that theory of outside pressure and a push from the steppes. However, the theory of pressure is the one most accepted in regards to the Great Migration—probably due to the prevalent dislike, and outright hatred, of anything that might "glorify" the

Germanic peoples; even though it is the truth—and it is therefore natural that when pieces are found that fit this pressure theory, they are the ones that are told. Contrarily, I view most of the great historical events in human history as a result of power vacuum. Power vacuums that are formed by this stagnation, and demise, of civilization that I have spoken of.

III. The Great Civilizations

The greatest of empires either die a very slow death, or a very quick and violent one. And so too, may I venture, it is for great men. The quick and violent death shows that there is a great opposition against it, and the resistance of force it had. The slow death shows tenacity, with values and foundations so strong that they are almost interminable. An example of this latter would be the Roman Republic and Empire. The Roman traditions still live on in the Catholic Church, for instance. And Rome served as a model and inspiration to medieval Europe. Really strong cultures show an almost ineradicable nature. Like in China, India, Persia, and even Egypt to a degree. And let us not forget Ancient Greece and Rome. China started to stagnate as a civilization after the rule of the Han dynasty almost two millennia ago—with a few invigorating injections from the north, such as the Jurchen Jin dynasty, the Mongol Yuan dynasty, and the Manchurian Qing dynasty. Also worthy of mention is what can be called the last Golden Age of China, with the native Chinese Ming dynasty. More specifically the Yongle Emperor and the Ming voyages. But still, these last 2000 years have been a steady decline there, and any real advancement and technology since then from China has been minimal. The legacy of their past splendour has lived on in the same manner as Roman culture has, however. It set the foundation for the northeast of continental Asia, and it even had an impact on and merged with Indian culture in Southeast Asia. Just as Rome did in large parts of Europe. In this same way, Persia also survived. Not on the same scale, however. With the Arab invasions and Islamization, it took a backseat, but nevertheless endured. Egyptian culture died out, but it has left such a strong impression that it can never really be forgotten. How can it, when they left some of the greatest man-made structures to constantly remind us? And then there is India, which is possibly the cradle of civilization itself. Its impact is so old and vast that we almost take it for granted and ignore it completely. And whether the Aryan (Indo-European) came from the Urheimat of the Pontic-Caspian steppes or Central Asia according to the Kurgan Hypothesis, or if it was Out of India, which is doubtful, it nevertheless had a profound impact on the cultures of both Europe and India. Proto-Greek civilization started to flourish in the 2nd millennia B.C. As did Vedic culture in India. Vedic culture produced the Vedas and Hinduism, which is Indian culture today, and the Indian culture stretched and spread down and into Indo-China and beyond. And the Bronze Age Greek culture, and the following Ancient Greek one, obviously had a massive impact on Europe. Thus, the foundation for both regions were set. The difference between Bronze Age and Ancient Greek is evident, however. Also, consider the stagnation of Bronze Age Greece into the Greek Dark Ages, and that the Dorian invasion (and a number of other peoples from different directions) resulted in a spectacular resurgence, or better to say a blossoming, into a magnitude of great achievements. These Dorians came from the north. Almost always from the north a reinvigoration of civilization, or way of life, comes. And from it springs forth the establishment of a master culture that resonates throughout the ages. A conquest and culture coming from the north is also true in China. China which, along with a few other empires in Asia, has been the only true contender to Europe these last few thousand years. Repeatedly, the tribes from the north, such as the Jurchen who formed the Jin dynasty, or the Mongols that formed the Yuan dynasty, invaded and ruled there. Yes, most of the powerful empires across Asia were created by invaders from the north. Like the Turk, or the Hun, for example. Incidentally, the Mongol, Turk, and even loosely the Korean and Japanese, are related to the Altaic language, and perhaps even genetically, in some way or other. It should also be noted that the Korean is just as advanced as his brethren on the large islands to the east of himself. Considering all this, one might say that the Altaic is the Aryan of Eastern Asia.

Exactly how far north the invading Dorians in Greece came from is unknown. They may have come from within Greece, actually, but then again we do not know where they came from at all. The *Return of the Heracleidae* the Greeks called this event—the return of the descendants of the demi-god Heracles—which illustrates how important and profound the change was. And it is no wonder that Sparta and Lacedaemonia was Dorian, really; their way of life so easily resembling that of the north, with their warrior cult and their laconic wit—reminiscent of the wit found in Norse mythology (quick, intelligent wit)—and the practice of infanticide to breed only the healthy and strong. Overall reminiscent of a stern and harsh lifestyle that was a fact of daily life in the north. The Dorians, Attics, and other Greeks achieved marvellous things, in any case. They withstood the great Persian Empire and later became its masters. And through the use of colonies they spread across much of the Mediterranean and Black Sea. Some even say that Rome itself was found by Aeneas and the Greeks of Troy, or at least so the Romans would have us, and themselves, believe—such was their reverence, awe, and respect for Ancient Greece. A Greece that generated a culture and developed sciences that are incomparable in history. Not counting the Modern Era, of course.

Part Three: A Recollection of Events

IV. The Northern Man

What is it about the north then? It seems quite self-evident, really. Where nature is hard and scarce, it puts more demand on man. And to survive, man has to meet those demands. He has to endure both physically and mentally. He has to device new methods and tools for his survival, and he has to learn the patterns of the tides and seasons more clearly in order to work better in coordination with nature. You cannot stop or conquer the weather, after all. Only to work with it, and anticipate and plan for it. He has to meet that challenge posed by nature or perish, and so a body that is adapted to the environment will emerge. A body that is taller, larger, and stronger so he can—and he has to—rely more on himself. One of the reasons for this is because there are fewer people in the north than in the south. Fewer because there is a smaller availability of food, and the lands are more course due the fjords, the heavier forestation, and the many swamps and wetlands. The lands are rough and sparse; and the men had not had the free time to deforest and drain the swamps yet either, naturally. With all of these considerations in such an environment, the intellect has to meet new demands as well. The increase in methods used and information needed requires better memory and higher intelligence to make it all work. The oceanic areas of Northern Europe and Northeastern Asia—like it is with the Japanese on their island nation separated and isolated by the sea and the north just like Scandinavia is—helped man become even more diverse. Taking to the sea for fish, trade, and even war and raiding. So, the northern man is just as proficient as those southern men, or perhaps even more when considering the harshness of the seas, and the North Sea is one of the harshest by far. As any a sailor could tell you and just did. The durability and versatility of the Germanic, and in particular the Viking, longboats is also a testament to that. The man of the north thus needed to be open-minded. Open to new ideas and solutions. Therefore, the spark of creativity was bred in him. Nature made him that way, and it is a result of his intelligence. This greater intelligence formed by the north was the enabler of further developments and advances than had ever been reached before. And so, when the progress of the south reached the north, it increased population there due to higher capacity and efficiency through improved farming techniques, housing, etc., and that in turn also increased leisure, which enabled individual focus on research and development that grew exponentially faster than ever before compared to that in the south, due to this higher intelligence. For 200 years now, Western Europe and the Anglo-American countries have had larger leaps of progress and greater technological advances than all of the previous history of mankind put together. We see the cumulative power of intelligence right there. And even though many inventions, and many of the most important pre-industrial ones, were discovered in southern lands, they were not fully utilized until they came into the hands of Northern Europeans. Gunpowder, for instance. Which was toyish, or had a very crude and limited use in military matters until the European got his hands on it and made proper projectile weapons with this new found force.

I say European, because the blending and mixing of races have left us, after the Migration Period, and even more so today, with a mix that is more Celto-Germanic, with a smaller mix of Latin. There isn't, and almost never was—even in the time when the Germanic tribes were largely isolated—something of a pure race in that sense. Is there such a notion even in nature? No. There aren't any clear lines in nature, life, and evolution. Only similarities. But there are purer races that have had less mixing and larger periods of isolation than others. And take note that those who today mock the National Socialist term of pure race are oblivious to the fact that the National

Socialists themselves were fully aware of the fact that there wasn't one. Especially not Germans in that day. But they had a national race nonetheless, a breed sort of, and when they spoke of pure race it was in regards to maintaining that breed of theirs. Or the breeding of purer Germanic elements. Such as that of the Nordic man. A future breed, a pure breed, a pure race to keep separate from others, keeping the differences that are there. To build on the Germanic instead of the experimentation of globalization and miscegeny. They wanted to keep the genes and blood that made us what we are. We don't judge others when they want that very thing. Don't the Chinese, the Arab, or even the mongrel Indian have that right, this very natural right, to do that? But not white men and especially not Germanic men it seems. What we want is to keep Germanic ethnicity there, just as we want the Hungarian, Basque, Finnish, Japanese, or any other people and nationalities to keep intact their culture, their blood, and their way of life if they so wish it, and not to have it forced down their throat while being indoctrinated and lied to about it.

Assuredly, the northern mind is very open and able to adapt and assimilate, while still keeping his values, clarity of mind, and keen perception of realities. This clarity, and learned caution from seeing that others are not as honest and good as him—this confrontation with reality in a world with lesser men—is why the northern man, and especially the more Germanic of Nordic men, are seen, and usually described, as cold and distant to strangers, but when one gets to know them after a while, they are described as honest, kind, and faithful. This is because of our trust. If, and only if, we see that you are more like us and not like the criminal and amoral, then we will embrace you like brothers. We are also described as more calm and collected, and less passionate—or red-blooded as they call the Latins and southerners—and therefore also somewhat less sympathetic. This is because we are not ruled by our emotions and feelings; we are ruled by clear intelligent thought. We certainly do not sympathize with those more criminally inclined, that is certain, but the sympathy of our own is just the same as that of others. Perhaps stronger. We are ruled by our minds and the reality of situations. By knowledge and information. We calculate the good versus the bad, and compare the offset. We see evidence of Germanic open-mindedness in many ways throughout history. And in our own time with our tolerance of multiculturalism and multiracialism it has become an undeniable fact and proof that will haunt the rest of mankind forever until the end of days. No other places on Earth will you find this: the importation of strangers and cultures. Westerners do not even know what actual racism is until they have gone to Africa or Asia. The ease of how the Germanic tribes and Vikings adopted customs and laws, and changed many of them for the better, is yet another example. Another trait that is readily attributed to northerners is naivety, and this comes from this openness, and the fact that this noble man measures everyone according to himself. Meaning that the honest and bright man thinks everyone else is the same as he is, and then treats them as such—as equals. Until the lesson is learned, that is. In older times, we knew that we were not the same as the southerners, and we did not deceive ourselves by listening to lies and propaganda to the enormous degree that we do today. A sure sign of some degeneration, but at least the naivety is still there. "At least" I say, as it is a sign of intelligence, but maybe I should rather say unfortunately, since it is one of these reasons why multiculturalism and immigration is so welcomed by us. It is in our nature, ingrained. It seems that this nature which enabled us to be victorious and triumphant in the past will be our undoing and downfall. For when one uses our strengths against ourselves, only then can we be destroyed. We are simply destroying ourselves. This destructive thinking originated from the aftermath of the Second World War, where we were taught through indoctrination and propaganda that the love of ourselves and our own survival was equal to that of evil—a definition of evil that involve comparisons with devils, hell, cataclysms, Ragnarok, and such things. And we are still taught from early age and throughout life, and from everywhere around us constantly, that we are evil. None are more hated than the white man today and this is because this hate is picked up by non-whites as well, as it is everywhere. From schoolbooks to television and radio. Although, no one hates the white man more than the white man himself, and he will continue to be his own greatest enemy if he continues to do so. It is the greatest lie ever told, and it was much anticipated. Even before the Second World War. One could even say the world wars were the revolt and uprising against these ideas, or in the least a reaction against the cultivation of such notions and propaganda.

V. Roman and Germanic Ways

The Roman Empire—which will be the term I use for both the Republic and the following Empire—as an institution, was complex and offered a great deal more than most other civilizations. One of the main reasons for this was the patronage system. Even from the earliest of time this system was in place. People left their old cities to come to Rome and take advantage of this system where patrons, usually wealthy and noble men, and their clients had a lot of political influence and power. This patronage was an extension of the family, sort of. This system was much reminiscent of the mafia organizations of Italy, or the activity of freemasons, where hierarchy, privilege, and duty is available and taken advantage of. They help one another, in other words. Mutually beneficent. Though, the patrons, and people on top, were obviously the ones who gained the most from it. The head of a *pater familia* had not only control of his own *gens* or family, and the patrons in it, but also all the *cliens*, the clients or *clientela*, of those as well. And so, he would wield immense power. Some patrons were so powerful that they waged war against other cities with their clientela and hirelings. The usual casus bellis were debt collections and other grievances. These wars were mostly sanctioned by Rome. This City of the Seven Hills enabled their private citizens to conduct their business, and profited from the extra trade, work, and taxes, and in turn they would also protect their patrons with Roman military might. Therefore, the patrons were free to do mostly anything they wanted to as long as it did not collide with Roman interests, and thus they could sit safely in Rome without worries. And with so many opportunities, because of the booming economy in Rome due to the concentration of these rich patrons there, lowlier people flocked to the great city in the hope of getting one of the jobs available there or becoming a client. A number of Roman institutions gave soldiers, priests and religions, and the general populace, i.e., the people, political influence through various seats of power. Like the military tribunes or the tribune of the plebs. The possibility of representation and influence were always some of the largest incentives for going to Rome, or to join the Roman Empire altogether.

One of the traits of these southern civilizations, which includes Rome, is their tackling of issues with greater numbers. Which is natural, since there are always more people in such climates. Climates that allow the poor and homeless to sleep outside and beg for meagre scraps of food to continue survival, and also procreate profusely without forethought or worry. It could be said that life in the north today has become just as easy as that of the south, with a welfare safety net that provides both a warm home and food no matter how hopeless a human being you are. We now also have southern immigrants and minorities here that are outbreeding the indigenous northern populations. Immigrants and minorities—who are the main beneficiaries of the welfare system today, and receive much more, with much smaller criteria, than actual citizens that are working and paying taxes, and that are pure-blooded descendants of the age old inhabitants of these lands. This will be discussed in greater detail in such chapters as *Immigration and Politics*.

A northern birth is planned and accounted for, and is given much needed education to survive like those before it, while in the south a life either thrives or perishes, lives or dies. Both ways have potential for breeding good, strong men. The south through higher mutational chance and genotype variation through numbers, but it has to have a mechanism of weeding out the weak—such as human competition and war—when nature does not. Unlike the north, where one has to have warmth and shelter, and to prepare, stock, and take account of food supplies. Work was needed in the north to survive. So, those men who made it there had also proved themselves in all respects. A consequence of this was that individuals had a greater importance and worth. Indeed, individualism/liberalism, democracy, and the notions of equality comes from Germanic thought. Germanic freemen had to be self-sufficient, and in doing so would exert more personal and individual freedom than those in warmer, more exotic lands. And this notion transferred into law, which in turn reflects their way of life. They were used to going their own way, by themselves. This self-sufficiency also established a respect for each other and furthered other notions such as politeness—a common trait of northerners—and also the doctrine of hospitality. This was extended to strangers, and through a failure to discern also included foreigners. As still seen in our behaviour today. Germanics convened in popular assemblies and all freemen were free to speak their mind and vote on all matters. Thus, all freemen were also equals. The sense of individuality and self-sufficiency is very telling of the state in which Italy and Germany in the Medieval Era were in. The Holy Roman Empire exerted dominance over both these countries, and then some, and was the institution that held them together and protected them. But the Holy Roman Empire was an elective institution, and the lords had a vote and say in matters through the Imperial Diet—at least earlier on. This was much like the old traditions. The HRE can be seen as a macrocosm of the Germanic assemblies: Where before it was freemen that voted, it was now the Imperial Estates and their princes and officials. And where a warlord or a king was elected in times of war and general emergencies, there was now an emperor. In the Diet they determined laws and courses of action, but otherwise the members of the HRE exercised a freedom and privilege like that of the freemen of old.

With only the working man surviving in the north, this industrious nature was carried on in the blood of man there throughout the many millennia. The collective nature in southern man is in the same way also bred in him. The threats there are due to other men, and not the weather and nature like it is primarily in the north, and therefore men who worked together survived. To work together efficiently in great numbers you need unquestioning obedience. You do not ask questions, simply. You just do what you are told. And so, the man who follows those steps in the south survives. This man is a soldier, and works in groups. Unlike in the north, where man is a warrior. Which are more effective individually, because he is larger and stronger than those in the south, and also because of his free thinking capacity, which is part of his nature. A capacity to analyse and question, to plan and speculate, that is part of the survival and thriving in the north. This also makes northern men better suited as leaders. A state with Germanic aristocracy and leadership ruling over a people in the lower strata that are southerners—workers and soldiers—is seen again and again in history as extremely effective. But this aristocracy is eventually outbred by the carefree southerner who by his natural behaviour multiply in great numbers in these soft climates. This is why the kingdoms of the Normans in southern Italy and Sicily, or the Crusader States and Cyprus in the Levant—places where Muslims, Christians, and rabble of all kinds were in plenty and unchecked—would in the long run not survive with only a small aristocratic warrior caste in control. An aristocracy that did not remain selective and particular when it came to their own, and did not even bother to breed among themselves or with other nobles. The warriors come to power in the first place because of their effectivity in battle. They had a larger stature; a fearless, clear, and calculating mind; a life of training and war; and expensive and superior weaponry and armour that makes them far deadlier than any mere levy, and even most knights and nobles. These warriors were far more dangerous, and were worth half a dozen soldiers in the best of situations. They had to be, due to their fewer numbers. This is why these warrior armies, and warrior bands, defeated most soldier armies they met. The Romans learned this the hard way in Germania. And in those days the Germanics had rather crude weaponry. Some of those Germanics even came to battle naked. As was tradition with some Celts as well.

VI. Celtic Man

One of the most constant threats to the Empire were always the Celts. Feared and respected throughout Europe, and of which the Gauls were most prominent. An army of Gauls under the command of Brennus occupied Rome in 390 B.C. The only non-Roman army to do so until the Visigoths almost exactly 800 years later. Ultimately it was a failure, though. The Romans mustered another army and threw the Gauls out of the city, and with the people and treasury still intact. A hundred years later another Brennus commanding an army of Gauls and Celts invaded the Balkans and Greece and made a marked impact there. Some of these even settled in Anatolia (Asia Minor). Later known as Galatians. Celtic culture, before and after these mentioned events, spread across all of Europe. From the Celtiberians of Spain, to the Brittonic tribes, among others, in Britain, and from there to the eastern shores of the Baltic Sea and then south to the Balkans and Asia Minor. Almost all of Europe, in other words. Today these remaining Celtic cultures are confined to the outer reaches of the British Isles. Why is that so? Easy answer is that the Roman culture and language was widely adopted by them. Today, the Latin languages are present in the most western of Europe in Portugal and Spain to the eastern parts of Europe in Romania—a namesake of Roman legacy itself. So, we know the impact Rome had, and the consequences. One of the reasons for such smooth transition was that the Celts in large parts joined the Roman Empire on their own accord. Even the respected and feared Gauls did—although Caesar's campaigns in Gaul certainly helped persuade any opposition. This is not to say that it wasn't without a fight almost always from some or other Celtic tribe or group. The Celts in their temperament and social structure was not that different from Roman ways; they were a very advanced people. They had metalworking that was renowned even in the most advanced of places. Their chainmails and their many types of swords were of superior quality and use compared to other European military goods—or anywhere else in the world for that matter. Even the Roman gladius was of Celtic, or Celtiberian, origin. The Celts were also excellent traders and producers of general goods, such as jewellery. They also had a reputation for excellent horsemanship. And not only that, but their horses were considered superior as well. Another testament to their knowhow of the horse is that they were one the first people to have made, and used, a solid saddle. The type they used was a four horned one. Celts were, when compared to the Germanic tribes, much less "barbaric"—as the Romans used to say—even though they still were very tribal and warring. The Celts, and Gauls especially, went from being a number one threat to becoming a source of admiration and inspiration to the Romans, and also their most powerful client states and dominions when they joined. Celtic lands were rich, and they supplied excellent soldiers to feed the ever growing Empire. The Celts also benefited greatly from the Romans, which was why they usually joined very willingly. The Germanic tribes were a constant threat for the Celts, for one. And by allying with Rome, they not only had one less enemy to worry about, but also gained a strong and steadfast ally. The Celts were, naturally, quite content with sharing the blood spilled against the Germanic tribes with the Romans. They also had a certain degree of representation in Rome, as most did in some way, and there were even Gallic nobles appointed as senators. Celts with their craftsmanship and industrious nature seem to have been more content with those activities instead of war. And let us not forget that of trade. The Celts were very diverse, and as such very similar to the Romans. Or at least somewhere in between the Roman and the Germanic. Celtic blood was surely not a detriment to the Empire. Rather the opposite.

VII. Germanic Migrations

What impact the Germanic Migrations had is incalculable. Where we give credit to Greeks, Romans, etc., we completely fail to give credit to the Germanic race. Before the Migration Period, much of Western Europe was Celto-Latin in both breeding and culture. When the Migration Period started, much of Western Europe was to be conquered and ruled by Germanic peoples. The Visigoths formed a kingdom in the Iberian Peninsula. In the northwest of

Iberia, the Suebi formed a kingdom. And the Franks in Gaul, or France, which is their namesake. The Ostrogoths in Italy—followed later on, and more dominantly, by the Lombards. And in the British Isles, the Saxons, Angles, and Jutes, led by the brothers Hengist and Horsa, settled and made several kingdoms stretching far into the north and even beyond Hadrian's Wall. In the Balkans, the Gepids put pressure on the Eastern Empire. The Western Empire collapsed completely, however. Left as the spiritual successor, and heir to that dominance, were the Franks. This also reflect the importance of Gaul itself to the Romans. It seems to me that power in Western Europe hinges on France. After all, it was after the conquest of Gaul that Rome catapulted into becoming the superpower it was, and France has, generally, ever since been the dominant power in Western Europe. There was also a Vandal kingdom, with the non-Germanic Alans—that had migrated out of the steppes from the north of Caucasus—as a junior part, in Northwestern Africa, with a capital in Carthage in the later stages, naturally. Most of these Germanic kingdoms only lasted a few hundred years, but they left a huge impact upon several of these nations. In Italy they had a firm grip and shaped the culture and ethnicity of the people there. This was mostly in the northern parts, and in the province of Lombardy that is their namesake, with the people there being very Germanic in appearance with a lighter complexion, blue or light eyes, and fair hair. The north of Italy was the most advanced and industrious part of Italy throughout the Medieval Period, and has been ever since. Even up to this day. This is why the Northern Italians feel so different and distant from their southern countrymen. So too it seems in Spain. Always the Germanics exerted a positive influence, such as on laws and social structure. Always a benefit of some kind. Until degeneration starts, that is. The Arabs and Moors were able to take most of the central and southern parts of Iberia, but they were never able to take the last vestiges in the north, where the Germanic tribes were the strongest and most pure. But let us not forget that this was also where the most ferocious tribes of the Celtiberians resided and offered the longest resistance in the peninsula during Roman times. Of which I count the Basques, too, or Vascones as they were called back then. A people which have fought hard throughout history for their continued existence, while preserving their language and culture. It is quite understandable that such a strong-willed people express separatist notions still today. Much as their ancestors did: holding on to that of their own. The French (the Franks)—even though they have a predominantly Latin language and consider themselves Latin—is very much a greater amalgam of Celtic blood and that Germanic Frankish blood that came over the Rhine. Seen especially in the parts outside of the French Riviera and lower Occitania that have more Latin, Basque, and let us not forget the Greek blood—in Massilia (Marseille) and other colonies—than the parts more isolated from the Mediterranean in the north of France. The Mare Nostrum (Our Sea in Latin) has always been the greatest connector in Southern Europe, with people travelling enormous distances from their homelands to establish colonies in far-flung places. Like the Phoenicians and Greeks. The seas and oceans were, and still are in a sense, the easiest and most efficient way of travel, after all.

VIII. Muslims and Slavs

The Muslim invasions were halted in the north of Spain. When the Reconquista took place, it was done by the Visigoths from these northern parts under the command of Pelagius—the founder of the Kingdom of Asturias (forerunner to the great Iberian kingdoms of the Medieval Age). When the Muslims overran Occitania prior to this, they were stopped in the north of France. Sicily and parts of Southern Italy was also conquered by the forces of the Caliphate, but were again stopped by the north and the mainland. I see this as proof that where the more pure Greek, Roman, Celtic, and Germanic blood were present, they correspondingly offered greater and greater resistance. Even hundreds of years later the Muslim forces, now with the Ottoman forces at the helm, failed when they met Germanic resistance and thus were stopped in German territory. The Siege of Vienna in 1529 comes to mind. And the same again with the Mongols. The Mongols were stopped in Croatia, and in Poland. Another place where the Mongols were stopped, sort of, were the Russian Principalities: states of Viking origin. And while you might argue that these countries are Slavic, there are a number of reasons why I count them the way I do. First of all, both Poland and Croatia border, or bordered, on German lands, which at that time was the Holy Roman Empire. Secondly, there was earlier—from the Dark Age, Viking Age, and Medieval times, and even earlier during and before the Migration Period—much mixing with Celts and Germanics among the Slavs. The Eastern Europe that we know the Slav for today were the lands of those two former groups, and several others. It was only after the migrations that the Slav became a player on the world scene and arose from great obscurity. Much of what was known about them before that time was that they lived on the fringes, and they were hunted for their use as slaves, mostly. Their primary use in slavery is attested by the word slave today. The word that the Slavs used for themselves was the autonym rendered as Slova, Slovo, Sloven, Slava, or Slavos and the many variants of these. This is why many Slavic places, cities, and countries have this similarity. Like Slovakia, Slovenia, Slavonia, and Slavuta. The derived ethnonym *sklabos*, which the Greeks called them, is from where Latin got the name *sclavus*. Therefore, due to the main use and prevalence of the

Slavs as slaves, which was earlier called *servus* (serf) in the Roman Empire, the name of the Slavic race began being used in the definition of their capacity and primary function. Slav was no longer a name of them as a people by the masters, but instead what they were used for, and that is how the much used word *slave* came into being. Most European languages experienced this change. For example, the earlier used word of *træl* (thrall) in the Norse language was replaced by *slave*, and that is the sole word for it still today. Greeks had the word *doulous*, before they switched to the use of *sklabos*.

IX. The Vikings

A second push from the north came with the Vikings, and their impact was no less than that of the earlier Germanic migrations. They expanded in all directions and made huge, and largely overlooked, contributions to history. Norwegian Vikings explored and sailed the North Sea and the Atlantic. They discovered Shetland, the Faroe Islands (Fær-øyene: the islands to travel to/of travel), and Iceland (albeit there were Celtic monks there when they arrived). Erik the Red, who was a famous warrior and berserker, had been outlawed first from Norway, and then from Iceland. One of his crimes was the abuse of berserkergang in holmgangs. In his exile from Iceland, he settled on Greenland—discovered just a few years before by Gunnbjørn Ulfsson and explored by Snæbjørn Galti at the end of the 9th century A.D.—and after his exile had expired on Iceland, he returned there to convince people to come to this land. For this task he took the lesson learned from the misleading name of Iceland and thus he came up with the more appealing name of Greenland. At one point, over 5000 Norsemen lived in Eiriksfjord and the surrounding areas during Erik's time, but a plague killed a great number of people, including Erik himself—and eventually they all left or died out much later in the 15th century. Erik the Red was about to set out on exploration further west, but on his way to the ships he fell off his horse and took it as a bad sign. His son Leif Erikson took the lead and was the first to discover the Americas. The many shores and lands they saw there in the New World they gave many names: Hellulaland, the land of shales; Markland, the land of plains; and Vinland, the land of wine (the Norse name indicates something fruitful, sweet, or rich, and not necessarily that of wine or grapes).

In the east, the Danish, and primarily the Swedish, Vikings were to do what most Vikings do: raid, settle, and conquer. The Eastern Vikings were most commonly known by the Greeks and Slavs as Varangians/Varjagar (Væring in Norse, meaning something like compatriot or companion), which is also used today when historically designating the Eastern Vikings. The etymology of the word Viking comes from the place of Viken, which corresponds to the place around Oslo and Skagerrak. The Vikings of the west that raided the British Isles and sailed throughout the North Sea were mainly from Viken and Norway. The Danes took part in both the east and west in large numbers, and probably the largest thereof, but they focused more on the Baltics, England, the Frisian Coast down into the English Channel, and the French coast and the rivers there. Swedish Vikings were from Ruslagen/Roslagen—the area around the ancient Norse centre of Uppsala in Sweden—and they called themselves Rus accordingly. This is from where the autonym Russian and Russia comes from. Much to the shame and discomfort of the Russians ever since, and especially today when they try to build nationalism from a Slavic perspective, but fail to see that it is mostly only their language that has some Slavic origin. The prevalence of fair hair and blue eyes across Russia and Ukraine (and Eastern Europe, in general) is from the Viking and earlier Germanic admixture, and they owe the formation of their states, and their rise out from obscurity, to them.

Part Three: A Recollection of Events

Under the leadership of Rurik, the Rus took all the lands in these northern stretches and made their capital at Holmgard, which is not far from Novgorod—another city founded by the Norse, whose name is derived from Nygard (New City). They founded a number of other cities, too, that still exist and still bear their Norse names even today. Some of these are: Aldeigjuborg (Old Ladoga), Pallteskja (Polotsk), Smaleskja (Smolensk), Sursdalar (Suzdal), Moramar (Murom), and Radstofa (Rostov). This new kingdom of theirs they called Gardarriki (loosely meaning the realm of cities/settlements). Which is quite a fitting name, considering the quantity and that they had established most of them. The Norse had brevity, and quite the wit, in their way of naming things. Seen again and again in their names and nicknames of themselves or places, and of the names in their mythology, stories, and legends. In the naming of anything they encountered, really, and it is very reminiscent of laconic phrasing.

A great tool for the Vikings were their longboats, which had a very shallow draft that enabled them to sail the great many rivers around Europe, yet were robust and large enough to traverse the roughest of seas and oceans, such as the North Sea, without any problems. This versatility was, naturally, used to great effect in all of their endeavours. When going between the rivers, the Vikings carried their boats on their shoulders. Quite a feat in itself. The later ruler Oleg, a relative of Rurik, led the Rus south and eventually conquered the lands there (Ukraine), following mainly the great river Dnieper, and then proceeded to move his capital there to Kiev (Kœnugardr, meaning the king's settlement/city of the king). The Rus had by then conquered and settled the lands which today comprise European Russia, Belarus, and Ukraine. They had contact with the Byzantines at Constantinople (Miklagard, meaning Great City), and even had a number of successful wars with them that resulted in some very favourable terms and treaties. In a very short amount of time the Rus had become masters of the east. So great were their martial abilities that it prompted the Byzantine emperor to establish a permanent contingent of these fearless warriors to have under his command. Aptly named the Varangian Guard. This was continually bolstered and replenished in numbers by the ever present Norsemen everywhere, and even Anglo-Saxons and Normans were inducted into the ranks. The Varangian Guard as an institution lasted for almost 300 years.

In the British Isles, Norwegian Vikings colonized the islands around Scotland and as far as Ireland and Man, and settled anywhere else they so pleased for that matter. Raiding was more common earlier on, but with Viking settlements and a large influx of Norsemen, a more prepared and organized resistance from the locals came about as time went by, turning the raids into wars. A great many Danes took part in the west as well, as said. The Great Heathen Army, with the sons of Ragnar Lodbrok in charge, swept across the Anglo-Saxon lands and changed them forever. Whether Ragnar Lodbrok and the later Great Heathen army was Norwegian or Danish, and to what extent, is unknown, but it seems that at least the most powerful of the leaders were Danish. It is not for nothing that the swathes of land these Vikings conquered and controlled—stretching north of York and as wide west as the Irish Sea and all the way down to London—were called the Danelaw. So great was the impact of these Vikings on England that English today is more Norse than Anglo-Saxon/Germanic. This is seen in the sentence structuring that is extremely similar to contemporary Nordic languages, and many words, a majority probably, are of clear Norse origin. The Danes continued to dominate and exert political pressure there, and even conquered England later on (England is Norse for the land of meadows, or meadowland) under the Danish king, Cnut the Great. Viking raids also plagued the Franks and the surrounding nations. It was so bad, in fact, that any and all efforts were made to stop it. The Franks forbade the sale of any and all Frankish weapons and armour to Vikings and any of their kind. Losing the arms race—the only advantage the Franks had at that point—was not something they could afford. It was slightly too late, though. Vikings loved Frankish swords and armour, and had already amassed a great deal of it through plunder and trade. Gange-Rolv (Rollo)—a man from my homelands of Møre, although the Danish wish him as one of theirs instead—was given Normandy as a buffer against the persistent raiding and outright wars with the Vikings. This was the final solution to that problem for the Franks, and it worked splendidly.

I have a small anecdote about Rollo. It is said that when Rollo was to swear fealty, the king of France demanded that he had to kiss his foot as a sign of submission. Rollo, however, refused to comply with such a humiliating act. Instead, he ordered one of his warriors to do it for him. The warrior did as commanded and he took the foot of the king and lifted it up to his mouth, which resulted in the king tumbling over. This story tells us so very much in such a small narrative: That Rollo, and Viking warlords in general, were so powerful that they could deny or demand anything due to their power and supremacy—seen by the fact that Rollo got away with rejecting submission, and that he still received the Normandy he had demanded. It also tells us that even Vikings warriors themselves were unfamiliar with prostrating themselves, and that the lowly Viking raider had no fear of, or saw or felt himself superior to, even a European king. The story itself is also very Norse in nature. It tells of someone trying to humiliate someone, but then it only backfires; Norse tales usually incorporate such amusing twists. The haughty have been ridiculed since ages past in the north, and even fairy tales and stories up to present day, excluding this now destroyed society we have, have incorporated this thinking, which stems from Germanic equality, and a meritocratic thinking where we despise and make fun of the weak and unworthy. Compare Norse mythology, folktales collected by Asbjørnsen & Moe, the Law of Jante, and works by Astrid Lindgren.

X. The Norse and the Normans

A hundred years later the Normans, as these now christened Francophone Vikings were called, would make a huge impact on history. One arguably as great as that of the Vikings on Europe. Normans, on account of their ferocity and martial skills, were granted lands in Southern Italy as a buffer against both the Byzantine hold there and against the Arabs. Early Norman mercenaries met the newly created Varangian Guard and suffered a heavy defeat at the hands of their cousins in the Battle of Cannae. But over time, more Normans came, and they prevailed against both the Byzantines and the Arabs, and even defeated a Pope, which subsequently found himself a prisoner until he gained a more favourable attitude toward his captors and their demands. Norman hold over Sicily, Apulia, Calabria, and Naples grew over a hundred years and eventually led to the creation of the Kingdom of Sicily—one of the great powers of its time. The Normans back in Normandy also had quite a rise themselves. When William the Bastard—a descendant of Gange-Rolv—came to power, he quickly made himself a force to be reckoned with. With a papal blessing in hand, he set his aims high: the conquest of England. He set out on this mission in the year 1066, and it coincided with the simultaneous invasion of England from another claimant named Harald Hardråde (Hard-ruler)—the king of Norway and the last great Viking. Hardråde had earlier in his life served in the Varangian Guard, where he had campaigned with them in Sicily and Italy, before he came back to Norway to claim his birthright. The

Anglo-Saxons, that were now a mix of these Germanics and Vikings, set out to York to meet the Norwegians in the field. The Anglo-Saxons were led by the newly elected king, Harold Godwinson—founder of a new royal dynasty, but the most powerful dynasty in England, and the Isles, at the time. Because of the hot summer weather, the Norwegians had foolishly left their chainmails and armour back at the beach with the ships. There they also left behind a third of the men to guard the boats, supplies, and equipment. The Norwegian army was taken by complete surprise by the Anglo-Saxons when crossing the river Derwent, and they tried taking up defensive position, but were overpowered. It is said that a huge Norse warrior or berserker, wielding a two-handed axe, held the bridge alone against the entire Anglo-Saxon army and cut down over three scores of men. He was only stopped when an Anglo-Saxon soldier thrust his spear into him through the slits under the bridge. This valiant stand had bought some time for the Norse reinforcements to arrive—these in full battle gear, led by Orre. Some of these were reportedly so exhausted by their hasty march from the beach that they collapsed, and some even died, upon arrival. Orre and his men—their arrival called Orre's Storm—made a small impact and held the ground for a while, but in the end it was too late. It was a bloody and hard-fought battle, with the Norwegian king being killed in action and a majority of his army wiped out. The few that survived made it back to the ships and sailed home. The dreams of England were given up and this usually marks the end of the Viking age, even though later Viking-like expeditions did take place. The Anglo-Saxons were victorious, but at what cost? They had lost more than 5000 men in the Battle of Stamford Bridge; this crossing of the river Derwent. William of Normandy had already set foot with an even greater army than the Norwegian invaders, and with heavy cavalry to boot. The Anglo-Saxons rushed to the south to meet them, and gathered what forces they could in the process. Less than a month later these armies clashed. The English king and a number of his kin fell in battle and William won the engagement. Any opposition left was crushed by the Normans, and the Norman duke was crowned on Christmas Day that same year as king of England. He was now, and forever, known as William the Conqueror. The descendants of Vikings settled in Normandy had vanquished the amalgam of Anglo-Saxons and Vikings settled in the Danelaw. A clash of Titans for sure. And the result of all this Germanic and Nordic struggle on the British Isles was the shaping of a people and a nation that would create the largest empire in history and a culture that would dominate the world right up to this day. These Anglo-Normans of the newly conquered England, and the Normans in France and Italy, heeded the call of the First Crusade (1096 – 1099) and contributed greatly to its success, and would continue to do so, furthering the Levantine enterprise of the Kingdom of Jerusalem and the other Crusader states.

The Norwegian kings Øystein, Sigurd, and Olaf—co-rulers, brothers, and descendants of Harald Hardråde—were engaged in domestic affairs during the First Crusade. To make up for it, Sigurd was later chosen to be the one among them go on crusade in support of the newly created Crusader states. He set out in 1107 for the Holy Land (Jorsalaland) with 60 ships and 5000 men to redeem himself and his country. He was the first European king—the very first king in history, when not counting the newly created king of Jerusalem—to go on crusade. He raided and looted great treasures in half a dozen or so Muslim settlements and cities all the way to Jerusalem (Jorsal). They harboured in Sicily and were greeted by the young count, Roger II—later to become king of Sicily—before sailing on directly to the Holy Lands. They landed in Acre (Akersborg) and were met by the first king of Jerusalem, Baldwin I, with a great welcome and feast, and the two kings rode together to the river Jordan and back. During the meet, Baldwin asked Sigurd if he would help with the capture of Sidon—a heavily fortified city of the Fatimids—to which Sigurd replied: "We have come in the service of Christ." They then set out to commence with the siege. The Norwegians mounted the daunting walls, and with surprising ease they obliterated the large garrison that was there. And just like that the city had been taken. Baldwin and the patriarch of Jerusalem, Ghibbelin of Arles, ordered a splinter of the cross to be taken and given to Sigurd in recognition of this most holy and glorious victory. The service to Christ had been fulfilled. Voyaging home, Sigurd sailed to Cyprus—then under Byzantine control, and later conquered by Anglo-Normans in the Third Crusade—and stayed there for a while before setting sail to Constantinople again. They anchored at a Greek port named Engilsnes to wait for better winds, in order to fully stretch the sails and make it look more spectacular when sailing into the harbour of Constantinople. And so they did. The ships sailed so close at entry that it looked like one big sail covering the sea. All the people saw the splendour and the Byzantine emperor, Alexios I, proceeded to open the city gates, with Sigurd riding in on horse through the Gold Tower Gate in front of his men. The King would spend some time there with the Emperor in the Great City before recommencing his voyage back to Norway. A majority of Sigurd's men would stay behind and take up service in the Varangian Guard and would not accompany their king home. Sigurd gave away some treasures and most of his ships, including the glorious ship figureheads, to the Emperor, and in return he was given the finest horses for his journey back to Norway. Sigurd travelled through the Balkans and Central Europe, and the many kingdoms there, and even met with the Holy Roman emperor, Lothar II, before eventually reaching Denmark. A trip that would take three years or so. In Denmark he was given ships by King Niels I and sailed back over Skagerrak and home. This is the story of how he came to be known as Sigurd the Crusader (Sigurd Jorsalfare, meaning the traveller to Jerusalem). In the entire Norwegian Crusade, not one battle was lost.

XI. Impact on the World

This is the importance of Celto-Germanic man—this purest extant descendant of the ancient Aryans of old. I have tried to show the significance he has had on history, and still has. Even today the Anglo-American countries, and the Nordic and Germanic countries in Europe, are still the most powerful and greatest. They are the least corrupt and most crime free, and the most inventive, productive, and cultured. It should be said, however, that in the recent decades the immigration and minorities have increasingly worsened those statistics, and it is getting worse by the year now. We can see how the Balkans or Greece are today, with the mixing of a massive variety of nationalities and races, and how it has worsened those places. This was what happened to Rome and all other great empires as well.

We can easily correlate how advanced a nation is today by how it has adapted to the current global status quo. With the Anglo-American sphere being the leader of the world, and with English being lingua franca, we see that it is repeatedly some nations—these nations who were historically great—that adapted the best and were able to integrate and work with this current world order. Taiwan, South Korea, and Japan has done very well. Nations that do not even have a population that can properly speak and understand English. When North Korea and China finally throws off the communist yoke, they are also likely to perform as good as their brethren—China has already committed to capitalism, albeit state capitalism, but they have done very well because of it. And all the extremely successful European countries like the Nordic nations, or Germany, Austria, and the Netherlands, all speak English fluently. However, speaking English is not a measure of success, or intelligence and ability, as I was trying to make a point of with South Korea and Japan. In India there are many who speak English, and they are not a successful nation in any way, really. And in Africa, too, English is commonly spoken and understood, and there they are still in a Stone Age in terms of culture, governance, etc., and even in regards to technology, when not counting the technology that the Western world has brought them. And brought the rest of the world for that matter. My point is that the countries that adapted to Western culture, values, and practices, and have succeeded in the same manner as the aforementioned European ones, have shown themselves capable and worthy.

The Third Position

Plato and Socrates

I. The Position of Plato

What more undervalued figure in history is there today than Plato? The man who set the basis for Western civilization as we know it. A man that the subsequent, and more credited (at least in recent times), Aristotle owed much if not all to. Plato, who tried to change the world with a messiah of his own: Socrates. And because of the fact that Socrates has lived and existed, it becomes so much harder to deny Plato's dialogues. Even in his own time Socrates was a famous person, and Plato used this for what it was worth. With such a solid anchoring in that persona, there was a lot to build on. In any case, what would Socrates be, if not for Plato today? Socrates did not write anything of his own. All we have is Plato, and a few other sources. And there is constant speculation on what is true in Plato's writings about Socrates. But what does it matter? Is this a sort of trial against Plato on behalf of Socrates? Why would Socrates care about that? If it had not been for Plato, Socrates would have been an obscure figure in history. And if Plato was indeed using Socrates for his own agenda, then what harm has been done? It did not tarnish the reputation of Socrates. Quite the opposite, really. And how are we to say that Socrates is not present in these writings? Plato was his pupil, after all. And a close and trusted one at that, and surely most of Plato's values came from his master. If but a small portion of his master's opinion and thinking is there in those writings, then that would be better than if we had none today at all.

Better it is to ask why there is such great wish to undermine the works of Plato. And when reading and understanding Plato you see it clearly: it stands almost in complete contrast to modern society.

Part Three: A Recollection of Events

Plato's Republic was intended as a polemic against the Athenians and the democratic city republics of old, and even more of a magnificent polemic it is today. This is why Plato is so reviled, hated, and ignored at present. He attacks equality/socialism, rule of money (capitalism), individualism, art in its corrupting capacity, and ignorance and lies. It is therefore not strange that society, then and now, show such hostility to Plato and his ideals. Or perhaps it was actually Socrates' society? After all, the Athenians did put him on trial and sentenced him to death. That is no coincidence to me. He spoke out on their corrupt, decadent, weak, and abominable society, and the people hated him for it.

Plato believed the state to be a reflection of the people, and that the brightest and strongest of the people must be prioritized and put in positions of government. They must also be encouraged and allowed to breed more, and more freely, than the lower classes. The lower classes must be discouraged to breed, and should instead be encouraged to benefit the strong elements in society through productivity and obedience. Plato repeatedly talks about the unequal capacity and ability of men, but there is also a socialistic element. Not in the manner of socialism of today, and especially not that of communism, but socialism where every healthy and strong citizen born is afforded the same opportunity to show his ability and skill as all others. A socialism where classes exist, but where all are born classless, and then divided into class according to their ability later in life. A meritocracy with class cooperation, and not class struggle and strife. A state where the people are the most important part of society; and along with good education, culture, and values this makes for a good state. And not vice versa in the case of communism, where the state is the most important thing above race or man, and where they think that brainwashing and indoctrination matter more than the vessel that contains it.

The Third Position

The common good takes place over the people. The common good being the best and brightest, and the furthering of it, in society. Therefore, no individual is allowed so much freedom that he can intentionally or unintentionally do harm to the people and the state. The people are free to compete, trade, till their lands, and reap the benefit of their work, certainly, but first and foremost for the good of society. Free enterprise and freedom for the individual as long as it benefits the state and its people. Plato allows trade for the main reason of being able to barter and buy goods that are not produced, or otherwise unavailable, in his utopian society. The upper classes are not allowed money or private property of any significance. No money, no houses, no lands, and no valuables. Everything these upper classes, called guardians, need is given and supplied by the state as a whole. This leaves the rulers of the state incorruptible by the fact that they are not allowed to have anything.

In this society the harmful arts, myths, tales of fiction, and other superstitious nonsense is done away with, but not completely if there is some use for it. Have gods if they serve as a good example. Have stories if they teach you right and wrong. Have myths if they show the noble virtues and set a basis for society. But first and foremost comes the people, and the state they collectively represent. In order to better the state and the people, you need the Good. And to find the Good, truth must be found to have a clear understanding and foundation for what that really is. To always question and find the truth, the Good, helps to weed out the faults and to locate problems so that society can change accordingly. Plato is known for his condemnation of art. The way I see it, you have to understand this in the context of the time he lived in. The poets and artists of his day were lousy and unskilled, and they were in a position to make a great impression on, and to sway, the public on anything and everything, and to such a degree that falsehoods and lies were commonplace and festered upon society. Much like art has become today, in many respects. Art where idealism is dead, and shock value, vulgarity, and incitement—on the verge of being pure rabble rousing—is everywhere. Shallow, superficial, and politically and publically harmful art for the ignorant masses. I think we would all, in essence, agree with Plato. Or at least understand why he has these opinions. Those not even able to understand his point of view are lousy historians and researchers, and even worse philosophers.

I venture that Plato and Plato's Socrates would have been atheists if they had lived today. Socrates denies being an atheist only because he could not prove the non-existence of gods—such silly proof that people persistently demand. You don't have to prove a negative, obviously, but the existence of gods was not seen as negative in those days. Therefore, Socrates worked around this and he shaped the gods in his image, and used them for the noble purpose of persuading the people instead. The use of religion was one of calculated politics. Populism, in a sense. Plato did pander to the masses. He sort of veils his Republic as something to be wanted and desired by all—and it should be, though—in order to convince people to take the right path and embrace this new state. He knows they are all shallow, ignorant, and selfish, and he needs to convince them somehow. Hence, the necessitous use of gods, for example.

What we all have to thank Plato's dialogues for is his dialectics: to dig and search for truth, to discuss what is true and what is false, and to stay on topic and avoid false rhetoric. Which may sound easy, but people constantly fall into these simple traps. Fallacies, as we call them today. And what else but rhetoric and fallacy is used in political debates today? The politicians are not even called out on it when they commit them. Not by the people, and not by the political moderators. A few opposing politicians have tried to, but the truth is that people are just too ignorant to understand—most do not even know what a fallacy is—and they are not able to differentiate between the words of meaning and those of none, or even handle simple definitions. This is why Plato continually talk about the sophists and their bad influence, because there was the same problem in his day with politics based on rhetoric, lies, and fallacies. The politicians of that time were almost exclusively trained in those horrid arts by the sophists. Not educated in what can be known, is known, and what is good and true. Nay, only trained in the art of swaying public sentiment in whatever devious way possible. Sound familiar? Yes, I'd say the sophists and their apprentices are a problem still.

II. Critique and Comparison

There are constant attacks on Plato from the philosophical, and even the scientific, communities. The philosophers usually accuse Plato of only arriving at the conclusions that he wants to, as if he magically conjured it up. What they actually have a difficulty with, and fail to see, is that it is the premises they have a problem with and dislike, and that this is why he arrives at those conclusions. In my political opinion, Plato's premises are well founded. The criticisms of Plato can therefore be attributed to political bias, and I see it as petty and presentismic.

One of these philosophical debacles, and common confusions, is between that of the Ideal and the ideal. The Ideal is something that is familiar. A common image that one person has learned in his situation and environment. Coming from the Idea: when you hear the word dog, you think of the one you are most familiar with or the one you liked the best. It serves as an insight into thought, and how that thought was formed. The Ideal is therefore very subjective and may vary greatly between different individuals, because of that difference of experience. Through the Ideal we do see function and definition, though, and this way we find the objective. See chapter *Dissociation and Ideal*. This is not the same as ideal, which is best defined as something that is best, better, good, or perfect in a general sense. A figure of speech.

Another of these problems is that these detractors fail to interpret in context. They are judging it by the time they live in, and not by the realities of Plato's time. Plato based his ideal society on a time where reality had empowered city-states to be the pinnacle of civilization. He also had to consider the power politics of the time. Therefore, many solutions were rooted in such premises: Having little or no riches in the city to make it worthless to conquer. Training the best soldiers and guardians in the world so that no other city-states would want to attack such a fierce state. Always try to stay out of wars and be neutral. If the state was threatened in some way, you would find allies by offering them all of the spoils so that they would be more willing to join the cause. The point I am making is that Plato was taking measures mostly according to the needs of his day, and not ours—how could he have? And calling Plato's conclusions intellectually dishonest when you do not agree with them is absurd. The fact of the matter is that it is purely a disagreement and a difference of world view and politics. A truth is very subjective unless dealing with conclusive proof and facts. It is therefore only your own embarrassing failure to properly analyse, and not the failure of these viewpoints and conclusions. And if you go by the science of today, and use it against Plato or people of times before such revelations and truths were available, or even possible, I see that as either despicably dishonest or idiotic. There are a few valid criticisms—or better to say clarifications—but not really aimed at Plato and of his fault. Only on some of his policies, which were well considered at the time they were made, but not today with modern science. Such as his breeding program. Children in Plato's city-state were born without a family name and were to grow up without parents, or the ones that were their biological ones at least. With unrestricted sex and promiscuity among the upper classes—no monogamy, in other words—it could have resulted in incest, since no one knew their parents and siblings. The children would presumably sleep in collectives or in assigned family houses. Not having a stable family life at such a young age may not be optimal. Well, not in a society such as our own, but in a good and proper society where everyone loves, teaches, and takes care of each other, as if they were their own—which they actually could be, and should be in mind and thought according to Plato's society—then it would perhaps work, and they may even be better off for it. This would lessen favouritism, such as nepotism, due to not knowing your blood and family, and everyone being a brother and sister in spirit. And how well deserved it would be, when rising through the ranks of society based only on your merits.

As for Plato's definition of Good, I see no problem with it. A Good is easily defined as what is always best for the survival of Plato's city-state. And so, it is logical and consistent that his Good follows that principle. But how expected and pathetic such criticisms are, when coming from contemporaries, or others, that praise or condone the lifestyle of today's society. A nihilistic society. A society that pollutes, overpopulates, and depletes resources for pure hedonism and egoism. A society that is destroying our only habitat. It is no wonder why these two greatly opposing views are so polarized and incompatible, and why these adherents of democracy (as was Plato's enemy as well) are so keen on falsifying the truth so that their unsustainable and all-destructive lifestyle may continue unopposed.

There are a great many comparisons made, even by praised and valued scholars, between Plato's ideal state and that of communism, but this is nothing but wishful thinking, and pretty shallow interpretations, on their part. Plato does not advocate equality, for one. And he does not advocate elimination of free enterprise or personal property for the people. He also does not believe in the importance of the state above the people. He believes, rather, that the state hinges on the people, and not the other way around. He believes in building society from the upper class and down, and the power of breeding the strong and intelligent. He believes that man and body shapes and creates ideas and states. And not the communist thinking that the state shapes mind and body, and in building on the poor specimens of the lowest classes. We have seen what such societies as those have become, and in most cases they have vanished completely due to their own unsustainability. Plato also believes in proper education, and in telling the truth, because it is not a threat to such a state. Unlike the communist state that lies and deceives, and keeps its people blissfully uneducated and unaware. When these "experts" see socialism and equate it with communism in Plato's Republic, they actually see social Darwinism. Which is fully in line with the notions of competition and free enterprise in his utopia, and also with his breeding program of the fittest. Plato saw in his time Sparta as the state most similar to his own, and in modern times it is actually fascism, or National Socialism to be more precise, that is the comparison. How extremely similar the society of Plato is to that of Hitler's, with free enterprise and competition, a breeding program, a guardian class—the SS, SA, and various organizations—and a hierarchical meritocracy. But why is this not remarked upon more then? Well, it is, and by quite a few, but it is not publicly stated, and it will never be accepted by society, either. And quite understandably so, because National Socialism is hated to such an absurd degree today that it will never be spoken about in any manner that may portray it in a good light. And they will lie, conceal information, and twist the truth for it to remain that way, because if you were to equate Plato with National Socialism, then you would intertwine the greatest and most influential thinker in history with it. And you would then also have to equate or compare feudalism and much of medieval Europe and Ancient Rome to it. These feudal systems, class systems, aristocracies, kingships, serfdom, mercantilism, or even the Church, that are much inspired by, and defended with, the teachings of Plato. Most of post-Hellenistic European history, in other words.

I think that Plato is the most brilliant man that has ever lived. I owe my enlightenment to him. He was a genius that no one has yet to match. I actually think he was too smart for his own good, as geniuses usually are, and therefore the common people cannot and will not understand him. Plato was a man of principle. He wanted to improve upon society, or construct a new, good, and ideal one. To better it, or to simply create it, if need be. This is the greatest thing that man does, in my mind. It is what makes man unique, and what separated him from the beast. It is evolution, really. To continually create more and more advanced societies, ways of life, that correct the problems and flaws of the previous ones.

Part Three: A Recollection of Events

Nietzsche and Germany

I. Description and Characterization

Nietzsche was the last of the great philosophers. After Schopenhauer's system thinking, there was not much left to do, in a sense. Schopenhauer had pinpointed all things, and where he had found an unknown, an x factor, he would resort to describing and assigning it to his theory of the *will*. This made the equation solvable, and this is one of the reasons why it can be said that he was one of the greatest metaphysicians to have ever lived. It had been all too fashionable in Schopenhauer's time, and before, to be thinking of societal structuring (note that Schopenhauer had no societal ideas or intentions) or developing philosophical systems—was this why Nietzsche focused more, and to a higher and higher degree throughout, on the individual instead of society, the collective, or the people? In any case, Nietzsche found his niche: he set about to unravel the secret of morals. This was to be his main study, and this is where he shines. Everything else is more or less a by-product of that. And when he plunged into the depths of right and wrong, he found the inner workings of the mind, and through this his psychological insight started concurrently. Nietzsche started this path of enlightenment after a near-death experience from illness, and Nietzsche did in fact characterize it as having died. Prior to these serious bouts of illness, he was struggling with increasingly poor health, and in the end it made him give up on his career of philology and retire. He travelled to Switzerland, Italy, and France and spent much of the rest of his life in the Mediterranean areas. This was when he had these frequent bouts of ill health, and it surely made him rethink and ponder life more deeply than he would have had the time, and inclination, to do earlier. I'm sure the seriousness of facing death, coupled with the knowledge that his father died young as well, made a massive impact on him—the latter of which he admittedly wrote about. So often the thought of being obliterated from existence is a mind-opening experience. One that grounds you to reality. At least that is how I know it, but I am sure that many a soul has had the opposite feeling and experience, and started grasping for the supernatural and promises of eternal life, when faced with such grim truths. But for Nietzsche, surely not. He was an atheist. His great inspiration Schopenhauer was also an atheist, and that is usually how it is for most thinking men. Nietzsche says that he had never had an inkling about notions of God or other supernatural entities, and he attributes his insights into moral relativism due to this early detachment from Christian values—which is exactly how I have experienced it myself. Earlier in his retirement and book writings he was much less vicious than later on. He was more understanding of both men and events. He states that his retirement made him re-evaluate everything, or gave him time to think on his previous learnings, and to study more, as he says. Re-evaluate his life, and life in general, I would call it. One prevalence throughout his writings is the characterization of himself as happy. He freely divulges to not having been happy as a child, but now he has found happiness, he says. It seems his adult life was surely not a happy one back in Germany. Still, he is happy now, he proclaims. Why does he need to convince us of this, and to what purpose? Could it be that he was only trying to convince himself? It seems to me that Nietzsche found an internal happiness instead of external happiness, which one must do when the external is not there. This man who almost met death, and lives in physical pain and agony with his affliction, and with a seemingly short time left of existence: such a man can do no else. He has to change his outlook on life, and refocus his energy and stop blaming himself. He is no longer the one at fault, but through this rationalization he takes on an even worse attitude. One of arrogance and elitism, which is the result of him telling himself that he is better, and better than everyone else. And that he thinks so is quite apparent in his writings. An example of this arrogance and conceitedness is his repeated mentions of his power and skill with women. Something that has not been attested at all, and seems to be the exact opposite of what was known of him then and now. There are also other boasts about himself. Like being a self-made man. But by his standards it could apply to anyone. He was sent to private school at young age and received an education that was available to very few. I fail to see how that is anything close to being self-made. Privileged I call that. Which is more like the opposite of self-made. His works, great that they are, was much accomplished with the help of his scribe and assistant Peter Gast (Heinrich Köselitz), who also had a lot of input on Nietzsche's ideas, and helped to compile and correct. Nietzsche does credit him a great deal, but it seems worth to mention that Nietzsche's books and writings were thus much helped. At least in the tedium of the physical process. I am by no means saying that any man in his time, or any others since, has risen to the peaks of insight and clarity as he has. The mental acuity and brilliance is all his, I am sure. It seems that this excess of things, like that of money, was there his whole life. He even says so himself that "there was never a shortage". Although, he says that about women as well so who knows what to believe?

When he took on this new thinking and found his happiness, and in a new place and locale, and then saw his previous life in Germany as unhappy, the association had been made: Germany is bad. Everything else is good. This is the truth he sees. But happiness was not found, it was created. In his mind. But it is there now, nevertheless. And he seems to revel in it. This suffering and unhappiness of his has been turned into happiness. He is happy with being unhappy. This *amor fati* he speaks of—*amor fati* meaning love of one's fate—is the act of him resigning himself to his fate, both past and future. To his circumstances. He needs to do this. He needs to embrace the past, the present, and the future for whatever it is. His health, mind, and happiness depends on it. And this he does. Unashamedly so, but so does any other man, in his defence. He repeatedly claims that he lacks resentment, bitterness, and ill will, as he calls it. Yet, all he does is resent. But not himself anymore. No, it is directed at almost all the factors of his former life, his former unhappiness. And who else is this directed at more than what was most central to his life prior to retirement: Germany, and everything German. Yes, even success was found outside Germany. Or at least a success that he found a happiness in, and appreciated. He desperately wants Germany to be this hellish hole that he felt his life was like while there, and he does everything in his might to distance himself from the German. He makes up the completely false and unfounded lie of being descended from Polish noblemen, for instance. The reason for this hate becomes blatantly obvious through the fact that he doesn't mention Austria at all. Only, and always, the German in Germany. This German who he had been around all his life. This picture, this Idea, of the German which he associates Germany with. Everything this German likes, he despises. With Wagner being the opium for the masses and greatest entertainment at that time, it is natural that Nietzsche would despise such artistry that would appeal to these "dumb" masses. In fact, Nietzsche goes so far as to call Wagner's music pandering, as if this was Wagner's intention, and that Wagner didn't like, or wanted to make, the music he made. "How awful", Nietzsche thinks, when even the lower classes have found a happiness and a passion he had not. He who was much more worthy than them. This elitism of his is rampant throughout most of his writings. If he would have had success with the great masses, I am sure it would have mellowed him greatly; or perhaps he could not have stood it all, being one of those panderers.

I concur with Nietzsche. I also think that *Thus Spoke Zarathustra* is his greatest work. By far. It is probably one of the greatest works in history. Other than that, the last part of *Beyond Good and Evil* and the first part of *Genealogy of Morals* are worth mentioned as being particularly brilliant. In all the rest of his writings, between glimpses of brilliance and his rather good maxims and the likes, there is a great deal of large and small venting of hot air. One problem I have with Nietzsche is that he has no mission or goal of some kind, and he only rarely states his point outright. It is as if he picks apart everything and everyone only to glorify himself and his vanity sometimes. He has no alternative proposals and conclusions for most of his attacks and criticisms, and he does not aim to change the world, beyond that small and narrow path he sets before us, that is. He dreams about a world that would revolve around his thinking and philosophy, but he does not have any precise way or plan for such a society or state. Despite all his faults, there is greatness, though. He gave us a profound insight into morals, and he was a fantastic poet. His unravelling of Christian and pre-Christian morals—the master-slave morality paradigm—is thorough and deep. Immoral and the Antichrist he called himself; the one who opposes Christ and Christian morals. His genealogy of morals—the good, bad, and evil— is enlightening and groundbreaking. It is clear that when Nietzsche started out, he associated the masters and master morality with the Greeks, the Romans, and all other ancient empires and their values. He saw it as the rule of the strong over the weak, the intelligent over the stupid, the noble over the peasant—an order of old. The order of nature, lacking in sympathy and devoid of notions of equality. A society where the ones who are better must rule over those who are not, and where man thinks and acts for himself, and sets his own goals and way of life instead of following blindly like sheep. But the strange thing is that Nietzsche hails the Caesars and Napoleons, even though they had plenty of sheep following them. It seems that populism is not a problem for Nietzsche, as long as it benefits the strong and superior. As it very well should be.

II. Falsities and Contradictions

There are many claims about Nietzsche today. One of the most absurd ones is that he was not a proponent of his own master morality, which is quite laughable for anyone who has read Nietzsche. Thinking such things only shows a shallow understanding of Nietzsche—the psychology of him—and his work. I'd call it wishful thinking, and an obvious effort to try to distance Nietzsche from National Socialist Germany. Reading Nietzsche, it is quite clear that he thought master morality was better. He always refers to the masters as being heroes and superior, and always speaks of the slaves in condescension. Nietzsche says, for instance, that pity has no place in a superior moral system, and since he identifies pity as being part of the slave/Christian morals, then the opposite of that is the master system. Nietzsche has only identified two systems, and he therefore has to think of master morals as better, and slave morals as inferior. If he supposedly preferred or condoned slave morality, then why would he undermine and paint slave morality or Christianity in the way that he did? After all, most of his books revolve around attacking Christianity, and the lower class, the commoner, the feeble, and the weak. In light of this, such speculative views make no sense. Maybe one would like to think that Nietzsche only thought about these things without having the slightest care about them, and with no purpose. People throughout time have worked on what they wanted to and that which they liked the most. They would have to, because motivation and joy are some of the most important attributes when developing expertise and perfection in the thing done. A motivation and drive due to a mission, design, or plan in mind. You would have me believe that Nietzsche spent months and years on these things, but that it meant nothing to him at all? Criticisms and viewpoints such as these, or whatever you call it, is nonsense and it is a true example of falsification of history. If Nietzsche sounds neutral in his work, it is because he is explaining the moral landscape thoroughly. He has to take an intellectually neutral stance, and has to look at it from both sides and explain in great detail about each of them, in order to be taken serious in this greatest work and achievement of his: the transvaluation of morals. It is clear that he favours the one over the other, though.

Nietzsche praises the great leaders and free spirits of history, and he compares himself to these repeatedly. Napoleon is an idol to him, and he worships him to no end. Nietzsche says that it was the German who stopped Napoleon from creating a European empire. This is where Nietzsche shows his a weakness as an historian—flattering as this accusation of his is, though—because he fails to account for the rest of Europe and their large contributions. The fact is that it was the British, and the French exploits in Russia and Spain, that undid Napoleon. Another fact is that none of those wanted, or would have accepted, a Napoleonic Europe. How could the strong Spanish pride in culture and language, brimming with nationalism as it is, have accepted a French dominance? Or even Britain for that matter, as the largest empire at the time, and for a long time after as well. Their nationalism, and that of many others including Italy, was not under the sway of, or even interested in, anything French. He attacks German nationalism, but in the Romans, the Greeks, the French, and pretty much everyone else he praises it. And when he says that Napoleonic Europe would have been above petty nationalism, he truly shows how rose-tinted his view on what he likes is, because Napoleon and the French Empire was utterly French, and there was no room for anything but that. When Nietzsche saw the formation of the German Empire and its domination of Central Europe along with Austria, and that it was on the precipice of uniting Europe under a German dominance and not a French one, he said nothing. And had someone asked him about it, he would not have wanted it so, and probably would have lashed out in angry ranting at how unworthy and culturally lacking the Germans were. Nietzsche had no dream of a united Europe free of nationalism. He only wished to see German power and dominance, and anything German, to vanish. Or at least change. Nietzsche shows his resentment and disdain for Germany again and again in ever more devious ways. He says he has more readers in Scandinavia and Russia than in Germany, and says this is "natural", and thus makes an inference that even there they are more advanced and cultured than in Germany. Which is wrong, and laughably wrong in the case of Russia.

To illustrate how advanced the Germans were, I feel compelled to clarify the massive contributions they have made. In truth, German technology has set the foundation for our modern world: Johan Philip Reis, first telephone; Karl Benz, first petrol engine and first car; Rudolf Diesel, first diesel engine; Karl Braun, shared Nobel prize for the first radio, and pioneered electronics and television technology; Karl Jatho, first flight; Focke-Wulf Fw 61, first helicopter; Hans von Ohain, first jet engine; Otto Hahn, first nuclear fission; Heinkel He 178, first jet plane; Konrad Zuse and the Z3, first computer; Wernher von Braun and the V2, first in space. All the things we think of when we think modern, really. And these are only a few. There are huge amounts of intellectual achievement credited to Germans, overall. A great many of these inventions that I have mentioned have been falsely claimed by the Americans, the English, and other nationals today. Such as the Wright brothers and their "first" flight. It is all lies. Or half-truths at best. It was the final defeat of Germany in the Second World War that enabled the Allies to promulgate their revised records on global and historical achievements. They rewrote history for the glorification of themselves. They probably didn't need to rewrite much of their own books, though, self-centred and myopic that such nations are. The true inventors, those first ones, these pioneers of German nationality, were buried under this large quantity of new books and media, and as time went by they were largely forgotten by this world that is now only digesting the politically correct. Victor's justice they call it: to falsify history and lie.

Therefore, even in Nietzsche's days it was an appallingly untrue statement that the Germans were without any achievements. He also says the German is without culture. He would have to say that wouldn't he? Because if he saw himself as cultured, and disliked everything German, the German would have to be without culture. If he had liked some of it, they would have some culture, naturally. So, he just dismisses it wholesale. And as he had read and appreciated a lot of foreign culture, and in particular French culture, which he loved the most—always these French who he greatly admires, Francophile as he is—he would necessarily call it the highest, or greatest, of cultures. When he has something good to say about Germans, he dismisses it later on by saying that they were of other nationalities, or of an older and long gone race of Germans. He will tell any lie and absurdity about them to justify his characterization of them. Rationalization at its best. The only one who believes what he says in that regard is probably him, and that is enough since he was mostly saying it for his own benefit, anyway. Yet, he cannot stop himself from talking about the Germans. Any Germans and all Germans. He dedicates more time to Germans, these objects of his loathing, from the intellectual to the lowly commoner, than anyone or anything else. Nietzsche thus fails to attribute how much Germans have influenced him. Or how much he owes them. His whole life was due to Germans and a German way of life. His schooling, his job, and his pension. And without these German artists and writers and thinkers he would not have had a starting point of discussion to then clarify where they were wrong; or right for that matter. But he seems to be somewhat oblivious to all that, and in any case he does not mention it. If they are German, he hates them all. Except those that he likes, which he has labelled as not being truly German. Everything from poets to philosophers, all despised. And if there was some of them he didn't despise at that time when illness gripped him for good, he probably would have eventually, because most of the other Germans he had the slightest of praise for earlier in life had withered away during those final years when his faculties were still intact. Which brings me to Schopenhauer. Nietzsche calls himself the first psychologist, yet many others before him, such as Plato, had a great understanding of the human mind. Schopenhauer also had a very profound insight into human behaviour, and it is not for nothing that many of the famous and pioneering psychologists throughout history read him. Nietzsche, however, no longer valued Schopenhauer at all. Once an inspiration and master to him, Nietzsche later on completely dismisses him in *Ecce Homo* as being wrong in everything he ever did. Nietzsche also complains that there are no great Germans left in his time, but he forgets that he himself is one those great Germans. The truth is that there were no truly great philosophers and thinkers at all in any nations in his time, and as for posterity it has been a desert wasteland ever since. Nietzsche, with his clarification of morals, conquered one of the last few bastions that were left to be conquered. Today, there is for the most part only the assertion of old beliefs, or statements of baseless, wishful thinking that the conditioned masses nod agreeingly with. And the answers that are yet to be found and uncovered are taboo in this current political environment and world, and thus they will not be embraced when revealed.

I am fully aware of the fact that I have fallen into Nietzsche's trap when I use the example of the great scientific advancements made in Germany against him, but how could I not? He has hedged himself against any attack conceivable in his voluminous writings. In this case I refer to, he says that the argument of the great scientific progress of Germany is not relevant, because he speaks of an entrepreneurial free spirit and mind so that fresh ideas and new culture, as he calls it, emerges. How many types of cultures, morals, and societies does he think that there can be? He himself has only identified the two moral systems of the master and slave. And what of culture? Is culture some sort of standard? I dare say the master does not need culture. Culture is for the slaves. This argument of scientific achievement is, in his opinion, an indication of one who has not properly read, or understood, his books and philosophy. Nietzsche resorts to an ad hominem just as easy as that. Nietzsche states repeatedly that there are no morals and no truths, yet he proclaims them all the time. Culture exists he says, and some are better or higher than others. But a richness of culture is not the same as technological progress and advancement, and we repeatedly see that intricate cultures with many rules and regulations sometimes stagnate completely due to that rigidity. Or what about his attacks on nationalism and how pointless he thinks it is? He attacks anything, really. Well, are those not his truths? He repeatedly proclaims his truths to be right, and that others are wrong. Those who do not agree with him therefore do not understand him and are just mistaken. He is a strange one that way—in that he doesn't analyse himself to any great extent, yet he calls himself a psychologist. He compares people and their beliefs, and says that they are influenced and interpreted by each other—plagiarizers he calls them. How can he be so certain in that? And he pokes holes in every truth there is, as if this was proof of having a brilliant mind or that you need one for it, or that it is some sort of glorious achievement to do so. One would have to be quite stupid not to find things in Plato's writing that are not wrong today. 2400 year old writings. Were they wrong at that time? No, they were some of the most profound truths uttered in that age, and still are. Such it is for most beliefs: they wither away and die lest they are not restructured, reinterpreted, or completely revised. This is why I find Nietzsche so arrogant. He thinks and finds everyone wrong, yet he does not clearly see that even his own findings may be very relative, and sometimes even incorrect. His critique of the character of other people and philosophers is also very peculiar, because he completely fails to attribute those faults he finds in others to himself.

His clarity is very blurry at times, and sometimes not there at all. For instance, he speaks of a degeneration of man and claims that it is the lack of following one's instinct that causes this. In other words, he says that the man who follows his instinct will be better off. Yet, this is not true. Today, we see that the hedonism and enormous luxury of excess food, leisure, and entertainment has made man worse. He has degenerated. And this is because of instinct. The instinct to stuff oneself with food and drink, to intoxicate oneself with alcohol and drugs, and to have a lazy, sedentary lifestyle. To seek the most amount of pleasure at all times. This is instinct. Animal instinct. We know that animals will do this if they are enabled to do so. So will humans. Animalistic humans. But a society of values, morals, and rules will help to keep this in check. What I think Nietzsche actually meant was that nature, and following and doing what was once natural for man, does not degenerate man. Instinct is a part of nature after all, as everything is, but it is also held in check by nature. They are opposing, or combative, forces. If one can simulate nature in human society, or a natural way of life and living for man, then one can stop the degeneration of man. This has nothing to do with instinct. Yes, you should identify what is instinctual so that you are aware of it. Some instincts are good, and some are bad. In nature they have their worth, but in society one has to compromise and find the best of both worlds.

III. Dionysus, Loki, and Downfall

Nietzsche does have great insight when his judgement and vision is not clouded. All that he is, good or bad, is why he has such great keenness. Such as his own resentment, which is probably why he was able to identify, and where he got the idea of, the *ressentiment* of the lower classes and Christians in his master-slave morality theory. This theory where the old master values of strength, strong will, pride, and bravery was turned on its head and was deemed not only bad, but turned into an evil, in order to surpass the previous notions of bad; and the slave morals and values of timidity, humility, and meekness, which the masters had called the bad, were now good. This was the reformation of values. Values still held today. The Christian values. And thus Nietzsche calls himself the Antichrist for the offensive connotation that it has, but also because none of his values are that of the Christian. Indeed, he did think, especially early on, that his values were the opposite of Christian values. Later on, however, his thinking takes on more of a rebellious and oppositional nature. Everything is wrong and everything is rejected, no matter what it is. Even states and governments are targets now. All authority is to be denounced. The few and precious individuals are to go their own way, and no morals and laws are to hold them back. He is quite banal in his later days, attributing former statements of his as "folly of youth", but it is instead his words later on in life that makes no sense and that is wholly contradictory. The reason for this is because he is no longer one of master morality, but has planted himself in the middle between master and slave by his spite, envy, anger, and rejection. He earlier praised social structure, empires, and great leaders. Now they are just an obstacle. He repeatedly compares himself to Dionysus—a demigod: one born of a human mother. And so, not quite man (slave), but not quite god (master), he, too, was torn between, and did not belong to, these worlds. Dionysus was quite ambiguous, and was worshipped as a god of self-indulgence, ecstasy, joy, and play, but he also had a shifty, more dangerous, and darker side. He could become resentful and angry, and was also seen as an androgynous character. He is very reminiscent of Loki in Norse mythology. A trickster god, much like Dionysus, and they are both shape-shifters, too. Loki was the joker and the unpredictable one in Åsgard. He was never much serious, although he was easily offended himself when he was made fun of. Loki tested any and all of the other gods whenever he could. Even Odin was subject to his mockery and foul tricks. But most of them were played on Thor. Thor was very prideful, powerful, and easily angered. The symbol of master morality. Loki always liked to point out how hypocritical or highfalutin the gods were with their stories and tales when they had shown very opposite behaviour on many occasions. Such as when Thor hid—or crouched in fear as Loki says—in the glove of Utgard-Loki (a jotun king) while they were in Jotunheim. I see this as very similar to Nietzsche's nature as well. In that he jokes around and makes fun of whatever he can, pointing out the flaws of others and how they are wrong. Loki is like a court jester to the gods and creates a lot of fun and games, but he also serves to always remind the gods of the flaws in themselves, and in their plans. And sometimes even seeks to sabotage them. Like a jester—a vicious little imp—that keeps the king and court in good spirits, but also grounded to earth. With a cruel tongue, he fearlessly speaks the truth and sets them straight. This is what Nietzsche is to us as well. He clearly points out the flaws, wherever he sees them, and while he does this, he plays around with words, and various other theatrics, to keep us entertained. He is still one of us, but has tired with our ways and now only seeks to amuse himself. Similar to Loki, and his fate. He also said too much, and distanced himself too far from the Æsir, and in the end he was to suffer bound up with poisons dripping in his eyes until the days of Ragnarok. I see it as quite the parallel. Nietzsche also started out, or gained entry, as one of the masters (the gods), but he gradually found no fun or comfort there either and started picking and tearing apart that existence. Does Nietzsche tell the truth in most things? Yes, as long as it's not one of those blatant hatreds of his. And even if Nietzsche, or anyone else, tells us how flawed and failed this or that is, one has to remember that nothing is truly perfect, and not everything is logical. There are always contradictions to be found, and it is quite impossible not to be a hypocrite in some way or other. Especially when judged through eyes that fail to see nuance, context, and specifics.

IV. Idealism and Realism

Nietzsche makes comparisons in his later days that make little sense. He says that Christian values and Platonic values are similar, or the same. And although it is true that Plato influenced the Medieval Era and feudalism to a high degree, it will still be hard to compare Plato's social Darwinist world with the egalitarian and altruistic Christian world of later and present time. The reason why Nietzsche compares Plato and Christianity is because the latter drew from the former. They have absolutely nothing in common otherwise. Plato is a master morality proponent just as Nietzsche is. What Nietzsche despises is that Plato and Socrates derived morals and values from their conclusions and ideals. In other words, they believed

The Third Position

that some things were absolutely right and wrong. Nietzsche is of the opinion that anyone who believes in morals and values, and their existence, is stupid. Especially if such a believer is a philosopher or intellectual. But the way Nietzsche attacks laws and morals only leaves us with a lawless and anarchic society. He even praises the criminal at one point. I would call Nietzsche amoral, and not immoral, because in his view there is no good or bad man. He says there is no virtue and no vice. This is obvious when one reads him. But what is his point then? It doesn't seem like he has a point, really. If he is advocating the destruction of morals, he is actually saying that people should stop valuing altogether, and this goes against nature. I would call this complete nihilism. Nihilism, which Nietzsche purportedly tried to prevent and warn us about.

Nietzsche also goes for the easy criticisms of Plato that all other would-be philosophers do: the Forms, and Being and Becoming. Which may not hold water, but they always fail to realize that these things are meant to illustrate and to help you understand the world—formulated in a very ancient setting a long, long time ago. They are not definite things. This should be fairly obvious, since it is Socrates who talks. Socrates, as we know, never claimed that he knew much, but he always tried to explain things when he was asked. "I know that I know nothing", to paraphrase Socrates. What a splendid vantage point that is. No wonder he had such powerful analytic capacity and insight. Philosophers in this modern age of Darwinism, atheism, and scientific wealth should be rather ashamed of themselves when they attack philosophers and thinkers that lived 2400 years ago of their faults. What one should focus on is what they were right about! These modern thinkers, most of them aren't right about anything in the slightest. Indeed, none of these modern philosophers have had any significance at all, really. And seeing that all other fields of science have had a profound rise in understanding and accumulated knowledge in modern times, then the failure of these philosophers is quite a spectacular one indeed, and thus their one and only true achievement, if one can call it that. Philosophy today has become nothing more than an esoteric activity, where they sit in their ivory towers, totally detached from reality and devoid of all practical thought, inventing terms and then building entire studies on them thereafter. I truly despise such people with all my heart. People who get paid for conjuring up fantasy which they then use as some sort of proof of time well spent. And these self-important and -proclaimed intellectuals and academicians even get praised for this. And no better, and probably worse, are the mathematicians, biologists, neuroscientists, and other assorted hacks of our day who try to do away with philosophy altogether, yet when they try to argument for their assertion of it as an artificial field of study, they fall flat on their face. So pathetically unintelligent are some of these people that they cannot even fathom the simplicity of the naturalistic fallacy. They also repeatedly stray onto the path of moral absolutism, and then obstinately and shamelessly deny it afterwards. It could be that some of these only do it for money and fame, riding the wave of the moral zeitgeist for all it's worth, which is even worse. Whatever the case is, they are either abnormally obtuse or they are cynical, moneygrubbing exploiters without a shred of integrity.

Nietzsche has a problem with idealism, that's for sure. German idealism, or Platonic idealism, it is of no difference to him. Which is probably why he develops this distaste for Plato later on in life. Seemingly, he thinks that idealism is in opposition to having a realistic perspective—as many repeatedly do. He says that too perfect and ambitious goals cloud our sense of reality. This idealistic thinking he also equates with Christianity and Christians, who are much too idealistic with their eternal life in heaven, and as such will suffer on Earth because of this priority set. Or that is to say, suffering is the prerequisite for gaining entrance to paradise. Schopenhauerian thinking he calls it. He says that Plato is also plagued with such thinking by not embracing the now and nature instead of the future and the transcendental, or a vision of a better existence. He says that Socrates' willingness to embrace death is comparative with the Christian thought of some future reward, such as life after death. I disagree. I would say that Socrates neatly ties up his life's work of preaching and teaching with that final act of bravery and calmness. It is difficult for me to understand how one can interpret the *Apology* any other way. Although, I do see the resemblance between Socrates and Jesus, with them both being martyrs to their cause. I am not so sure that Jesus was a willing or aware martyr, though. Nietzsche thinks of the present, and life on Earth, as realism. And that of idealism as a future of rewards, or that of the beyond. Nietzsche has stopped suffering, and now only finds joy and pleasure in his life. Such a mind-set, to me, is also idealistic. Although, there are many definitions, and a whole range of different classifications can be used. Does Nietzsche fall for such an easy trick of linguistics? Does he fail to see actuality of use, beyond association of words? Everything does seem to be rather black or white with him. One word that is not to his liking and he eschews it. Nietzsche identifies with the Romans, because of their practical thinking and way of life, and with the sophists, who were also practical, in a sense. But he does not see how Rome was very idealistic, and very inspired and influenced by the Greeks. The Roman had to be idealistic, in my opinion, by going as readily into war and death as he did. Presumably, it was the loss of idealism that caused the Empire to buckle under. Nietzsche praises the sophists later on, which coincide with his new found hatred of Plato. He sees the sophists as practical and realistic, but even Plato would agree in that respect. The purpose of the sophists was to balance out idealism with realism. What Plato loathed about them was their telling of lies, and their rejection of truth and the Good, and not just for them being rhetoricians per se. The sophists are not worth much by themselves. An equilibrium is best, such as Greek idealism balanced out with the realism of the Romans—realities of life such as war, greed, power, and betrayal. If one is idealistic, could one not also be realistic? If I were to plan for a good future, may I not also live well in the moment and before set time?

I am sure Nietzsche was aware of this, and what he tried to do away with was the resignation to the various ills of life. Meaning that he wanted people to strive and better their situation. He wants them to want and lust, which is the drive needed to make that beneficial change, and not to wait for it in some fictional place beyond the clouds. Nietzsche celebrates individual joy more and more throughout, and as he does, he moves away from master morality. The master has to rule, after all. And not only himself, but the lands and the people. The master has to be idealistic. He has to plan for the future. Yes, the future on Earth and not the one in the Elysian Fields. The master can enjoy himself, yes. But he should, and has to, suffer hard physical and mental work, too. He cannot be a soft, dim-witted weakling. And he cannot, and should not, concern himself with the joy of individuals. The master must build the state. He must preserve the order and structure of a Good society. And as we all know, Nietzsche does not seem too concerned with matters of statesmanship and governance. He is only interested in the individual, the superior individuals, and as such it is a selfish interest. He says all are selfish, but having a concern for the people, the state, and mankind, and to live for the continued survival and success of your own kind, is clearly less selfish than the joys of just a single life—the latter of which is pointless and goes against nature. Perhaps he has resigned himself to fate like that of the Christians (Catholics), with this world being run by the great masses who only think in terms of slave morality and thus he believes that getting back to the old structure is now impossible. But that, too, seems doubtful, because he repeatedly, although vaguely, mentions an overthrow of morals and society. A new empire, as he states.

V. Prophecy of a New Empire

Nietzsche speaks of a man who will bring about change. A ruler which will create a new empire and invert the Christian morals, and that will be vilified and portrayed as the Devil himself. An empire of master morality. It is an incredibly exact prophecy he foretells. This is National Socialist Germany. And who else but Hitler is described as the most evil man in history and the Devil incarnate? Even though Stalin killed more men in his time, he is still not called such names. Stalin is barely mentioned at all today—not that there is much memorable about him. Or what about Mao? He thrones the statistics by far. And keep in mind that the people these two communists killed were their own. A legacy of the repeated failure of communism is that the people of these states died—apart from those just murdered for being an "enemy" of the state—while trying to implement collectivism, industrialization, and other absurdities without having any knowhow and knowledge, or able people, to draw up plans and properly implement them. And there is no point in industrializing just for the sake of industrializing, without a market or need for it. They were destined to fail, really, because communism is rooted in ignorance. One only needs to read the *Communist Manifesto* to realize that. And it is worth reading it, if only for the many laughs it provides. Never in my life have I read such baseless drivel. It is as if the author(s) did not have any knowledge of the world and history at all—at least not of a sane and rational kind. Ultimately, communism managed to kill upwards of 150 million (R.J. Rummel) people. If one were to the blame the National Socialists for all the casualties in the entire European theatre of the Second World War, one would not even count 40 million, probably. But this is purely a hypothetical, because it takes two to tango and the Allies and Russia have much of that blood on their hands. When the Russians systematically killed Ukrainians in the Holodomor, which killed upwards to 7.5 million people, there wasn't much of an outcry. So, when fewer people died in the Holocaust—political terrorists, criminals, prisoners of war, and people of all nationalities and races—in these war camps in Germany, due mainly to starvation and disease (as in all wars), and it garnered a bigger reaction and condemnation, then it is not strange that people question how truly biased and dishonest the holders of these views are. And it is perfectly easy to explain, because the communists and the social democratic countries today are not that different from each other. They both believe in an equality, of sorts, and in globalization and the system of slave morality. So, when the fascists and National Socialists entered the world scene—with their third alternative in politics—and with a completely different moral system and societal order, it is quite easy to understand the reactions against them then and now. And with completely opposite viewpoints, they quite naturally have the strongest of hate for each other. But this hate manifested itself much more strongly in the ruling and dominant slave system. After all, they had, and still have, a monopoly on what is good and evil.

Would Nietzsche have approved of this new empire then? It seems to me he would have to. When he spoke of it, he was comparing it to the coming of a new Napoleonic Empire. One that would unify Europe. So, yes, he was right in that sense. But would he have thought it would be a German empire? I doubt that. But maybe, just maybe, all his scornful lambasting of the Germans was done to set them on the right path. Like a mother who is strict and overbearing, because she only wants the best for her children; he does not want to spoil the German by giving them too much, or unwarranted, praise. And in doing so, he might have wanted them to excel, and to rise to his challenge to bring about this new change. Nietzsche wrote in German, after all. And he was German in most manners. As Nietzsche hated himself, he hated the German, and he would also then love them in the same way he loved himself—at least it seems that way to me. And who else but the German would accept Nietzsche? They were one of the few capable of understanding what Nietzsche talked about; and certainly not any of these other races or nations that he says he prefers, but in truth he knows little of except sheer superficialities and what he reads in books. Who else, but an intelligent and open-minded people like the Germans? Nietzsche says the Germans are ever changing and easily swayed (open-minded), and then later says they are single minded. A contradiction in my mind. Single minded sheep he calls the German. They talk and think in the same manner. Nietzsche's thoughts of individualism was much disgusted by this. But surely they cannot have been as single minded as he painted them to be, when looking at the great breakthroughs made by independent mind and thought there. The way he rationalizes away these facts is known to us, however. Germany's military successes is also not an impressive feat to him. He may even have been a bit offended, when the French, who he adores so much, was so utterly defeated by the Germans in the Franco-Prussian War. A war that led to the unification and creation of the German Empire. He claims the Germans are proponents of Christian morals, and when they are ready to revolt and cause upheaval, he sees a lack of culture in them. But Nietzsche is wrong. The reformation was in fact an expression of Germanic individualism. As opposed to the collective thinking of Catholicism. The German, with his intelligence and open mind, is always ready for change. Ready to ascend to and embrace the higher truth whenever it reveals itself, and he has the courage to do it. The capacity for new and more information is how a change of mind occurs. Capacity of information is intelligence. Therefore, if the Germans were to change their ideas and embrace new ones more readily, then it is due to intelligence, and not a lack of culture. If stubbornness and blind devotion to religion and tradition is culture, then better we would be without it. The people of the south behaves that way. Catholic and Roman, the two fused into one, as they still are after thousands of years without much change. The leisurely and passionate life, which he found in the south, probably made Nietzsche sympathetic to it, because he had now found some happiness, as opposed to the working and striving German life, but he fails to see that this existence is not one of a master morality or that of *Zarathustra*, because one has to work, build, and improve for anything and everything. Whether it is mental or physical activity, doesn't matter. It was these southerners who made, and still maintain, the Christian moral system that Nietzsche despises. This is because it is convenient to them. Not much work keeping with it, and too much of a hassle to change. Or hassle? I should rather say unable. These southerners are set in their ways just like the native in the jungle, who has also had his traditions, habits, and rules for many millennia without much change—they see no other way, simply. This Nietzsche praises? I doubt it. Nietzsche loved science. He loved truth. He despises religion and the feebleness of older times. He saw German naivety and open-mindedness as a flaw, but he did not realize that this is the character of intelligence. And with their intelligence, the Germans saw right through his lashing out at them. They saw his character flaw for what it was, but appreciated the critique, nonetheless. They embraced it, took it to heart, and revelled in it, as he did with his own misery. His greatest gift to them was his tough love. He set an ideal to them, and they faithfully followed. He, who hated idealism. At least on the surface of it.

VI. Anti-Semitism

Nietzsche never cared much for anti-Semitism. There seems to be many reasons why. He mainly saw the anti-Semitism in the German as a weakness and poor excuse. As envy of the richer and more privileged Jew. The Jew did, after all, behave in the selfish way that Nietzsche so often praises. Another reason why he likes the Jew is because he doesn't see lying as something immoral, as the Christian does. Nietzsche detests Christian values, and inverts them whenever he can, and embraces that opposite. The lying, deceiving, stealing, and exploiting that the Jew does is a good, and certainly not a problem, for Nietzsche. He admires the Jew and his survival. A survival helped by their modus operandi. The Jews operated, and still does, in a way that is very reminiscent of the way freemasons did. A privileged society that protect their own, which enables them, by this preferential treatment, to profit. The Jew treats his synagogue as the freemason treats his lodge: a place where they gather and conspire, and form new acquaintances and connections to further their dealings with each other. Judaism is freemasonry, in simple terms. And where freemasonry was much hated for such practices, the Jews were, and are, hated for that very reason. This used to be common knowledge. People knew these details. Today, however, their way of operating has been covered up, and any talk or critique of Jews, Judaism, or Israel is shut up with the label of anti-Semitism. And mentioning these very well-known truths of old will immediately garner you the label of being a conspiracy theorist—another technique of trivializing and silencing any opposition. Be sure, it is all part of the grand scheme of political correctness. When the German was taken advantage of and tried to use Christian morals against this as a preventive measure and defence, Nietzsche would certainly have to disapprove. He supported such action, after all—this exploitation of the weak. Whoever does that is stronger in his eyes. Laws and morals are to be circumvented. And this the National Socialists did. In the exact manner as the Jews. They turned the tables on them. As for the racial issue, there never really was one. It was always, and only, just a natural reaction to the organized mafia-like businesses and activities of the Jews, and that of Judaism. The hate for the Jew was as a group or people, and not as a race. And as Nietzsche probably saw in his day, and as all Germans have always been aware of, is that the Jew, the Ashkenazi Jew to be precise, which is the only Jew to be truly successful—the European and now American Jew, and it is they who still dominate among the Jewish types—is actually Germanic in blood and genes. Long suspected and known was this due to their fair skin and hair, and the prevalent blue eyes. This genetic reality has been attested today with gene mapping. The National Socialists were well aware of this. Like they were about the racial realities in general; they wanted a pure race, but never actually claimed that they had one. There is a big difference between those two things. Which is ignored today and propagandized to no end to make it seem like the National Socialists, and all others in that time, were stupid. As Göring said: "I decide who is a Jew and who is Aryan!" Or at least it has been attributed to him. In any case, it reflects the National Socialist thinking. Anyone could be a German, and even the hated Jew could, if only he showed his loyalty and commitment. But most of them never did. Quite the opposite. Which is why they were imprisoned. Why racial classifications were not of great interest to Nietzsche is based on that same reasoning as the National Socialists had: what is most important is ability and merit.

The Third Position

Would Nietzsche approve of National Socialist Germany? The answer would have to be yes. If not, he would have to go against all of his teachings. The German had risen to Nietzsche's challenge. But where Nietzsche prophesied that this empire would last for a long time, he failed to see the parallels in the Napoleonic Empire with the adversity and opposition it garnered, and even more so in how difficult it would be to operate with a new moral system to boot, without the world starting to hate you. Which was exactly what happened. The entire world turned against Germany and did not stop until it was smashed to pieces. One could say that Germany and everything German was actually annihilated in that war. Only the language and a few other notions survived.

One of the consequences of slave morals, according to Nietzsche, and it is hard to disagree, is that with it also came the degeneration of man. This is why he speaks of the Overman (Übermensch), the one that will continue on the path of evolution towards higher intelligence and a more refined body. Or the Last Man, who stands at the threshold of extinction. Anything below the Overman was the Underman (Untermensch). This latter would be to the Overman what ape is to man. A source of shame, ridicule, and laughter. But Nietzsche also says that man as a whole may not be degenerating. He speculates that it might only be the priests—those firmest holders of slave morality—that is on the wrong path, this path to extinction. He may very well be right, and in any case, if only a few are to digress from slave morality and stay on the path of the master and nature, and to overcome and rise, they will eventually take over again once the inferior majority have lost out, or just self-terminated.

Part Three: A Recollection of Events

The Causation of the World Wars

I. Precursor

After the Austro-Prussian War, and the closely followed Franco-Prussian War, Europe had stabilized. The victory of Prussia in those wars finally enabled the reunification of the Germans, which had been lost when Napoleon forced the dissolution of the Holy Roman Empire. Much trauma was caused by that event. The Holy Roman Empire had not only been the guarantor, but the extension, of the German people for over 800 years. After it ended, a power vacuum formed, and a struggle ensued that caused much spectacle and upheaval. The Holy Roman Empire itself was in many respects the spiritual successor of the Roman Empire, and thus the stabilizing force of Europe, after the Carolingian Empire, and after the Frankish dominance had waned. The muscle of the HRE, in combination and cooperation with the intellectual and spiritual power of the papacy, preserved the territorial integrity and safety of the nations and people in Europe; they were the stewards of Europe. The legacy of this German institution was that it enabled the rise of Europe. The ravages throughout Europe by the French kings, and Napoleon later on, led to the weakening of the glue that bound not only Germans together, but much of the Italians and other people as well. And in the end it finally broke. With the old structure gone, a huge power vacuum was left behind. And as there was no force or will to reinstitute the HRE, nationalism and unification efforts instead took over. The Italians and Germans didn't really have a rise or emergence of nationalism and nationalistic sense, they already had that in the HRE. That was their state and their homeland. The extent of the HRE was such that it stretched from the Netherlands to the Baltics, and from the Danish border and deep into the middle of Italy, and sometimes it even comprised much, if not all, of Italy. The HRE was a German and Italian state proper, with a small amount of other peoples, e.g. the Czech. This "rise" of nationalism was nothing but the fallout of having the HRE dismantled and fractured. Germans did not suddenly wish to become united, they only wished to be reunited.

When Prussia was finally able to consolidate its power throughout much of Germany from the grip of the Austrian Empire in the Austro-Prussian War, and then the French in the Franco-Prussian War, the German reunion, a union that was lost after the dissolution of the HRE, was finally achieved. During the Austro-Prussian War, the newly unified Kingdom of Italy joined in, and despite their very poor efforts, the honourable Prussians were loyal and true to the Italian cause of unification, and with Prussian victory achieved, the Teutons pressed the Italian claim for the return of the province of Veneto. Such was the nobility and brotherly love of the Prussian that he would further the unification of Italy before he had undertaken his own German one. One may say that this was merely coincidence, but one has to take into account how selfish and treacherous nations were in that period (this period after the loss of the stabilizing force of the HRE and the weakening of the papacy and religion). This behaviour persisted all the way up to the end of the Second World War, and therefore the Prussian conduct was remarkable at the time. An example of this selfishness and treachery was the French promise, or better to say deal, in granting assistance to the Kingdom of Sardinia in the struggle of Italian unification. The price the French had set was a large tract of land in Savoy and a smaller piece in Nice; certainly not selfless and noble. The rather insubstantial gain of Lombardy, made in the Second Italian War of Independence with French help, could not be considered a good trade, but it did consolidate the power of the Kingdom of Sardinia, and as such facilitated the subsequent unification of Italian lands under them. Rome and the papacy was the final piece in a united Italy, but the French had guaranteed papal territorial integrity and blocked that path. However, with the utter defeat of the French in the Franco-Prussian War, the way to Rome was open. With these two wars—the Austro-Prussian and the Franco-Prussian—the German had not only finalized the unification of his own country, but that of Italy as well.

This reassembly of order in the former Holy Roman Empire was quite swift, as you see. And the powers of the day certainly noticed it, and grumbled much at it. Many had appreciated the complete loss of cohesion and structure in Europe. They hoped for a disintegrated Europe to profit on, and to do so unopposed from all sides and in all corners. The British Empire was the main culprit in this, but the Americans and the Russians were also very happy with this new world order. It backfired, however, and where there were only small and powerless states in the former HRE, there were now two very powerful nations taking their place instead—namely, the Kingdom of Italy and the German Empire. Austria was not broken either despite these defeats. But she had suffered setbacks, and cracks were forming that were threatening the foundation. The state restructured, and with the 1867 Compromise, this once German nation was now a dual monarchy with the Hungarians being in control of their own half. Thus, the Austro-Hungarian Empire came into existence, and the northern half of the Balkans was stabilized as a result. The southern part of the Balkans, however, were continuing to ever spiral ever more out of control. The powder keg of Europe, as it was called, had first seen its independence wars against the Ottoman Empire in Greece. And with the relative success achieved there, it served as an inspiration to the rest of the various nationalities in the Turkish territories. War by war flamed up in the Balkans, and one by one the nations there eventually liberated themselves.

There was peace in Western Europe for over 40 years after the conclusion of the wars that had resulted in the German Unification. A truly remarkable achievement and a testament to the righteousness of those disputes, the validity in the borders finalized and the treaties that were concluded, and finally in the general contentment thereof. The new order was a success.

II. Build Up to War

The French were so offended by their utter military failures, and having to give back Elsass-Lothringen to the Germans, that they turned absolutely insane with rage and thoughts of revenge. This even after the Prussians had only settled for half of Elsass-Lothringen. This half of which was overwhelmingly German. Besides, the entire province had always been part of the HRE. The horrendous defeat of France, in a war that they had started, and the glorious and complete victory of the Prussians and the German Confederates, made the terms in the Treaty of Frankfurt extremely mild, lenient, and forgiving. And perhaps this was the problem with it, because the French were not broken. At least not in spirit, and they were insistent on having another deadly war no matter what. They started the Franco-Prussian War, and they lost it and did not pay the price for instigating it. They suffered no condemnation for it either, as opposed to what others have had to endure for starting wars—how hypocritical and biased the telling of history is. And now the French were dead set on starting another one, of which they also managed to avoid any blame for. They set out to ally themselves with the Russians and the British Empire, and then they awaited the opportunity to strike. There was an enormous gearing up for war because of this

French revanchism. Both military and naval buildup shot through the roof. The French had learned from the Franco-Prussian War that even with having superior gear they could still suffer extreme defeat. And so, they doubled down on everything. Germany and Austro-Hungary became increasingly isolated on all sides. Everyone wanted the successful German nations to crumble. The Germans had the best military in the world, the best intelligentsia, and now their nations were becoming the industrial powerhouses of the world as well. Even the U.S. felt that their trade and industry suffered. The bullying of the German states had thus started, and everyone was in on it. In the southeast, the Ottoman Empire felt threatened in the Balkans, with the British and French support for the Greek and Romanian independence movements there. The Entente also wanted a large piece of the pie in the Middle East at the expense of the Turk. And the Russians wanted lands in the Caucasus and in the northeast of the Balkans, and worked to create Bulgarian and Serbian buffer states—Pan-Slavic interests always compelled the Russian to exert hegemony in the Balkans, one way or another. The fronts were thus set. On all sides the German was met with a cold shoulder, and therefore quite justifiably expected to be attacked sooner or later.

The Balkans right before the First World War had experienced two wars that had reduced the Turkish territories in mainland Europe to the small portion that surrounds Istanbul today. The Balkan Wars also resulted in even more friction regarding the borders of these newly expanded and created states in the south of the Balkans. Bulgaria found herself betrayed by her previous allies, and in her fight to retain some of the borders she had gained and was promised in the war, she lost even more. Serbia had grown immensely, and with her newfound victories, her confidence had grown as well, and she turned towards Austro-Hungary with a hungry and irredentist look: Serbia set her sights on gaining all the lands that any Serbs resided in, and then some. In Austro-Hungary itself there were many nationalist movements, and with the awakening going on in the Balkans, and their success, there was now more hope for the nationalist minorities than ever before. Austro-Hungary had to tame the Balkan situation somehow, and in any case the friction between the countries there proved an untenable and unstable situation overall. The Balkans had to be dealt with. It was only a matter of time before the tension would ignite and cause the powder keg of Europe to explode. Which it eventually did: The Austrian Archduke was shot in Sarajevo by a Serbian nationalist, with ties to Serbia and the government there. It was deemed that the Serbian threat had to be neutralized, and the Austro-Hungarians finally had the casus belli they were looking for to intervene. An ultimatum was thus issued. It was not severe, or meant to be unacceptable, as is claimed today. The fact that the Serbs accepted all but one point in it is proof of that.

With Russian guarantees to Serbia, and the French alliance to the Russian, and to the British Empire as well, they had all intertwined their fate with that of Serbia. Russia mobilized and the threat was unleashed. It was now only a matter of time before France would use their alliance with Russia to enact their long-awaited vengeance, and then the British Empire would come to the aid of their ally France, or on the pretext of "protecting" Belgium—which always gets involved when there is war between France and Germany, due to its location. Germany declared war on Russia in response to the aggressive measures taken, and then on her ally France shortly after. Britain, of course, did not fail to come to the aid of France on that pretext mentioned. Italy and the U.S. declared themselves neutral, but would later join the war on the Entente's side when they saw that it had become a stalemate, which only meant that time was on the Entente's side and they greedily recognized the profit to be had by having a seat at the victor's table.

Part Three: A Recollection of Events

In the east the Russians suffered heavy defeats and revolution eventually flared up. Later on they were completely defeated militarily and their revolution had resulted in a communist takeover. After several hesitations on peace terms, which cost them dearly, they finally settled. Germany had proposed marvellous terms and had shown their good intentions for a diverse Europe. The Treaty of Brest-Litovsk negotiated the release and guarantee of the states of Finland, Ukraine, Estonia, and Latvia—freeing all these long trodden-upon peoples—while Lithuania and Russian Poland would be incorporated into the German Empire as protectorates. Also, a payment later on was made by the Russians to the Germans as compensation for the nationalizing of German owned businesses and industries in Russia by the communists. All in all, the Germans had freed much, if not almost all, of the East European nations. Which have always been espoused as the noble goal and aim of the Allies, and repeatedly been used as pretexts for war, but they never really did accomplish it, or even bothered with seeing it to actual fruition like the Germans did. For instance, the Allied used the pretext of protecting Poland in the Second World War when they declared war (yes, they declared war first), but Poland never got her old borders back, and she was under the thumb of the Soviet Union when they ended the war and concluded the treaties. The Treaty of Brest-Litovsk also unified Romania with Bessarabia (Moldova and Ukrainian Bessarabia) and the Bulgarians got some lands with Bulgarian majorities back. Eastern and Central Europe had been stabilized, with more people, groups, nations, and territories having self-determination than ever before. Unsurprisingly, this is very little talked and told about today. Or not at all, truth be told.

The Entente was not much pleased with this, of course—not being the liberators. And they had no interest in freeing people if they could not profit from it. They wanted to break all Germans in Europe and their industry and economy. Only then would there be a point for the Entente to have a diverse Europe that they could freely and unhindered spread their market into. The Entente was not in a war to protect or free anyone, and this is clearly seen by their adoption of total war—unrelenting war until the enemy was broken completely. This is easily understood with their real motives known and not in the context of the ones they proclaimed. These latter which make no sense when you compare them with what was done during and after. The Central Powers offered peace several times, and even when they had clearly done better in the war. They even offered a return to status quo with the entire Entente as a whole, before they finally had to conclude peace with the Russians. Such was the unrelenting warmongering of the French and the British, and it was this that gave the world war(s) the scope—the massive amount of casualties and destruction—it had. The two German states stood pretty much alone, with only minor and weak allies, against the whole world that had been turned, and mostly forced, against them by the powerful British Empire as chief instigator. The Central Powers were ultimately doomed to lose. The Germans never really understood that the Entente was fighting to destroy everything German completely, and to reduce them to mere puppets, until after the end of the war. Had the Germans known this, the war may have been fought even more intensely, and perhaps that is why the Second World War turned into such a polarized and hard fought war. The German had learned, and refused to be pushed aside and reduced by the Allies as had formerly happened, and happened again at the end of WW2.

The Allies sought to carve up the entire Austro-Hungarian Empire, the Ottoman Empire, and large parts of Germany. All the minor states in Austro-Hungary were released and gained very large territories compared to the actual ethnicity that was there. Hungary proper was absolutely destroyed and a national trauma was imposed on them. Hungary lost 2/3 of her lands and population, and 1/3 of all Hungarians suddenly found themselves being inhabitants in one of these strange and newly created countries. The magnitude of that loss is truly soul-rending. What great crime was committed by the Entente—they had shown their true colours. As for many of the newly freed states by the Germans in Eastern Europe and the lands there, they were abandoned and forgot about—left to be gobbled up unrestricted by the commies in Russia. This pretext of freeing people is truly laughable. Especially when considering the imposition of these harsh treaties on the Central Powers that realigned borders and left those people suffering under new, alien governments. Always this double standard. What shameless liars!

III. Aims and Treaties

It is speculated and told today that the treaties imposed on Germany were too lenient. In particular the one after the First World War, but if you compare it to the previously mentioned Treaty of Frankfurt that was imposed upon the French after the Franco-Prussian War, then that is obviously not true. The ones imposed on Germany, Austria, and Hungary were some of the harshest in modern history, and were absolutely vile and abominable. Germany had to reduce her military and navy to a bare minimum of existence with a set number of 100 000 soldiers and a severely limited navy. She was not even allowed to have an air force, and the restrictions on the armaments of the navy and army pretty much made the German military useless. Another part of it was that it severely destroyed the industry and economy of Germany, too. As it would have done to any nation, because military production is a great driver and employer in all state industries. And accompanying this destruction of German industry was a massive war indemnity, which was intended to be the last nail in the coffin for the German economy. This totalled an amount of 132 billion gold marks. The Entente even had an estimate and plan to demand the deranged sum of 269 billion marks, but some of the more sensible British argued against it. By comparison, the war indemnity that Germany imposed on France after the Franco-Prussian War was just a mere 5 billion francs. Or the compensation for the communist nationalization of German owned industries, properties, and assets in Russia was set at 6 billion marks. John Maynard Keynes—the father of modern economics—said that the war reparations were just too absurdly high, and that Germany would never be able to pay them. To add insult to injury a war guilt clause was also supplemented that placed the entire blame of the war on Germany. The war reparations, and the Treaty of Versailles as a whole, imposed by the Entente, was completely nuts and it reeked of a hatred and retribution of a torturous and ignoble kind. Most of which was due to the French and their insistence on the harshest and most life denying measures against the German. Their shameful defeat in the Franco-Prussian War had left them with a psychological scar similar to that of a superiority complex. One that would only be reinforced by yet another extremely humiliating defeat in the Battle of France. This is still lingering in the mental condition of the French to this day, and it seems as if French pride and honour has been permanently damaged. Or it has been completely eliminated rather, and thus non-existent, and that is why he behaves the way he does. He has had no real opportunity to repair or reinforce this honour and pride either, and he will suffer this until the day he reverses it. In the Treaty of Versailles, Germany was stripped of all her colonies, and she also lost Elsass-Lothringen and large parts of her lands in Prussia, resulting in what was left there becoming a German exclave. Those Prussian lands that were handed over to the brand new Polish state had a majority of German inhabitants, and there was no justification for giving them to Poland other than the plan for them to have access to the sea. Yes, this is actually the justification! And it is still the justification told today, without anyone lifting as much as an eyebrow when told. What strange notions of justice there are, and how much they vary from circumstance to circumstance. The justification for giving Transylvania to Romania was that there was an "overwhelming" majority of Romanians in those lands, which is not true. The truth is they may have constituted, overall, a little bit more than half. Going by that standard they therefore had no right taking away lands that had overwhelming German majorities—which was most, if not all, of the lands they took away after the First World War. In any case, Transylvania and the other losses for Hungary had always been Hungarian lands. The Romanian peasants were allowed access to them, and to live there, by the Hungarians. Had the Hungarians known that this was the practice of how lands would be allocated and designated, then there would have been no Romanians there at all. They would, first of all, not have been allowed to enter, and secondly, they would have been driven away or exterminated. It may seem severe, but this is the consequence of the Allied agenda. Which is most likely why the Turks committed the Armenian Genocide as well. They had to rid themselves of the concentrations of Armenians to remove the perception that they were Armenian lands. Even after this the Allies tried to impose upon the Turks the Treaty of Sèvres, which would have left the Turks with less than a quarter of the territory they have today (unfathomable). But where they failed there, they succeeded in much of their plans for Central Europe. Which was always their main objective. The outcome of the First World War was a tragedy, really, and any historian and learned man understands what absurdly extreme terms were imposed and the consequences they would have. Four empires succumbed, and the industry and economy throughout the lands of those empires were shattered—

much to the delight of the profiteers. The Austro-Hungarian industry, for instance, was reliant upon the specializations and resources of each different region as a whole, and with the fractioning of these, and their loss of ties and the dependency on each other, they were bankrupted. This served the British, the U.S., and partly the French well, and they had an extreme economic prosperity after the war, which they would not see again until after the Second World War. Which, again, was the result of the same thing: war profits and enormous indemnities collected coupled with shattered markets to take over and dominate in. This post-WW1 prosperity was called the Roaring Twenties and it had a profound impact on the countries that were left most unaffected by the war, and which had profited the most by it, namely the U.S. and the British Empire. They had succeeded in destroying the largest economy in the world—the two German economies combined—and also the French one, which was an added bonus. New markets lay open throughout Europe for them to exploit and profit from unhindered. The Entente had managed to bring the entire world into conflict—a war that was the second deadliest in modern history in terms of casualties, and the massive destruction had laid waste to glorious Europe—in order to achieve their goal. And at that costly price they succeeded with the only true objective they had: to destroy German prosperity and their means thereof, which was the one, only, and ultimate threat to the monopoly and hegemony of the Allies. They certainly didn't want freedom of trade, or just freedom, in general. Competition, economic competition, to them was only wanted when they were not outcompeted and surpassed by someone who produced better goods, or did it more efficiently.

Part Three: A Recollection of Events

IV. A War of Contention

The behaviour and treatment of the Entente toward their allies served to alienate them, and sow hatred and mistrust. Italy, for example, was betrayed at the end of the First World War, when the promises made to her for her entry in said war was not upheld. These promises in the London Pact, made by the Entente to Italy, were actually very small concessions, but even worse than them breaking the treaty was that it showed the Entente having no regard for other European nations at all. For instance, Greek islands were not demanded returned to Greece from Italy in exchange for the acknowledgement of the irredentist claims made by Italy along the Adriatic Coast. In hindsight, the London Pact can be seen for what it was, however: a mere ruse to get just another sap to fight the war for them—making a bloody and destructive conflict even more so. Knowing that, we realize why no demands were made on the Italians in this treaty, as it was only meant to lure Italy into the war and was never intended to be fulfilled by the Entente. All in all, the Entente antagonized and polarized most of Europe with WW1. Another failure by the Entente was that they did not take into account the power of the human spirit and will. Or more precisely, the power of the German spirit and will, and the resurgence of Germany. And what a massive and powerful resurgence it was. It took everyone by surprise and it became quite the source of admiration. Despite what you may read today, it actually did take everyone by surprise, yes. No one foresaw or anticipated it at all. Germany was a completely broken nation after the First World War, and stayed that way for 25 years until she was finally saved. What turned it around was Hitler and the National Socialist policies. They came to power in 1933, and in an extremely short time they eliminated the rampant unemployment and rebuilt the entire industry and economy. Almost all of the wrongs were righted, one after another. Even the unification of Austria and Germany came about, thus finally (re)uniting those two German nations and people—only to be separated and denied that again after WW2. The Germans were happy, healthy, and had a job and money. Life had been restored in Germany and the people loved Hitler for it, and many still do. But not all of the wrongs were to be permitted rectified by the Allies. They still refused to give back Danzig and the Polish Corridor, and they were willing to instigate another world war for it. The Polish, too, were antagonistic, and always had been since that proud independence they gained after WW1, but the confidence from having won great victories on the battlefield against the Russians made the Poles blindingly arrogant. First of all, they thought the Germans would never be willing to actually go to war, and secondly, they never thought they could be defeated as easily as they were by the Germans. The Polish were offered several deals by the Germans. Even a fair exchange of lands in East Prussia for that in West Prussia, in order to eliminate the exclave problem for Germany. The Poles were even offered an alliance, and economic and industrial cooperation. Instead, they blatantly dismissed it all and even provoked Germany further by having pogroms against Germans in Poland. Germany declaring war and invading Poland was the only option left, really. The Poles thought they could compare a fight against Russia with Germany, but a German soldier—due to the military equipment, training, leadership, and overall military efficiency, and their blood—was worth 10 Russians (as we know from the WW2 Eastern Front) and the Polish quickly found that out. What caused the defeat and poor statistics for the Germans on the Eastern Front in the later parts of that war was the massive lend lease from the Allies to the Soviet Union, and the systematic destruction of German industry, which caused military collapse due to a lack of food and materials. A consequence of this latter was that it also affected civilians and prisoners, and caused starvation and disease that resulted in millions of deaths in the prison and war camps throughout the Reich. This was the fault of the Allies. Although, today they would have you believe a number of things. The Red Cross report that was made during WW2 speaks the real truth, however. What more objective source than the Red Cross can you get?

The Allies therefore proceeded to declare war on Germany to protect that small scrap of land in Poland, and again causing a massive global war. In many ways it was WW1 all over again—a war that was also fought over some backyard plot that nobody in the world cared about, or could even point out on a map. But instead of Russia being aggressive, starting a war, and bringing her allies into battle, it was Poland. The Allies declared war shortly after the German attack on Poland, and the new world war had started. Their hypocrisy truly shined in that war. They let the Soviet Union get away with invasions, such as the pathetic effort in the Winter War against Finland after the outbreak of WW2, and that of murder all across Eurasia, which resulted in over 60 million deaths (R.J. Rummel) from the rise of communism in Russia until the dissolution, with Stalin being the prime offender during this period. Yes, communism in Russia alone has probably resulted in more deaths than the highest estimates of WW2—a war caused and conducted by many parties across the globe. The Holodomor genocide in Ukraine is never talked about today, but then again, neither is the Armenian Genocide. Only the Holocaust seems to matter—mainly caused by disease and starvation—and only the Jewish deaths are talked about in that. China today is acting just as absurd, when it talks about Japanese war crimes, but it always forgets the almost 75 million (R.J. Rummel) that died because of communism there. All in all, communism has killed close to 150 million (R.J. Rummel) people worldwide, and most of these were their own people! Meaning internal struggles and direct causes of communism. Purges, ethnic cleansing, and all kind of mayhem and murder. The Red Terror as it was called in Russia. Stalin and the other communist cronies in Russia cleared and cleansed the lands of any and all people they could. Tatars, Ukrainians, Cossacks, Romanians, Poles, Estonians, Latvians, Lithuanians, Finns, Ingrians, Ugrians, Ingush, Chechens, Greeks, Germans, Manchurians, Koreans, and the list goes on and on. It is stomach-turning to think that the Russians got away with these mass killings in the tens of millions that was committed mostly in peacetime, but the Germans still have to bend their head in shame of deaths not even exceeding 10 million that died in wartime due to starvation and disease. If the Allies like and liked portraying themselves as the good side, then how can they justify allying themselves with the Soviet Union, which is undoubtedly the worst state that has ever existed in history. With Communist China as a close runner-up.

V. Hypocrisy and Propaganda

The same tricks that the Allies tried and used in the First World War were given another go in WW2. To lure Ireland into the war, they promised the return of Northern Ireland—that offer was an admission on their part that Northern Ireland was a valid claim by Ireland and rightfully hers. It did not work, however. Perhaps the Irish had learned from history. Another concession the British should have made, but did not make until after the Second World War, was the allocation of lands to the Jews. This solution was much wanted by Hitler so that he could deport the Jews and get rid of their destabilizing and detrimental effect on society. Many lands were proposed, like that of Madagascar, but the British, and the Allies altogether, absolutely refused to part with any lands. The British, as the Russians were and still are today, were completely obsessed with their lands, and this despite them owning about ¼ of it throughout the globe in their heyday. That small piece of land in Palestine, those lands that Israel occupy today, would have done much for the situation. The Allies later on realized that if they gave away that land, it would aggregate Jews there, and whatever stems from Jews, which is why they parted with it after WW2. But it also enabled the Allies to wash their hands of the whole situation and to reflect away any labels of anti-Semitism, and thus also enabling them to use it on others. The U.S., which wanted to get into the action to profit and divert away public attention from domestic problems—now that Russia and Britain were in the war they could not really lose—successfully managed to provoke the Japanese with trade embargoes and a hateful rhetoric that made the Japanese compelled to attack. They had no other option to such hostility. The U.S. was also hostile to Germany right from the get-go. This despite the U.S. declaring themselves neutral. Just as they did in the First World War. In both world wars they broke that pledge of neutrality, and actively and malevolently engaged in the assistance of the Allied side. The word of the U.S. has always been untrustworthy, though, as it is a nation built on a foreign policy of lying and deceiving. And it sure has benefited them greatly, having conducted some of the largest land grabs in history, or at least in the modern era. Surpassed perhaps only by the Russians in Siberia, the Far East, and North America. The American expansionist plan at the expense of Mexico and other states was called Manifest Destiny. I find it strange that the Lebensraum the Germans wanted is as badmouthed as it is, when it is the exact same thing as Manifest Destiny, and I dare say the Lebensraum theory is directly inspired by it. Just as the Japanese expansions were. The U.S. served as a source of inspiration in how you could just take what resources and lands you wanted, and easily get away with it.

Consequence free, and without any condemnation from the global community. The hypocrisy is strong, however, and the U.S. repeatedly berated colonial powers, and came to the "defence" of other nations who were at war or lost territories. The signing of the Atlantic Charter was another hypocrite act, but even worse it was for the British Empire. This charter would state such things as guaranteeing the right of self-determination, territorial adjustments being in accordance with the native people, and that the U.S. and British Empire would not seek any territorial gains for themselves. Obviously, the right of self-determination was not fulfilled after the war throughout the British Empire in India, Africa, or anywhere else for that matter. As for territorial adjustments, they did adjust the borders after WW2, without any consent or consideration of the people in those areas. Such as most of Eastern Germany, which was annexed by the Soviet Union and their Polish communist puppet state. As for territorial expansion, the U.S. broke that promise by taking a number of islands in the Pacific. These were the main points of the charter that the signatories violated so blatantly. It was all lies, in other words. They lied and deceived repeatedly throughout the war, and with any means available. Hitler had remarked upon the intensive and effective propaganda in WW1 by the Entente, with portrayals of the Germans as barbarians and calling them Huns, and the spread of ludicrous stories like Germans killing babies and impaling them on bayonets. WW2 would be no different. The Japanese would be depicted as rats and sub-humans, and the Germans and National Socialists as evil. The Jews made up stories about people being flayed and their skin turned into lampshades, or human fat used for soap. Any absurdity imaginable. And it is easy to count them all as fake and staged, because the fact is that nothing of it has ever been proven, and they have actually been proven wrong in most cases—which includes all these I mentioned above. These accusations were always third-hand accounts from mostly Jews and other biased sources, and as such would not hold up as evidence at all. This kind of propaganda is still spewed, though, and can even be found in ostensibly serious school books and history books.

VI. Defeat and Aftermath

The Axis, and the Japanese in the Sino-Chinese War, were eventually defeated. And truth is that they never really had any chance to begin with. They didn't have the resources, or the strategic locations, that were needed. The Allies had an abundance of oil and lay safely hidden away from the theatres of war. They also had control of the seas and managed to turn the entire world against the Axis, or at least deny any trade to them. The Soviet state nearly collapsed and was close to defeat, but in the last minute a massive amount of supplies came from the Allies in the form of food, trucks, tanks, and aircraft, and along with it also came much needed help from military, industrial, and social advisors that managed to make that backwards country somewhat functional. The Russians even got whole ships and trains. The list is just enormous. Stalin later said that the help from the Allies was the sole factor that changed the winds of war in Russia—his begging and pleading for help from Roosevelt and Churchill had finally paid off. Considering all this material and money, this modern day manna, it is actually surprising that the Russians did not do better. Even all the way up the very moment of German capitulation, the Russian advance was slow and amateurish. Germans at that time were operating without fuel, a navy, and an air force, while being overwhelmingly outgunned and outmanned. In the Pacific, the Americans were really not doing all that great either, despite their superiority in everything from resources to manpower. Just as Japan was on the verge of complete defeat, and about to capitulate, the U.S.—the self-appointed defender of all that is good—decided to incinerate over 250 000 civilian men, women, and children with their atom bombs to "speed up" the process. In retrospect, it only looks like a show of force and a need to set a historical milestone, of sorts. The U.S. and the Jews had started working on the bomb as soon as they got the idea that it was conceivable. It has been told again and again that it was an arms race to make the first atom bomb and that Germany somehow started that race, but the truth is that Germany never actually had nuclear weapons research. This the Allies knew full and well. What the Germans did have was nuclear energy research, and they even built a nuclear reactor at Haigerloch and had somewhat successful tests and runs. The Germans were not as insidious as the Allies were, and they never had any atomic weapon plans, even though they were aware of its destructive potential. The Allies levelled cities all over Germany, such as the infamous firebombing of Dresden, and targeted civilians again and again, which resulted in hundreds of thousands of deaths. Hitler and the Germans, however, refrained throughout the war from using any kind of weapons of mass destruction and the likes—not including the V1 and V2 rockets, which was a response and retaliation for said Allied bombings. The death toll in the Blitz (the bombing of England by Germany) does not even come close to 1/10 of the casualties inflicted on civilians in Germany by the Allied bombings.

After the capitulation of the Germans, the Allies finally exposed themselves for what they were. They systematically stole and plundered everything they came over and could find. They had established specialized departments for this task and they even had a name for it: Operation Paperclip. The Allies assessed and measured up everything and shipped it out of Germany. They even tore down entire factories and rebuilt them brick by brick in their own countries. Intellectual property was shamelessly appropriated, and it was never

Part Three: A Recollection of Events

restored to their proper owners. The German intelligentsia was also treated as mere goods, and the cream of the crop was picked out and taken away. The Space Race was a direct result of this. Wernher von Braun, the chief architect of the V1 and V2 rockets, was a leading figure at NASA—instrumental, really—and the birth of modern rocketry in Russia and the U.S. was solely possible due to the German engineers that were coerced into working for them. Work which the Allies had to rely on being done exclusively by these Germans for decades. The Allies stole and plundered everything they could get their hands on. Even the private property of ordinary Germans were taken. It is altogether the largest theft ever made, and it is incalculable. It is so large that it overshadows any plunder in history to this day, and even out-value most, and probably all, of them combined. With such pillaging also came rape and slaughter, and the Allies managed to set an historical record there, too. German women were systematically raped day by day, for years and years. Although, it should be said that it was mostly the Russians, uncivilized and immoral as they are, that committed this—sanctioned by Stalin. The slaughter and slavery was equally done by all the Allies, though. First of these crimes to mention was the population transfer of the Germans from Prussia, and the east in general, which resulted in the displacement of almost 15 million Germans in total! Such were the Allies and the goodness of their heart; and that declaration for the protection and self-determination of people in their homelands. The death toll for the expulsion of the Germans was over 2.2 million people, and this is only counting the actual forced relocation. Along with this transfer was also a number of other people, which pushes the total number of people expelled in this event up into the 20 million range. In this new reduced Germany came the institution of slavery on a scale that hasn't been seen in a long time. Germans were forced to work without pay and for meagre amounts of food. So meagre that there was starvation for half a decade. An estimated half a million Germans died in this artificial starvation. It must be concluded that it was deliberate and planned, because there are written reports and statistics that the Allies had full stocks of food lying around untouched, and there were a number of protests and inquiries from concerned and noble souls on the Allied side as to why these reserves were left untouched while people were dying. There was no good reason for it, because there was no shortage of food, nor an expected one—the Allied food production was rising steadily and without problems. It is therefore no argument that those supplies would be for emergency military use only. The revenge taken upon Germany by the Allies, especially by the French and the Jews, was thus even greater than the one they exacted after WW1. So much wealth and intellectual property was stolen, and so many people forced into bondage, that it propelled the Allies, and in particular the unharmed U.S., into heights never before achieved by them. Even the Soviet Union suddenly had an economic rise never before experienced. This lasted into the 1970s and at one point the Soviet GDP was over half that of the U.S. If you use a modern comparison, that would be as strong as China is to the U.S. today. And this without the use of a billion strong slave army to do their bidding, as China does. This huge economic rise to dominance is nothing more than a testament to the crime they had committed and to the extremely advanced technological, industrial, and intellectual power that was taken from Germany. This, and the denazification that followed, was told to be another Purim by the Jews—the biblical event where the Jews in Babylon and Persia would kill 75 000 Persians in one swift stroke. It is doubtful the Jews had that much control after WW2, but I can see the comparison in scope at least.

    The decimated Germany and Japan managed to overcome these horrendous events, however. With the brilliance that made them such powerful nations in the past, they turned their focus and strength inwards and built up the second and third largest economies in the world. Economic miracles not seen before or after—not counting Hitler's Germany. They both had used the lesson learned from National Socialist Germany, which in turn had based theirs on the principle of mixed economy, and an active fiscal policy, by Keynes. And the world followed. All of the largest economies today are built and run on the bases set by Keynes.

The absurdity in the restrictions of the peace treaties imposed on the Germans and Japanese are still seen today. For instance, in the Japanese constitution war is illegal, and in the German one it is not allowed to declare war. Free nations? I guess we are all free nations, but some are freer than others—paraphrasing that repentant socialist and communist George Orwell. In Germany, and throughout Europe for that matter, a ban has been implemented on pretty much anything nationalistic. We also have this thing they call hate speech, which means that if you love yourself and your own, you are hateful. Therefore, we are taught day and night how hateful and evil we are. And if loving yourself and your own is hateful, logic dictates that hating yourself and your own, and embracing everything and everyone alien, would have to be love. All this paved the way for the immigration of any and all cultures and ethnicities. The destruction of Europe never really ended as such.

Part Four: Problematique of Particulars

'Do you know, my son,
with what little understanding the world is ruled?"
– Pope Julius III

Part Four: Problematique of Particulars

Society and Leadership

I. Natural Inequality

The egalitarianism of today is an absolute abomination. It is unnatural and a hindrance to the mechanisms of competition and evolution. It is a hindrance to society itself, really. It aims to keep the great man down, and elevates the botched and bungled. A sort of reverse evolution. Instead of fostering greatness and building life on that, you instead reward weakness and inferiority, which always involves taking from other people. Yes, even the large middle class must pitch in to elevate these unwanted and unneeded wretches. Earlier in the history of man, these incapable and weak people did petty work for payment amounting to nothing more than a meal, and a roof over their head. For them to get a house, and a family to boot, was an absurd idea, but today they thrive and multiply without thought or concern. With the abundance of wealth and leisure time given to them, there are no longer any restraints on them in any regards. And they are certainly not bettering themselves, either. Where they already were the lowest of low, they now stoop even lower. They spend their excess of money on massive amounts of unhealthy foods and recreational drugs, and their laziness and need for entertainment plants them firmly in front of the television screen. Their low prospects, due to the lack of intellect and their poor physical fitness—which is ever worsening—makes them useless in any but the simplest of jobs. This they know, and they naturally have no illusions about their place in society. Their ambitions are therefore limited, or non-existent. And even if they are not employed in these low-end jobs and simply retreat from any productive living at all, they will still get their bread and butter. In their unemployment they find themselves just as well supplied to take care of themselves, and then some, thanks to social security and welfare. The restraints of time and resources on them have been lifted, and they wallow about in the pleasures of sex, booze, drugs, overeating, and inactivity. The choice to have children is no longer one of serious consideration for them, either. Why would they not? After all, they have nothing else to do and plenty of resources to spare.

And we see the results of these kind of policies, with the lower classes outbreeding not only the upper classes, but the middle classes as well. The upper class, or that of the intelligentsia at least, have purposeful lives with important work. The decision for them to have offspring is a great one. One that impacts their work and time. And with women's equality and them having a career of their own, that decision just got harder. This is the same with the middle class, albeit to a lesser degree; the greater quantity of free time for the middle classes enable them to be more prolific. We see, therefore, that the higher the worth of the individual in society is, the lesser their procreation becomes. A complete inversion of what would be ideal. In pre-modern times the lower class was in the least privileged position, and were usually servants to the upper classes, which then in turn freed up the time and duties for their masters. The upper class women were not employed or otherwise involved with having a career either, and this enabled them to devote themselves to running the house and have children. Therefore, in the old order we see the upper class enabled to have children. And a great many. The wealth of the upper class was used to educate these better and more capable blood lines of society. This wealth was also spread out among the children when the parents died, enabling them to continue the cycle. Some call it unfair, but as I see it, for you to call someone spoiled or privileged, when they or their family have done better than you and yours, is just another slave mentality. The middle class had more work and less comfort, but because of that they gained the drive and ambition to be successful and better so that they, too, could rise to the living standard of the upper class. Thus, the whole of society worked harder to improve their situation. Even the lower classes. Especially the lower classes. Where they today do not strive and struggle, they earlier had to work hard physically, and also better themselves mentally. And they would be motivated to do so because of that existence imposed upon them otherwise. Just as it would be in nature—meaning that in nature you have to work to survive. The meagre existence of the lower class, back then, was not like that of the "poor" today. During those times they had little or no money, and to earn that they had to work around the clock. Each and every day. This left the thought of getting married, or starting a family, out of the question.

Equality? There should only be equal rights and opportunities from birth, and equality in the eyes of the law. We should give men and women of all classes the possibility to rise and hold any position in society according to his own merit and ability. We do not need any more equality than that. Imposed and unnatural equality, when and where there is natural inequality, is absolutely damaging to society and man. As such, we do not need socialism. And we do not need ethnic or racial uniformity, either—although it is useful and beneficial. Only a common culture, and then we will judge man on an individual basis. In short, a society enabling the best to prosper, to rise to a position of their worth, and then to pass on the genes that gave them their skills and their capacity for learning and hardship. This was the basis and foundation that the British Empire was built, prospered, grew, and thrived on—a true testament to how powerful a proper social structure is.

II. Hierarchy, Class, and Leadership

The need for hierarchy and leadership is an obvious one. We find this truth in nature and the social groups there. And man is no exception. The origin of nobles in society came about as a result of individuals or families that showed abilities and qualities that separated and elevated them above the common people. Through competition and strife, and the following victories and successes, they would be granted higher positions in society than others—a hierarchy is built. The wolf pack needs a leader, but the selection in nature is not as sophisticated as the one in human groups. This is because man is intellectual and relies more on his mental capacity and ability rather than primarily that of a physical superiority. The elevation of individuals in a group is a basic evolutionary rule, because if the pack did not let the individuals that are the fittest and best have priority in procreation and food, it would not reward the better genes and the expression of those genes. And when I say let them, I mean that the weak let the strong dominate because of what the strong will do to the weak if not. The weak cannot do much about it unless they organize, which more intelligent life does. Like man does. Armed and organized, the weak then invert the natural order, and in this totalitarian slave society that follows, man degenerates.

Nobility and a higher class is born through the dominance of the strong and capable. And with a proper system in place, they may lead their kin to greater and greater achievements. But alas the system almost always buckles under in the end. Either from internal or external forces, or a combination of both. One of the pitfalls of the noble class is that of an inborn perception of a natural right, or perceived justified right, to be considered better just because one was born from betters. This is nothing but arrogance, and natural superiority is thus supplanted by pedigree and the privilege of education and training—this false thought that it is birthright, and not merit and achievement, that entitles the noble to positions of power and leadership in society. And when a complacency and lack of understanding as to why they are there, or what their duties are to the state, goes hand in hand with this, their fate is sealed. Over time, the nobility grow lax, lazy, weak, and fat from a lack of challenge, competition, and need to do anything. For when they earlier had to employ underlings and servants to ease their burdens, they now have too many and they themselves are left with little work. Or none at all, and reduced to mere figureheads. And when they are left unchallenged and without a clear purpose or function, their bodies and their blood weaken successive generations, which results in that deterioration of the nobility. Their intelligence and their physical prowess dwindle, and the results and consequences of that follow: the state is badly governed, wars are lost, fiscal mismanagement, and all sorts of evil due to poor statecraft emerge. This degradation of society is identified in Plato's Five Regimes. It is the corruption of the people, the loss of value, the changing of values, or the wrong values. The turning away from the Good. Moral degradation, in other words. The end result is the disintegration of society from a lack of food or incessant strife, or the people simply dying out or migrating. Or an overthrow of government, a revolution, or succumbing to an outside force by way of conquest or annihilation. We see the examples of fallen civilizations throughout history. Societies that stagnate, ossify, crumble, and collapse. The Spartans and their timocracy is a good example of a system that failed to account for a number of factors as time went by. The main one being that their system was built around the concept of the existence of only small city-states. Thus, their encounters with the larger empires later in time, and their failure to adapt in a number of other ways, proved their undoing. To prevent this rigidity necessitates that the leadership and higher classes must not only be better educated, multi-faceted, and diverse, but they must also endure the hardship of the people, and that of the world. They should be better in much of everything, if not all, and must at least be equal in all manners to that of the common people and in accordance with the common norms. The Platonic Noble Lie should be the guideline for the class system. Just because one is born of nobles should not entitle one to be a noble. Merit and ability is the only measure and justification for nobility.

In the Germanic tribes the kings were elected. The need for a unified leadership in war was the main reason for this. The Romans also knew this, which is why they had the dictator system. The efficiency of a superior noble to hold the reins during crisis meant the difference between victory and defeat. Hesitation and bickering could be catastrophic. The need to make unpopular decisions, and a willingness to take drastic actions and measures, proved instrumental to success. Therefore, removing the bureaucracy and the power of the popular assemblies were a necessary evil. In perilous times the autocracy was increasingly permanent. When the system of a strict hierarchy with an autocratic figure of unlimited power on top proved so successful, it also become accepted by the masses. Results are proof after all. This was how the transformation of a Roman Republic into a Roman Empire happened; the investiture of an autocrat proved much more peaceful than the earlier Roman civil wars. When Augustus gained firm control, and the wars were won, a period of unprecedented peace started: the Pax Romana. Time and time again we see this pattern of absolute rule in human history—it could just as easily have been the emperors of China or Persia mentioned.

Part Four: Problematique of Particulars

III. Governance and Society

Autocracy take many forms, and of varying degrees. The worst of examples are the tyrannies of the Greek states, where foreign armies were invited at the behest of the tyrants to subjugate the people by force and rule as a police state. They may have started as popular rulers, but it was the people's rejection (both nobility and commoner) of them that required outside forces to maintain control. The word tyrant, which in Greek times simply meant ruler of the city, is today used by democratic propaganda to label dictatorships in modern times, and a great many have been labelled as such by these detractors. Any autocracy today is readily dismissed by the democracies. Which is probably just as well, because most of them, if not all, seem to be of the communist or far left varieties. As for the (constitutional) monarchies, they have relinquished almost all political power. Modern monarchs, in the West at least, are heads of state without much of a function—mostly used for diplomatic missions and being commander-in-chiefs during war. They are also supposed to be apolitical, although they seem to be very much in line with the liberal agenda almost always. One good function that they do have is that they act as representatives of the people to safeguard against tyranny and veto unpopular decisions, and a known face and figure for the people to rally behind during crises—like the tribune of the plebs in Roman times. They are a fourth branch of government, in a sense. I should say fifth, but the media seems to have outplayed its role as a critical voice of anything. The main interest of the media today is money, and certainly not truth. Closely connected with the media are the celebrities and the wealthy. These are treated as royalty despite their only achievements being self-interest and egoism. In the republics they act as substitutes for the monarchy, and they do also, almost unfailingly, take the side of the people and the liberal agenda.

Not without reason of course, since they, too, depend on the people for their position. Calling them part of the elite is not without due—worthless as they mostly are, though—and they are like the old nobility in a great many respects. For one, their celebrity status and riches are inherited, and they are recognized by the public instantly by their family names, and by their connections to other famous people, and they love them for it. People today go out of their way to venerate and celebrate these famous and wealthy people. Being rich in the United States makes you more important and better than the commoner. This thinking is built and enforced from the ground up either through propaganda or through the thought that if you were to become successful, then you would want that treatment yourself. Or a combination of the two. Another part of this belief is that Americans think of themselves as self-made and hardworking, and that they therefore deserve what comes to them in terms of success and wealth—that they are not given anything like the aristocrats and nobles of the European monarchies. Yet, this is not true at all. More people are born into wealth and fame today in the U.S. than anywhere else. And they are certainly many more, and have a larger share of the wealth, when compared to the aristocratic nations of older times—even in the era of feudalism the common people were richer than they are now. However, there is also a greater middle class in the U.S. and Western Europe than in any other period of time, and this justifies a larger upper class. Although, the middle class has been diminishing greatly compared to what it was in the 60s and all the way up to the 90s. And the gap is now ever widening across the world.

This upper class, this elite, is not superior at all. The more the common people can relate to them and identify with them, the more they will support them. People today adore and celebrate mediocrity, or normality as they call it. The hyper-individualism of today—where you celebrate yourself egoistically and hedonistically—is the reason for this way of thinking. They celebrate themselves and those that are alike themselves. The whole term elite is ironical. This elite can never be compared to, or even take the position and have the responsibilities of, nobility. They would simply not be capable enough. If superior individuals are needed today, the intelligentsia would fit that description and fill that role. Whether the people would ever accept their rule and input is another question. The current elite will not be easily and voluntarily supplanted, though, having their fingers and influence deep inside government and politics, and being heavily involved in various masonic-like organizations to protect their interests and power. Self-serving in the same way as all masonic organizations are: to help their own kind to the top, and offer them positions and power for the good of their group.

So, what will this new structure of society, this new people, and this new state be like? As I have mentioned before, the Noble Lie of Plato is a good template. Assuming you are familiar with Plato. As everyone should be, in my opinion. And what an awful name the Noble Lie is for something that is only an ideal and an honest plan for social structure. Indeed, I think it is one of the most noble and just principles that men could follow. In a single word it is summed up: meritocracy.

Immigration and Politics

I. The Destruction of the West

Democracy and free speech is a thing of the past. Today, these terms are masquerading under an old definition that is no longer true. It has become so bad that most right-wing political stances have become taboo, or just plain banned. Yes, banned. Another show of deterioration is that in some countries you are not allowed to question religion anymore—reversing the secularization and atheism that was steadily on the rise before—and if you talk about ethnicities, the race card is used. Or more precisely, if they are religions and ethnicities that are not native to a nation, or just minorities, then they are off-limits. However, you are free to talk negatively about, and be outright hostile to, the native people, strangely enough. The religious are protected and given special rights and privileges: segregation; physical/genital mutilation; certain foods (given to them for free at the expense of the state); free with pay during work hours to pray; a number of extra holidays; not having to follow laws and regulations, such as required uniform clothing for government officials; special government funding for their religious organizations and their places of worship; etc. Anything that their wild imagination can conjure up. And it is all protected and guaranteed by the Western states. Yes, genital cutting being a state approved and protected right. What absurdity. The ethnic minorities also get their special rights. Such as the special protection of, and proliferation rights for, their language, culture, and so on. They also have a number of social benefits that is not available to the native people and the majority. In addition, these minorities jump on the religious bandwagon for the extra rights there. All this has, in effect, made the native majority a second class people in their own homeland and country. It doesn't matter that these minorities are born and raised in the nation either, because even if they are, they will still get special privileges.

Third World immigrants are often called welfare tourists, and that is what they are, really. They heard that there was a nice and hefty welfare check for them to collect—that is handed out to all immigrants in Scandinavia and other European countries, and in the Anglosphere as well—and so they moved. At least to stay for a while, and in any case they have no interest to mix with the indigenous population, thankfully. They are like the tourist who goes on vacation for the nice weather and to live well, except that the tourist actually pays for himself and he is usually respectful of the nation and the people he visits. The non-immigrant minorities do this exploiting as well, and they can collect whatever they want and wish for, because they are so "repressed", and they have it so "tough" and "bad". Truth is that these people are richer than most impoverished whites today. But those no one gives a flying fig about—those who are the actual citizens and our blood brethren.

Have you ever wondered why no one ever asks if someone is a Sikh, Hindu, or Shinto? That it because no one has had any bad experiences with them. Just like how someone does not question some nationalities, but then for some they do. If you are disliked by people there is a reason, and that is because you are bothersome and a nuisance, and not because of "racism" or religious "intolerance".

These immigrants came to the Western world not out of need, but out of greed and sloth, mostly. They knew the money, housing, and privileges they would get, without having to work for it. Not even that minimum of having to learn the native language. And why should they, when they are free to flock together in ghettos with their own kind. Ghettos where the inhabitants have a middle class income paid for by the state. The crime and rape prevalent there, and the rise of it in the Western countries in general, sure warrants the label of ghetto. Crimes committed against the native inhabitants, as the statistics show. Another thing the immigrants are allowed to do is to get their relatives to join them in their new found welfare paradise—called family reunion—which includes uncles, cousins, and all kind of family relations. These, in turn, will have their relatives join them. This means that if you let one immigrant in, then a few years later an entire family tree will have entered the country. And quite a few of them are not related at all, actually, and lied and deceived their way in. To question these immigrant practices, or immigration at all, will earn you a label. Racist and National Socialist are the most common ones. And just like that, they have shut down the discussion with a fallacy before it has even begun. This is their main tactic, usually. They even use those same labels when discussing religion. Labels that make absolutely no sense in that regard. Yes, they actually call you a racist today if you are against certain religions.

A fallacy made by people constantly is that if you are against immigration, they think you are completely against immigration—any and all. Which is just another false dilemma: you are either with us or against us. In reality, those who are against immigration only want more rigorous criteria and rules, and to lessen it. They do not want to stop anyone from either coming into, or going out of, the country. They only want more scrutiny.

Minorities, and especially the immigrant minorities, are nothing but a huge drain on the economy. 40 years of this experiment, and the statistics from it, has proven this, and that data has finally been able to reach the public. Not that it was needed, though, because by now society has become so corrupt and criminal that even the blind have noticed. A majority of immigrants and minorities are always unemployed and contribute little to society, even as a whole. They are also a much larger drain on the economy of the state than the average citizen. This is because they gather in their ghettos, and then they revert into that state of living they have where they came from: murder, rape, theft, armed robbery, drugs, and crime of any kind. They also do not work, and they don't care to, either. They just collect their food stamps and welfare checks, and if they need some extra money, they just resort to this criminal activity mentioned. And when not doing that, they hang around shops and street corners all day and harass people. Yes, grown men actually do this. If you can call them men. This is also where they turn into gangs, and this gang warfare is nothing but these bums fighting. Vandalism of private and public property is also rampant in these areas, which is not seen in society elsewhere at all, and it is on such a scale that it makes these areas look like warzones; or they actually are warzones, dangerous as it is for outsiders to walk into—the Western man is now an outsider in his own country. The consequence of all this criminal and uncivilized behaviour in these ghettos is that the public services are required to spend extreme amounts of money there, as compared to a normal neighbourhood. The police, fire department, medical services and ambulances, social services, you name it. This is now a massive drain and strain on the economy.

The reason why people resort to violence so spontaneously and easily in some societies is not directly because of culture. It is simply the fact that they are so dumb and ignorant that they are not able to resolve a dispute by logic or any other means, and this is if they even know what the dispute is about—dimwits lose track in discussions pretty quickly, and that is an undeniable fact. This spontaneous violence is not to be confused with organized forms of violent dispute, such as wars, or duels and holmgangs. War is usually a dispute regarding who should have this or that, and such disputes are unresolvable without actual fighting. Duels and holmgangs are of a similar nature. Only that they take the form of who is this or that instead, and a judge or an elder may be unable to make a ruling in either favour. A challenge then goes from mental dominance into physical dominance. All these civilized forms are different from the savage ones, in that they adhere to rules of engagement and honourable principles. Not all wars, but almost all. Seen by the fact that they knew it was coming and therefore had time to prepare. And if one part is badly outnumbered, or whatever else, and is surely doomed, it is still a civilized struggle. Civilized disputes are set up, and then resolved by the parts that are full and well knowing of what is going on, which does include covert state operations since it is a part of the game of nations. Savage disputes, however, are done in hiding, and are usually unexpected and spontaneous. This is because these feeble minds have little concept of honour and integrity, and usually have none, and therefore act purely on emotion. They are blinded with rage and see no other way than to eliminate what opposes them by any means possible—like an animal out of control— which is easiest done by surprise and in a furtive manner. And if they do not care about getting caught, or when there is no risk in being caught, or simply that they do it to make a statement, you will see it openly. Such unlawful killings, in any case, are properly termed murder. We thereby define the unlawful as that which isn't sanctioned by state and society.

Politically, this immigration is nothing but the import of voter cattle. And just like cattle they do not know anything about democracy or freedom, other than the fact that they will vote for anything that will benefit them, and thus being the voter cattle for the political parties that cater to them, or what they believe in—these beliefs which they drag with them from whence they came, and in doing so, they will eventually regress the society that they have newly infested into one that is like their place of origin.

Another way to exploit the Western world is through this imposed hate of ourselves and through the sympathetic notions we are told we should have for every kind of pathetic nation and race across the world. This exploitation is now being attempted in the form of claiming restitution or compensation for having been in slavery, or a colony, or occupied, or in a previous war with, etc. Such absurd claims obviously comes mostly from sub-Sahara. People in Roman or Greek times would laugh about such a notion as restitution for slavery. Where do such claims end then? Is every war or injustice a matter of restitution? If that is so, the Irish can claim restitution for the slavery that many of them were sold into, or even claim it from the Scandinavians because of what the Vikings did. Every war, every event, and every instance that can be found is open for such claims then. It will never end. Instead, let the past be the past. A war or disagreement is either resolved right after it is concluded, or should be left as a part of history and not some pressing agenda at any sudden or opportune moment. That is not to say that righteous disputes are not allowed to be upheld throughout the years, decades, and centuries, though. The point is that you cannot conjure up a cause from history—that has never been a matter of dispute or a problem before—just because you suddenly and greedily see a way to profit from it.

II. Rhetoric and Information Control

Islam—the religion of peace? Yes, the most peaceful on Earth apparently. Joined in line by Judaism. What loving bombs and wars they have in the Levantine. No one dares to say this, though. It is, in fact, classified as hate speech and illegal in some countries, gaining you jail time and a fine. That's "free speech" for ya. Besides, uttering such statements and truths as these will make the far left send out their goon squads, these Red Front Fighters of the modern era, to harass you; trash your house; beat you up; target and beat up your family; get you fired from your job by political pressuring; and sometimes they will outright kill you and your family. This is already happening. And not only for having anti-Islam opinions, but anti-left opinions as well. This is free speech and democracy? Political freedom and representation? The right-wing, and anyone not on board with the "program", are not allowed to be heard anymore, and are completely gag-tied. The left are frothing at their mouths like rabid dogs, looking to sink their teeth into anyone that crosses their path. Thankfully, their snarling and howling make it easy to beware them. Labels and associative comparisons are the weapons of the left—that of pure rhetoric. These leftists associate any and all political perspectives they do not hold themselves with something and anything than can be viewed as negative. And if it isn't negative they make it negative by lying. Any policy change that the political opposition want is called hateful. "Haters" these people on the left call others, when it is actually they who refuse to discuss, listen, debate, cooperate, compromise, or even let an opposition exist. These leftists—that are so intolerant and hateful of people that do not agree with them—call others intolerant and haters? Hypocrites are what they are. They also lash out pre-emptively to label first. Even when unfounded. Best they label others of all the things they subconsciously know that they are—a sort of psychological projection. Desperately they try to own a use of a word and thereby distance themselves from it; because how could anyone possibly dare to accuse someone of a thing that they have already said first? That would be a rhetorical misfire, certainly. You can, however, explain how and why such tactics are used. People are much more susceptive to that. Logic and truth are always better, even if the people at first are too stupid to realize. Disrupting the weak and nonsensical associations that have been rhetorically planted there is the most important thing. And you can trust that these faulty associations are there. The Pavlovian people of the modern age act purely on the input given to them by society and the media, and they are utterly devoid of reflection on life or their beliefs. Thankfully, this is also the tool with which a correction can be made.

The profiteering of the military-industrial complex goes hand in hand with the triumphalism and victor's justice of the state. This painting of yourself as good, all battles lost as glorious heroic defeats, and one's own survival as majestic and divine. And painting your enemy and previous enemies as outright evil. This has been the way for the last two world wars, and every large war since then. It has been common throughout history, too, but in modern times, where we are supposed to be above such things, it is just as prevalent, or even more so. This only shows that the majority of people are susceptible to it, and therefore the practice will not stop. No, it absolutely cannot stop due to that fact. Otherwise, the enemy will win the hearts and minds of the population and thus the war is lost before it even started. We can see examples of such a failure to maintain propaganda for the state, and against the enemy, in the modern media of the Western world today. It is driving a wedge between all the political and social groups of society, and cohesion is lost. Nationalism and patriotism is downplayed more and more, and thus the whole existence of the nation, and our civilization, is threatened.

Modern media is absolutely destructive and a disease upon society, and it does this because it thrives on an ever more sick and polarized society. Media profits from sensation and big and scandalous news, and the corruption and destruction of society is therefore only a source for further sensational news that brings on ever more profit for them. In a society where peace and harmony prevails, a free and private press that hungers greedily for money will just make up, or even instigate, any problem or event to start the snowballing of such evils. And when the news and media, in general, get more and more tabloid and sensationalist, with yellow journalism as standard practice—which undeniably is the reality now in the West—and starts to veer from the path of the responsibility in educating and informing the public, the people will suffer for it. With this loss, the people become dumber and dumber, which again serves the media and perpetuates the problem. The people are also to blame because they treat their news as they would with any indulgence, such as overeating or the lack of exercise: They only want what makes them feel good or stimulates them in some way. Even when it is positively harmful. And they may not know this, or realize this, until it is too late.

There is a control of flow of information in regards to association and value, or rather the reassociation—a reclaiming and reassignment—of value. I call this hypocrite propaganda. The current political agenda allows extreme left-wing ideologies to flourish openly, while simultaneously distancing themselves from it. At the same time it has a complete ban on certain right-wing ideologies, and it is getting more and more restricting every day. This is pushing politics more and more to the left. The further the extreme left is accepted and general politics are transplanted in that direction, the more alien the right-wing becomes, and the consequence is that this makes all right-wing politics seen as more and more extreme by political comparison. To further exacerbate the problem, the left embraces right-wing politics and makes them their own, and by lying and deception if need be. Distorting history and politics so that it looks like it was always left, or rather that it was never on the right. Like they did with environmentalism and animal welfare, which was first implemented by the National Socialists and were revolutionary in their time. And it was the conservatives that were fiscal conservatives at first—conserving (a conservation of) money by spending less and avoiding budget deficits—but this the left has also appropriated to themselves. Although, this was quite easy considering how the American conservatives strayed far from that path of their usual sensible economic state policies. The left calls the right selfish and elitist because those on the right are not social altruists and do not cater to the weak and useless, but the truth is that the left is just as obsessed with money today as the right is, and they need even more of it, if they are to have enough to distribute among all those wretches of theirs—that voter cattle bought and paid for. Actually, the American left today is spending more than has ever been done by any government before them. More money technically means a need to produce more, and more production means more pollution and a greater loss of precious resources. I'd say that this is as selfish and mindless as can be, and in stark contrast to many of the principles the left espouse.

Other Destructive Policies

I. Overpopulation and Pollution

What need is there of this absurd quantity of people on Earth, as it is today? This great breeding of the unworthy—the feeble and weak willed. What purpose does this serve, other than to power the illusion of a growing economy and a reason for a continued need for more food? It only leads to more pollution and ever diminishing resources. Ultimately, for what? What is the great goal of mankind in doing that? It is nothing but mere hedonism and self-serving individualism with no thought or concern for the future at all. These insufferable gluttons and egoists spit on the continuation of their own, or any others, only to maximize their "happiness". It does not further mankind at all. Indeed, it may spell its doom. Global warming is a problem today, and there is little indication that it is not largely caused by humans. The whole structure of human society on Earth needs to change if we are to survive as a species. We need to reintegrate the people with the state and let this hyper-individualism die out. We need to let the weak, stupid, and poor suffer, and certainly not let them mooch. And we need to stop them from breeding. Completely, preferably.

We need to let the middle class—the ones that are sufficiently capable and qualitative as breeding material—take over as the largest contributor of birthing. And finally we need to enable the top echelons of society—the superior few—to reach their potential and breed unrestrained. These superior few, this upper class that is to be the new noble class, must be superior in intelligence and physically fit to be considered proper specimens. Those who fail in either respect must fall to the middle class. When this population control has been implemented, a reduction of emission levels will follow the decline. And immediate results will be seen if we remove from the great many undeserving the privilege of having a high resource consumption. If all this is done in time, the environment will hopefully return to normal and global warming will be reduced. This normalcy may take hundreds of years to return to, though. These things I have just mentioned are imperative that we do, as the Earth is all we currently have, and there is no other option of an alternative habitat in sight. This overpopulation is one that pertains to certain parts of the world, and it is they who are the largest problem in the long run. The Western world should do the least to restrict population growth. In fact, we should encourage it so that we aren't outbred and displaced by immigrants coming here from those overcrowded places. We must encourage growth among ourselves and halt immigration if we are to stop the democide of our people. We should not, and cannot, fix the whole world from just the West at the expense of our own survival, while everyone else in the world are breeding like rats. If any part of mankind should absolutely and undeniably survive, it should be that part which had the greatest progress, and which contributed most to it. Which is the West, and certainly not Africa, or most of the Middle East and Southern Asia.

The promiscuity of the modern age is, in part, enabled by the medical advances we have made. No longer is there a worry about having children when we have prevention and abortion available to us. And the worry about sexually transmitted disease is also gone because of cures and antibiotics. What remarkable, and some would say outright repulsive, manifestations of such consequence free sex is seen today. And consequence is the key word here, because whenever there is a lack of consequence, all seriousness goes with it. The most peculiar pornography that man has ever made is produced in our age, and in greater quantities than ever. This lack of consequences has also made its way into the public, in general. Sex is no longer taboo. Not even the most depraved of sexual acts. Another consequence of having cures for these STD's is that they flourish, and with the massive use of antibiotics to combat this epidemic, it has resulted in these sexual diseases becoming resistant to treatment. In other words, the sexual diseases are on the rise and a serious threat again. This means that we cannot let this go on freely and uncontrolled. These spreaders of disease have to be severely punished and removed from society in some way, so that they do not pose a threat to public health.

The pervasive moral Christian agenda, and people being over-emotional and over-sensitive, has caused other failures of choice and selection in society. For instance, we let the mentally challenged and genetically diseased live, and even procreate! People choose to keep such kids, even when they are informed by the doctor and given opportunity to spare themselves, and most importantly the people and the state, of the enormous resources that is spent on them. These mental and physical deficients, and their kind, do not contribute back, and they have no value to humankind whatsoever—if they breed it is rather the opposite. Why spend all these resources, which amount to many times that of the regular citizen? There are citizens who could have been raised to a position, living a life according to their worth and ability through investing in education and an actual worthwhile job, with the reallocation of that money and effort. Instead, it was wasted for nothing. It makes no sense. To better the individual, or having a better individual, is to better man as a whole, and the state as well. But what do you think happens to humanity and the state when you foster mental and physical retardation?

A right to have children? Should it be a right? Should you not at least show yourself more worthy to have them than others? It is quite obvious that we cannot allow the overpopulation to continue, and thus the universal right to breed has to be curbed. It is either the eventual destruction of Earth—the foundation of life, and ultimately the destruction of mankind if it should perish—or a serious effort to harmonize with Earth instead; to achieve a sustainable system and a symbiosis of man and habitat.

II. The Insanity of Nuclear Weapons

Where else but in the land of selfishness could such a weapon as the nuclear bomb have been thought up. The land of the free and the home of the brave—what laughable hypocrisy that really is. What freedom is this then? The freedom to do exactly as you want? What bravery is there in having such a weapon, so that no proper military engagement will be had? And by having this threat, no nation and people will dare to match this military in production or size in the first place, lest they be nuked. And what bravery is there in launching such a weapon? A weapon that destroys everything, and leaves a place uninhabitable for years and years. The fallout and aftereffects are horrible, and can travel vast geographical distances. What a thuggish, brutish weapon. This they use as an ultimatum: it is either my way, or the highway. And what a highway it is. Like children at play the world used to be, where rules are agreed upon as we go along. All kids are allowed in the play, but some are better than others, of course. But then comes this stupid, unsophisticated lower class kid and with him he carries a big stick. These are his terms: play according to my rules, or else. And if the children refuse, he smashes everything and breaks up the game and play. And you can be sure that he will come back and ruin everything if play is recommenced. What choice is there then? Only one. To play with the bully and according to his rules. And so, the children are allowed back into play, but they are not happy and perhaps the game is not to their liking at all anymore.

There is no choice, however, and if they want any sort of fun and play, then this is what they get.

A weapon to stop all wars, they say. But this is not true, though, is it? Wars are still numerous and bloody. One may even contend that there are even more wars, and that the wars take a greater toll, than during colonial times. Also, weapons manufacturers are doing just as good as ever, and the military-industrial complexes are larger than ever. China is sure proof of that. So, what is nuclear weaponry then? It is the end of concerted wars. Wars of whole nations and alliances versus other nations and alliances. The elimination of concerted struggle. Where nature has its natural selection through competition and strife, man made up his own game of selection when he became master of the Earth. With no threat from nature or animals, he turned against other men. And naturally so, because these men were now the holders of lands, fortunes, and riches. Earlier, a competition, struggle, and striving was a gamble of one's life, but the hydrogen-firecracker-plaything makes it so that it is dead certain that you, and everyone else, lose in the process. There are no winners in such a game. It is not part of the game at all, anti-game as it is. It only makes sure that no one should take up a proper game, and as such it eliminates competition, natural selection, and the survival of the fittest.

These nuclear armed nations, gangsters that they are, work together so that no others should have their power, or match their power. Once in a while they let a new member into their mafia, but only the bosses on top carry the big guns. The big guns that sway the whole mafia to do their bidding.

The largest supply of nuclear weapons are found in the U.S. and Russia. And the latter has even more than the former. And why is it that these two nations are experts on doom and villainy? Truth is that it fits perfectly with their mind-set. The U.S., as we all know, has been on the path to global mastery ever since it came into being, and these last 100 years they have assumed that position quite easily and comfortably, taking much pride in it. The Russians match that pride of the U.S. with their relatively long and colourful history. Then there's the geopolitical position, the sheer size of their country, and the ambitions that result from this. And there are ambitions for sure. The incidents in Georgia and Crimea at the start of this new millennium is proof of that. And that incessant and continued use of power politics by the Russians is felt by everyone today. Just like it was back in the days of Communist Russia. The worship of the all-powerful state, even at the expense of any and all people—in good communist fashion—helps enable this further. The Russians today are fanatically obsessed and absurdly conceited with their mass murdering Stalinism, communism, and their general history of tyranny and that imposed poverty and despairing hardship on the common citizen, and it is utterly pathetic and extremely hypocritical that they have the gall to spew forth accusations of nationalism and fanaticism in others, let alone any societal criticism at all.

III. Differentiating Ideologies

People have great trouble understanding the difference between National Socialism and communism today, and they compare the two repeatedly. This is because people are so ignorant that they only compare the thought, or even the word, of socialism in them. National Socialism is one of class cooperation, private ownership, free enterprise, hierarchy (Führer principle), and the promotion of culture and race. Communism is one of class struggle, no private ownership, no free enterprise and thus state ownership, committee ruling, and the destruction of as much culture as they can, except for the little they need for the cohesion of the state. Communists also do not believe in race and racial differences, or even individual differences. They believe that they can shape any man into what they want, and manipulate and use nature in any way they need. In National Socialism the people live in harmony with nature, and is a part of it and dependent on it. They recognize genetics and evolution, and see the truth and reality of nature. In communism they believe that propaganda and lies should control the population and even alter the perception of reality. The term political correctness is a communist originated term and was put to use in order to let the state control what you can and cannot say, and what you can and cannot think. The similarity with communism is thus not to be found in National Socialism at all, but actually in the liberal and social democratic nations of today. Which means most, if not all, of the Western world.

Communism is just another wave of *ressentiment* in the way that Christianity was—a revolt of the lower classes against the ruling class. The loss of importance in Christianity, and the industrialization and rise of the importance of the worker, were two factors that contributed to the rise of communism. With it also came the usual hate and attack on everyone not part of the new order, i.e., the old paradigm and regime. The pre-communist example of this was the French Revolution, where the king, aristocrats, and everyone part of the old order were hunted down and executed by the rebelling lower and middle class. And with it, chaos ensued and stability was not achieved until the mob had placed an emperor on top. That is how it always goes: The Greek aristocracy was overthrown and disenfranchised by the people and their tyrant, and the Roman senate and the patricians were overthrown by the people and their emperor. Aristocracy and meritocracy, the rule of the few and able, is overthrown by the people and instead they place a single individual in charge to equalize everyone. Like democracy or socialism. And that of communism. This is not the same as hierarchy and kingships and the like. The slave controlled system of democracy, socialism, and communism is one of the people, and a single individual, or a few, that is installed by them to rule. In the master controlled system the power is divided among the nobles and the ruling elite, and the people in general have little say in matters. Obviously this is a struggle back and forth and very blurred at times, but that is the division, as a rule. The empires and states of ancient times, the feudalism in medieval times, and most types of fascism, were such master systems, and their authoritarian power was not necessarily derived by the people, but through their own power and ability, as opposed to the slave systems. Worth to note is that authoritarian today means anything that goes against the people—a rhetorical device in the same way as the use of the word tyrant or dictator by the left—but democracy is just as authoritarian, tyrannical, and hateful towards the capable and superior man (the noble) as meritocracy would be to the inferior and incapable man (the people). Authoritarianism is therefore not an indicator of something, or even a commonality between those that have it, because there are many different ways of obtaining and holding authoritarian power. Simply said, there are many different types of authoritarianisms.

When communism emerged, and its violence and ignorance festered upon society, a reaction to that action arose. This was fascism, which combined modernity with the old values. And to effectively combat this new threat it had to be just as ruthless and violent as these communist were. The Rotfrontkämpferbund, for instance—which was the paramilitary wing of the communists and socialists in Germany—necessitated the creation of the SA by the National Socialists. This was the same in all countries that were plagued with communism. In Italy the communists also caused havoc, and the fascist Blackshirts were created. The bloody Russian Civil War was another such struggle, with the communists winning and causing horrendous amounts of suffering, and the deaths of tens upon tens of millions of people for decades—the Red Terror had been unleashed and it exposed communism for what it truly was.

Part Four: Problematique of Particulars

Masonic Institution of the Jew

I. The Rise of the Jew in Europe

The continual watering down of Jewish blood with German blood made the Ashkenazi essentially a German. When you see the light and fair European Jew compared to the dark and swarthy Jew from non-European countries and the Slavic lands, it is pretty obvious. Therefore, what we know now for a fact through gene research was not an awfully difficult thing to see, and it was much known and talked about even in olden days. I will speak of the Jewish development in Germany, since that was where most Jews lived in Europe and especially where the most successful ones lived. These Jews almost always married Germans, or Germanics, diluting their blood with stronger blood. This miscegenation started at first with the children of such a union being ½ German, and when these married another German their children would be ¾, and the next were 5/6, and then 7/8, and so on, and so on. Although, this only in the scenario where they exclusively married German—those who intermarried between other Jews would still retain a bit more Jewish blood than that. But over time they would still be predominantly German through the fact that they more often than not did marry German, or Jews that were now predominantly German in blood and not Semitic. Some of these Jews married German noblemen and ladies. Some Jews married German commoners. Doesn't matter in the end. And when the Jew acquired Germanic blood to better themselves—with blood and genes as the basis of all advancement in nature—and also built a masonic organization around his religion— religion then and now being a sacred and untouchable institution— they had managed to create a state within the state. They had money and power, and with that it further enabled them to take better educations and to privilege them in other ways, in order to perpetuate their scheming. They had built a new aristocracy, in a sense, but one that was still faulty in many ways. It suffered, and still suffer, from the foundations it was built on: their religion and the traces of Semitic blood still in them. And there is also that life of comfort that only served to weaken them physically and physiologically. Another problem they have is that they tend to be exclusive to each other, and that they have to be inclusive of each other, and therefore they don't really better themselves. They just keep to themselves, and give each other better opportunities than those outside this system. Such a system would rot if it had not had the advantage that the Jews in Europe had: to continually mix in outside blood—this very superior and valuable European blood. This elevated the European Jews, and with money and opportunities to go with this better blood, it would produce good results, naturally. Results very close to that of Europeans who had money and connections—who were much fewer in numbers than these moneyed and privileged Jews. It is strange that the Jews have not done better, actually. Just think what results such a system and institution of preferentialism—as the Jews had and still have—would have, if based upon Aryan men!

II. The Overprivileged Jew

Jews today are even more advantaged than they were back in the Middle Ages. In the U.S. they dominate most of the important positions in percentages that is in the tens, twenties, and even into the extremes, while only constituting 2% of the population. This is because of their money that gets them into places such as better schools and elite clubs, and the power and connections gained from that get them into positions and jobs. They are the last aristocracy on Earth, really. The common excuse for why the Jews "deserve" this is their high intelligence. It is said by them that they have the highest intelligence measured among all people. But is that really true? First of all: What is a Jew then? Did they include Sephardic and Eastern European Jews? Of course they didn't. They only measured American and Ashkenazi Jews, and in particular the learned ones of those, and that is how they get these results they want and need. Results that they use for various purposes and justification when necessary. They have measured the intelligence of Europeans and East Asians as well, but this is also not a correct or specific measure. How can one lump together all those groups like that? How fair is it to measure and group the Slav, in particular the ill-schooled and brainwashed Russian, with an ethnic German, Englishman, or Scandinavian? Or grouping the commies in China with the enlightened people in South Korea or Japan in the case of East Asians? Also, if the method you use is that you only measure a small percentage of Jews—probably only hundreds of thousands, and probably a million or some at most—that are the ones who are most successful due to a number of reasons, it would not be fair to compare that with statistics in the hundreds of millions, and into over a billion. As mentioned, this intelligence measure is just a defence of their organizational and participating activity in the state and that masonic way that they thrive and benefit on. It is strange to me that while we managed to rid ourselves of this behaviour to a high degree in the freemasons and other fraternal organizations—mostly because of enforcing open registries and transparency—it is circumvented in the case of the Jew. Circumvented by having accusations made against the inquirer. We cannot ask why one would hire, or have an inordinate amount of, Jews in this or that job or office, because that would be "racist" or "anti-Semitic". As if being Jewish today has anything to do with race. And as if reacting to the unwarranted preferential treatment of a people or a group is racism. The Jews get a double pass today. The first one is the racial/ethnic/people status they have. Or falsely claim, which I have already explained why. The second one is that of religion.

III. Exploitation and Palestine

All religions today are sacred, and more than they have ever been it seems. In this age where science has unravelled all the truths of the Universe, and all the lies of religion, panic has ensued and the religious have started to pressure, lobby, and even threaten in order to gain more protection and privileges. To preserve their organizations and institutions they are working tirelessly with propaganda of any and all extreme kinds to retain their religious power—this power being the spiritual monopoly on the salvation of the soul, and the entry into paradise. This goes for the Catholics, Muslims, and Jews, but the latter two are especially fanatic. Buddhism is naturally not so threatened, because of its atheistic nature. Neither is Hinduism, due to the exotic flavour in its polytheism and its perceived strangeness and likeability around the globe, and also because of its connection with the Indian national identity, which makes it strong there. Shintoism can also be counted out on the same grounds as Hinduism. Overall, it's the Abrahamic religions that have the most to lose, and that is why it is they who adamantly fight atheism, and even science, the most. Atheism and science goes hand in hand, really. You can't have one and not the other, without looking like a complete buffoon.

Only the racial minorities get as much protection as the religious. The Jews are thus well shielded—this double pass I spoke of. Better than most other groups. This, even though the Jews aren't a race of people, or even an ethnicity or anything like it. Being a Jew today—and has been for several thousands of years—only indicates religious designation and denomination in the same way as being called a

Muslim would. The Arabs have had a hard time playing the race card, or the religious card, in the same manner as the Jews have. Perhaps that's because the Muslims and Arabs today are so utterly unlikeable, which makes any attempt by them to gain sympathy futile. A better example than the Arabs would be the Chechens, because of their vulnerability and smaller numbers. But of course, it always helps to have control over the media. And if you do not, then you cannot expect anyone would care if they are not aware of you, or that you even exist. If the media influence and the protection as a religious group fail, they turn to that joker card of theirs, which is anti-Semitism. This is a stronger version of the regular race card, because it conjures up not only notions of racism alone, but any kind of images or associations—in particular those of the last world war—and if they are not there, then you can be damn sure they will plant them there. By force and coercion if necessary. It always astounds me that what the Jews blame the Germans for doing in that war is the exact same thing that they have been doing, and are still are doing, in Israel and Palestine with the Arabs. Displacement, ghettos, war, and killing as a consequence of that. By expanding upon the land given to them by the government of Britain and the U.S.—which the Jews lobbied heavily for through their contacts and briberies—they have in fact shown themselves to be just as land hungry as the Germans who wanted their Polish, or should I say German, Corridor and Danzig back, which was just a small portion of what Germany lost in the first place. The Jews blame the Germans for the killing of their kind, but the Jews have no qualms about killing Arabs, it seems; and the Arabs are to them like how the Germans felt about the Jews. Although, where the German attacked the Jew primarily because of his criminal activities, the Jew only sees the Arab as Untermensch, and with basically no justification for it as well since they are both Semitic people. That the Jew now thinks himself better than the Arab is delightfully ironic, and this would be pure racism as per a proper definition of that word. Differentiation due to very real and factual differences between the stronger and weaker races warrants the use of the word racialism instead. Millions of Arabs have suffered at the hands of Jews and under Israel for over half a century now. Do I care much for the Arab? No more than the Jew I'd say. Which means just about nil. In fact, I see them both as detrimental to society and therefore a threat.

I really do not see why you have to be either for or against something if you like or dislike one or the other. This false dilemma is continually committed today. You have to side with either the Jew or the Arab, the U.S. or Russia/China, the liberal or conservative, etc., when it is quite possible to dislike and oppose all in that list. Although, I would not say that I am hostile to the good ol' U.S. of A., her values, or conservatives, in general. I would call them a necessary evil, or a lesser or two evils, in light of the alternatives in this day and age.

It is the lying and hypocrisy of the Jew that is so intolerable. This region once called Palestine, and the Arab speaking people there, are in the eyes of the Israelis and Jews no more. Palestine is shrinking day by day and year by year. Israel is unremittent with their propaganda, though. There is no validity in a Palestine, they say, because there isn't a people called Palestinian. By that logic, Israel shouldn't exist either, because there isn't an Israeli or a Jewish people. Saying that there doesn't exist anything called Palestinian is like saying there isn't something called Texan. Or American even, because one can just as easily say that Americans are, or were, British or any other people that migrated there. The logic is just nuts. It is irrelevant and a play on words. The designation of a people in a location does not have any bearing on whether or not they should be living there. And they have lived there for a thousand years or more now. And designating them simply as Arabs, and then designating Israel as a non-Arab land, is just as bad. May as well designate all English speakers as English then, and maybe all those would have to move to England.

IV. Manipulation and Deception

How do you expect people not to question Jewish intentions when they have—and have had for a long time now—control of the largest media corporations in the world? They also have a lot of power through their ownership and influence in the book and literature business; and also through their dominance in the academic strata, which they hold mostly in the U.S. and Britain, but that is enough since that is where the flow of power and information stems from today. For instance, if you have Jews writing all the books and producing all the other media on the Second World War, or the wars that Israel are involved with, then how can you expect that people will believe you to be objective at all? Or when Jewish writers translate texts, and annotate and comment to such a degree that makes the reader almost vomit. Texts which they thereby show themselves having no capability of objectively assessing or understanding.

For example, Walter Kaufmann is peddled as the prime authority on Nietzsche today, but how can we expect truthful representation when Nietzschean thought and master morality is exactly that of National Socialism, or fascism and aristocracy, without the strict racialism, obviously. And we see what happened when Mr. Kaufmann tried to give us insights: he perverted much of it. Such people are so blinded by their values and identity that it paints everything they do. I am not saying that this is not right to do, but it is absolutely wrong if you actually claim, and portray yourself as, being objective and analytical, and this they most often do.

These many lies the Jew commits constantly, and he uses his Jewish connections to spread these lies. He lies to himself and to the world. This is the reason for the accusation of the Jew being a liar and deceiver, and this accusation did not just emerge out of nowhere to find an audience nodding agreeingly because they are mere bigots. Stereotypes, the old stereotypes, are based on truth, after all.

> *"They have not acquired a perfect mastery of the art of lying; they lie so clumsily and ineptly that anyone who is just a little observant can easily detect it." – Martin Luther*

Calling yourself the chosen people in light of the fact that there isn't a thing called a Jewish people, and that religion and God is only a delusion of the mind, is particularly offensive and aggravating. It implies that God only loves the Jews, or that the Jews are the only worthy people. Only when the Jew stops calling himself, and seeing himself as, a Jew and starts identifying as one of the nation instead, can there be acceptance. Just like it is with everyone else. Move to Ireland and be Irish. Move to Germany and be German. And not the opposite. Do not move to Italy, for instance, and be a Jew, Muslim, Arab, Iranian, Turk, or whatever. The Jew has to stop his activities and that favouritism of his own. This is the source for the contempt they meet in all societies they inhabit. This is the same contempt as the freemasons garnered, or the aristocracies in Europe when they no longer had any function or purpose. It is merely the reaction to a very real injustice.

Having said that, it should be remembered that a lot of Jews have done this already, and have more or less distanced themselves from

Judaism as an identity, and more importantly, as a worldly benefit. It is therefore pretty obvious that I am only speaking about those that fit the criteria of the things I have mentioned, which is perhaps only a minority of Jews. To think otherwise is just another fallacy and false dilemma: that you are either for or against. Earlier in time when people were criticizing the Jews, it was apparent that they did not speak of all Jews, but only those who dabbled in these masonic activities. No one ever attacked the Jew for just being a descendant of a Jew, or a Jew by blood. Although, I am sure that quite a few have been mistaken for one of these masonic ones on account of being a Jew—a generalization and a failure to discern for sure—but perhaps they should blame their Jew brethren for that, since it was they who made all Jews look bad in the first place. And besides, the Jews did that exact same thing with the Germans after WW2—a label and stereotype that they have been stuck with ever since.

Atheism and Religion

I. Past and Present

I find the word atheism somewhat insulting and strange because the word itself presupposes the existence of deity. *A* means without and *theos/theism* means god/godhood. Therefore, this term designates someone as without god. This is an odd notion to me, since we know that we need to teach people about gods, or about the word of God, in order to know god(s). This then tells us that the default is rather the non-existence of gods.

Religion is a product of the mind that served as an instrument to find an explanation for the things that it was unable to understand in an earlier age. In a time where there were no answers, and when the intelligent creature wanted and absolutely needed answers, religion would soothe and comfort him. And it worked. Religions gave the answers that—in their time and culture—would best explain the world. Through religion, strife and bickering was avoided by uniformity and agreement; order and structure was instituted. And this institution man thrived on. As he always does—man craves order. Man, intelligent man, wants to organize and systemize his life, his surroundings, and his world. But as the world changes and our knowledge increases, our values change with it, and when new findings arise that make more sense, and are truer, we have to adapt accordingly. A truth is not eternal, so to speak, and that is usually the problem of religion: when it is dogmatic and inflexible and it fails to conform and modify itself with time and discovery. What is the need for religion today then? We have a lot more answers, after all. And we have better hypotheses than religion in cases where we do not exactly know or have proof. This childish attitude of making up explanations for what we do not understand is over. We can know. We have explanations for most phenomena in the Universe. Just open a book or go through the many digital sources of today. Most of the answers are out there.

As I briefly mentioned, what religion did early on was to uniform opinions and values in society—to create a cohesion of the people. People without any connection to each other, in some or other form, do not feel any solidarity or mutual responsibility. Or even worse, a lack of cohesion and belonging creates dislike, hate, and loathing, and in the end it will fracture society. Although, this does not necessitate that there needs to be a great similarity for this cohesion to be there. Only that there is some sort of kinship, equality, or commonality. Equality under the law, or a respect and tolerance of other beliefs with freedom of religion, for instance. From the earliest of time, religion was quite accepting, open, and free. In pre-Christian Rome there was freedom of worship, and there was a god for anything one might need one for, and temples and shrines for each of them, too. One cohesive factor in such a society was in being reverent to the gods through respect of worship, and letting other people believe in what they wanted. The logic was simple: If one cannot be sure which of the gods are real or more powerful, then one may as well treat them all, and their followers, as if they may be. And when the acolytes of one religion or god did better than others, it followed that there may be truth and power in it. The Romans practiced this thinking to the full. They incorporated a number of deities from other nations and people, and conflated a number of them with their own. Such a high reverence of the gods, coupled with a high tolerance of each other's beliefs, was quite unique.

In the Western world today it is not easy to find something comparable to the religious tolerance that existed before the rise of the Abrahamic religions. It was the written word that dogmatized and perpetuated truth, and it was this that made the new religions so intolerant and hateful. Yes, the Abrahamic religions are religions of hate, and certainly not of love. What I mean by this is that this love of theirs is not a universal love, and it is just as selfish as any other definitions of love; they love themselves and those of their own. Yes, even Christianity is hateful. Although, the Protestants and the New Testament are certainly the most accepting of these, and I'd say that they are almost as tolerant as Buddhism. The intolerance lies mostly with Islam, Judaism, and Catholicism—the largest denominations of Abrahamic religion. This God of theirs is one of same origin and similar character. They share this god and yet they still fight as if it was of importance to anything. Quite laughable, really. Tragicomic as it is. And they even fight within themselves, such as in Islam with the Sunni and Shia. Sectarianism as this is pettier and more hostile than completely different religions were to each other in the old pre-Judeo-Christian times. Like the pantheonic Greek, Roman, and Germanic religions, for instance. Have these followers of God so little pride in anything at all that this is the only thing they can find and hold on to?

These religious practices and customs of the Semites are quite offensive, to say the least. The Jews and the Muslims with the circumcisions of males, and girls in Islam, is quite despicable. Cutting away flesh. Cutting away flesh and sowing them back up. It is sacrilege. A sacrilege against nature. What a vile and abominable thing we see through this that religion can be. And then there is the non-optional, or signifying, clothing they wear. From the skullcap of the Jew to the efforts of trying to completely cover up females in Islam with burkas and niqabs. There is also the ritualizing over food in the form of halal and kosher. This they must have, and demand to have, with threats of violent aggression and acts of murder. Such is their lunacy. This is what we have come to then, with modern society returning to the barbaric slaughtering practices of old, where the animal suffers without much purpose, and certainly of no need. This has become so widespread and accepted, with the infestation of these people all across Europe, that these slaughtering and butchering practices are now being done pre-emptively in order to cater to the religious. And the rest of us do not have a say and are barely informed about these products. All of this is done because the religious want to have their religion "respected", and the consequence is that atheists and non-religious are now being fed religious food that is prayed over and harvested and cultivated according to their practices, and not ours. In other words, it is now we who are the ones being disrespected and stigmatized, but no one cares about that. As if atheists and others, or just Westerners, are not of any importance, because we are only heathens that do not have any values or culture and believe in nothing. Which is a massive lie, and one told often it seems. Formerly we had regulations in place that were based on sane, principled, and purposeful meaning. And we also have, or used to have until this immigration happened, the great value of respecting each other, with rights such as freedom of speech; freedom of religion; political freedom; the right to a have a say in matters, to be heard, and to vote; the rule of law; equality under the law; habeas corpus; environmental protection; animal protection; and regulations for the industry and the economy. Meaning that we cared for both the animal and environment, and for the citizen first and foremost, and the state and the people bowed to no special and privileged groups. Yes, freedom, law, and order is the culture and the values of the West—modern civilization. This freedom is not the equivalent to being free of any laws and to do whatever you want, or lacking a restraint or restrictions, or that we are free from values and principles; and this they constantly fail to realize. We have had a gargantuan crime and rape wave caused by Muslims and Africans and their immigration to Europe, and this tells us that they cannot have such civilized concepts as we do. They are just too dim-witted and incapable of understanding them and living by them. This is most likely why these states and nations need collectivism and tyranny, because it is the only thing that can keep any semblance of law and order there. All of the Western values and our culture are now being trampled and spat upon by the religious, the minorities, and their cronies on the left: the liberals, the anarchists, and the communists. Bizarrely enough, these latter have always been entrenched in the atheist stance and should be thoroughly opposed to any religion. Why they are not anymore is because the left and religious have always been of the masses and for the masses—one of slave morality and uprising—and the most stupid and uneducated are always to be found there. A few things have brought the whole of the left-wing and religion together: The first reason is capitalism, with the rich being their common enemy. The second one is that they are so ignorant and uneducated that they do not even know the bases of their political stance or beliefs. This, coupled with the manipulation of the religious priests and leftist firebrands, is what drove these people into these lowest of low ideologies and religions. These groups on the left, and the religious, are a dying breed as their lies—which is what all their beliefs and ideology is based on—are now being exposed by science and truth. In their desperation they have therefore banded together. Everywhere in the Western world, religion is becoming more fanatic than it has been in hundreds and hundreds of years. Much of it caused by the immigration of other races and their religions. There are also signs of this in places such as Turkey, which had made great strides in secularization after the fall of the Ottoman Empire. Religion has shown its true colours again: being the opposing force and enemy of civilization and progress. Not only that, but I think it extremely childish to fantasize about God, heaven, and whatnot. It only shows of a desperate need in a person and society to escape from the real world, with this promise of a better and eternal life after death, and as such it is mostly embraced by the weak, the failed, and the unintelligent.

II. Arianism and the Reformation

Even early on the Germanics found fault with Christianity and were mostly Arian in conviction. Why this is so is quite clear when we look at the inner nature of Catholicism. The Catholics had Jesus die for their sins, and sinning is accepted by them as everyone is sinful. In the Catholic faith, one is born a sinner and no man is free from sin. They sin throughout life and have to continually take confession, and to repent and pay indulgence for it. Such thinking excuses sin and sinful behaviour because they resign themselves to it as a fact of life, since "everybody" is doing it. This is why Catholic countries have more crime than Protestant ones. The thought of eternal sin was not acceptable to Germanic man, however. He who is honest, noble, and idealistic.

Catholicism from the earliest of days was built on a Roman foundation. A religion for the masses, for the people. And where the Roman Empire was aristocratic and hierarchical, so was Catholicism, but this hierarchy was one that was utterly populist and benevolent. Always for the "love" of the people. On top of this hierarchy we find a pope with the old imperial title of Pontifex Maximus, which was the highest office of priesthood in Rome. Furthermore, these new Christian priests now donned the imperial colours and symbols.

When the Roman Empire crumbled, the Christians picked up the pieces and made themselves a transcendental empire from what was left. No longer an empire of the Earth, but one of the soul, the heavens, and afterlife. They filled the role of religion in all the former Roman regions, and connected these regions and people together in this new, albeit familiar, system. Rome now worked as a mediator and separate power apart from that of nation and state. But Rome still set the rules and laws, and all had to play their game. The use and adherence of the widespread Roman law from earlier was replaced by Christian laws, or at least a code, and these rules and values had much of the same consequence as law. Those left out of this establishment and these customs, or outright rejected them, quickly found themselves with enemies now bearing the cross. The Germanic invaders and their kingdoms that sprang up in, and after, the Migration Period found it much easier to establish themselves and survive when playing ball with the papacy. There was an obstacle, however. The early Germanics were of the Arian persuasion rather than the Catholic one. This Arianism was a very early take on Christendom, and had been practiced among the aristocracy and the emperors themselves. Arian, the founder of this sect, did not believe in the trinity of God. He said that Jesus was subordinate and not a part of God; the son of God was a created, mortal being. How easily the Germanics, and aristocrats, took to Arianism instead of Catholicism is an early indicator of the gap between the north and south, and that of the noble and the petty commoner. A gap in blood and intelligence. Arianism was a much more realistic, earthly, and natural denomination than the Christianity we know today. It was one that was much closer to the older religions and less fantastical. Simply, more believable to an educated and intelligent man. Even though the Arian heresy was stamped out, this rift between the north and south, and the aristocracy and the plebeians, would continue on until the final breach with the coming of the Reformation.

The Reformation was the revolt of Germanic man against Rome and Catholicism, and not a return to Christian values per se. It was the Germanic man making Christianity better so that he could live with it, and not those flawed and lowly values of the Catholic institution. The Protestant man has Jesus' life and death on the cross to serve as an example and idol, and not as a sacrifice and martyr. Germanic man is much too prideful for that. He in his greatness sees that he can become godlike himself, and will therefore attempt to emulate Christ. Germanic man sees himself as divine. This is why he does not need a church or clergy to talk to God, because his goodness and godlike being allows him to talk to God (and the gods) on his own—Protestantism was born. This Germanic way of thinking is, for example, why Nietzsche says he is Antichrist. The opposite of Christ. He, too, is godlike, but in an atheistic way, obviously. Although, I doubt that Nietzsche would agree. My point is that only a Germanic mind can think this way. Germanic man needs either or. Either slave morality or master morality, but he needs them in perfect and intelligent forms. This was why he changed Christianity, or Catholicism, into Protestantism. It was just more palatable to him, as Arianism was. Germanic man always takes a thing and makes it better. He even had a better variant of master morality. Romans always looked up to the Germanic men of their time and praised their culture extensively—the only exception being their excessive drinking. The Romans, too, had master morality, but the Germanics had perfected it. It was not ruled by emotion and was free of the sympathy for, and the rabble rousing of, the masses. The Romans had always been susceptible to this. When they threw out their last king, Tarquinius Superbus, it signified their first step away from nobility and aristocracy. Roman history was an ever gradual change from a master morality into slave morality after that—albeit extremely slow, due to the magnificently ingenious governmental structure and system that was in place, in some form or another, from monarchical times.

III. Need and Use of Religion

In the temperate zones that allow for large populations, there is always some power input from the large masses, or some overthrow to enable that. This collective nature of theirs is one that comes from their numbers, which in turn stems from this ease of living there. In other words, it is a direct cause of a lazy and struggle-free life. This laziness leads to a lack of contemplation and also a lack of disagreement and strife among people. They resign themselves to whatever may be, as long as they are left in peace, more or less, to live their lives. These commoners have no ideals and no principles. They merely conform to whatever is in place. It is not even a cowardice either, as it is just their subconscious behaviour. They resign themselves to fate, sort of. Whatever that fate is. Empires and religions come and go without the masses not really caring the least about them, and without them knowing anything about them and why they are there. Such lax people prefer emperors and rulers of great territories. And they will gladly institute such rule, because when there is only one large empire, it diminishes war and conflict—they want the Pax Romana and other such times of peace. And even if tyrants come to power and great injustices are committed, they will accept it, because wars are more destructive and more costly in terms of life and suffering than what any tyrant can do. Although, Mao and Stalin seems to prove me wrong with the combined murder of 135 million (R.J. Rummel) of their own people, which is more than the two world wars put together. Much more. In any case, the great empires of Rome, China, Persia, and those in India rested on the pillar of this collective mind-set, and this is the reason why they still are as they are. The people there simply do not care, and haven't got the slightest inkling of what is going on. They only care about their peace and their life. However, given their ignorance, they are also unaware of how life can be bettered, and few if any of them have the capacity to even dream about that, and if by chance they did dream, they would not have the means and ability to conjure up the plan to build a state, nation, or world accordingly. Only the worst of hardship will compel them with the bothersome task of uprising, and even though it frequently happens, it usually fails. Their best hope for success is to find the capable few that can; they have to find some noble men willing to lead them.

In the Germanic lands every man was a freeman, and as such every man was a noble. He was free, because he had to be. This I have talked about earlier and should not warrant any further explanation—see chapter *Roman and Germanic Ways*. When we see that the very Celtic nations of Ireland and France held on to Catholicism after the Reformation, it becomes clear to us why, and how, the Celtic man so easily joined, and found his place in, the Roman Empire in the first place: he must have had some of this Mediterranean temperament. Although, know that the roots of Catholicism were set early and are very deep in Ireland—meaning that it may have been tradition that persisted, and not due to the mind-set of said people. Catholicism also served as a symbol of opposition to, and difference of, the English, which have been their greatest threat and hated enemy for hundreds of years. Almost a millennia, actually. This collective nature and thinking—seen in the people of these populous places—is why they so easily adopt slave morality and any institutions that embody such thinking. Which Catholicism was, or is. Opposed to this collective is the individual and individualism. This was present in the aristocracy, nobility, and in the Germanic man that embraced Arianism and Protestantism. This German Christianity lastly devolved into deism. Which is a type of Christianity that is devoid of the supernatural and of miracles, and finds proof and a basis for the creator in nature instead. This is almost a complete reversal back into that of the old gods and the old pantheon, where Thor, for instance, was the manifestation of lightning and thunder. Or the various fertility gods, and gods of wine or song, that were indicative of the fruitful, of birth and life, ecstasy, etc. That is to say, a belief that has returned to the logical again, and is relatable. This deism does not resign the soul and life to fate and helplessness; God helps the one who helps himself. Or more precisely: nature helps the one who helps himself. Which is the process of nature, life, and evolution itself, and that is why it is natural that the oldest of human ways would be based upon this, and why man tends to revert back to this, time and time again. Especially the clear-sighted man.

One was not blessed by the old gods, one was only acknowledged by them. If a warrior did well in battle, he was worthy and entered Valhalla. Thus, he had to prove himself, and he could not expect any help or blessing from the gods. This thinking is similar to the Protestant thinking in becoming as good as Jesus. It is the affirmation of action and deed, and of life. Such a man lives life to the full and in accordance with his values and principles. The afterlife to the Germanic and Protestant man is one of remembrance and legacy. Unlike the Catholic or Muslim who only lives for paradise, which is why they have such horrifying behaviour. Or the Jew, who lives only for Earthly life, and this is why he indulges shamelessly and without worry. Which is not much better. He doesn't care about Earthly posterity, or reputation and setting examples. But the Germanic man does—he needs both idealism and realism. He needs high ideals and ambition. No, he sets and creates high ideals and ambition, and he also needs to make them happen in his life. To see them come to fruition. And he has. The world is proof of that. Religion was just a tool for him, and a fact of life, in the past. One that he improved much upon, in order to make it more natural and better for society and the state. We do not need religion anymore, however. It is no

Part Four: Problematique of Particulars

longer a fact of life that we have to work with, or around, and it has no function or use for our mental state anymore, either.

Language, Writing, and Culture

The nature of language is one of constant abbreviation and higher understanding, Nietzsche says. And how true that may be. There surely is a need and continued competitive progression in being able to say something in the shortest amount of time so that a danger may be averted. The faster I can explain and warn about the green monstrous troll that is about to club my friend on the head, the faster my friend can react to it. There is also less work and effort involved, when we are quick to be understood, or understood at all. This is why we create and collect words for increasingly specified things. Loanwords, for example, is such a thing. Although, I would say that it is better to create a word within, and out of, your own language than using one that does not come naturally or has evolved naturally. This is because a word usually evolves from the actions involved or taken in it, and therefore they will have some connection to each other, which will help the logic of the language. A loanword may not have this.

To be understood we have to normalize words then, and this is how language comes into being, and even how they separate. In given areas the people will become uniform if they are connected and dependent on each other. The written word, and a common tongue, can directly influence and make a language uniform, but this can also hinder and stifle the natural evolution of a language. Earlier when the written word and language standardizations were not common and implemented, the natural evolution of language occurred in areas without the impact of such corrections—these "right" and "proper" ways of a language—and thus they were free to branch out, develop, and meld, naturally and accordingly.

Part Four: Problematique of Particulars

The Latinization and Arabization of language would not have happened if it was not for the fact that there was an almost complete vacuum of writing in the places where these spread. The proof of the power in a written language is how readily accepted these languages were in their time, and how widespread they are today. And we can see how much more uniform Arabic is than the Latin languages, due to having a standardized book early on that was culturally important and integral to their lives. The Romans never had such a powerful tool until the spread of the Bible and by then the great Latin languages had grown apart from Latin. Latin had not even kept up in the homeland. Latin had become too old-fashioned and detached, and the chaos and the undermining of the Roman Empire during the Migration Period had sealed its fate as a standard. By the time the Roman Catholic Church had been firmly established, and could assert itself as the successor of the Roman Empire and its culture, it was already too late.

The Frankish Empire, and its successors, dominated Europe for centuries, and even over a millennia, and it is therefore not for naught that the common tongue was the Frankish language, which is where the name of lingua franca derives—this word may also mean bridge language, and not just common tongue. The actual lingua franca was less Frankish than the name suggests, however. Understand that it was named so because of the importance to be able to communicate with the Franks, because of their power and dominance in Europe. With this loss of Roman cultural dominance, Latin took a backseat to the other cultural powers of its day. And even though the Romans still dominated religious life and tried to force a Latin language on all Christians, they were not able to supplant the many languages in Europe. What the Roman Church did instead, with its monks, missionaries, and general dominance of the written word, was to make Latin the common alphabet and phonetic standard, and this was embraced throughout Western Europe. The dedication and reach of the Catholic Church is seen in the history of Iceland, for example, with Gaelic monks already living there when the Norse first set foot, which is also the reason why the Norse took up writing and used the Latin script as early and readily as they did there, adapting it to their own language. The literature from Iceland is remarkably rich and plentiful for such a small and out of the way place. Cultures that were strong and sophisticated were therefore not supplanted by the forces of Latinization and Arabization, and only adapted and filled the gaps where they were lacking.

Script and writing is only a vessel, though, and without any content the vessel is useless. When we see the profound impact that Islamization and Arabization had on almost all places it dominated, we must assume that it brought with it a lot of appreciated value to the people there. But we must also not forget that all of Northern Africa and the Middle East were left in a power, cultural, and stability vacuum left by the loss of control by the Western and Eastern Roman Empire that was much caused by the concurrent migrations and invasions of the Germanic peoples during the Migration Period. Not a stone was left unturned by the Germanics in the Western Roman Empire. Everywhere from Spain and Morocco to Libya, Sicily, into Italy, and indeed all of the lands there that the Arabs so easily swept across later on. The Eastern Roman Empire also suffered its share of encroachment, and not only from the north in the Balkans and in their holdings in Italy, but also from the east and south where the Sassanid Empire—also just before the Arab invasions—took Egypt (to be reconquered by the Byzantines and then lost again to the Arabs shortly after) and also a great deal of the Middle East and Asia Minor. This sapping of strength all across the Imperial lands was surely the greatest factor in how swiftly and unhindered the Arab conquests were made. But there was probably also a great deal of culture that was offered to the conquered by the Arabs. Seeing the Arab conquests in view of the climate zones that they came to conquer and hold, it becomes clear to us that their expertise in desert warfare in these areas was crucial. And as these climates shape the culture and the people there, we may assume that the conquered masses found great similarities and commonalities in their new lords, and perhaps also some useful changes and innovations in what they brought with them. And greatest of all was the implementation of written law. Which had probably not been properly executed since the fracturing of the Roman empires in the Migration Period. Or maybe even as far back as the divide of the Western and Eastern halves.

This was not the case with the Germanic areas. And they were also not threatened, or at least not intimidated, by wars. The culture, and social structure, of the lands inhabited by the Germanic peoples were so strong that they were very hard to convert properly, and the values of the Catholic Church were also very hard to maintain among them if implemented. It is not coincidence that the Protestantism that spread across Europe originated, and manifested itself most strongly, in these Germanic lands. In the lands with more Celtic blood we see that they did not react in quite the same way. Which is probably why the Roman Empire were able to have the Celts submit and join their empire much more readily than the Germanics. The few Celtic fringes that were left unconquered by the Romans were Caledonia (Scotland) and Hibernia (Ireland). Some argument that it was the weather that made them stop, but why did the Romans bother with Germania then? The climate on the outskirts of the British Isles are far milder than in Central Europe, after all. Although, the richness of the Germanic lands were arguably greater than that of Caledonia and Hibernia, and this may explain the attempts at invading Germania, and perhaps also why plans and efforts in conquering the rest of the British Isles were put on hold and then scrapped. What these places did have in common were densely forested areas, which made them easy to fight guerrilla wars in, and the warriors in these regions utilized such tactics constantly—making them very hard to conquer and control. Not counting the ferocity of Germanic warriors, which were a force to be reckoned with—the Romans found out the hard way, and in the end they decided it was best to stop poking the beast for fear of enraging it.

Again and again throughout history we see that Germanic lands and people are different. With the rise of Protestantism we saw it take a hold in most of the Germanic lands: in Scandinavia, in the lands in the north of the Holy Roman Empire, the Netherlands except Flanders, England, and much of Switzerland. In the lower parts of the Holy Roman Empire and in France, where Germanic blood was very prevalent, there was also a great following and uprising. This resistance and clash of beliefs is explained by the simple fact that Germanic people were used to personal freedom, and a say and a vote in society through popular assemblies. The submission to the absolute authority of the Catholic Church was therefore untenable.

Since Mediterranean peoples and the Celts are more submissive—in that they follow rules more unquestioningly and are less independent in thought and person—they will not revolt in the same degree, or for the same cause. This may not sound as great an attribute, but when one identifies this as unquestioning discipline and adherence to law and rule, one then realizes how the Roman Empire was able to become the greatest empire the world has ever seen.

This small chapter should serve to illustrate how important culture is. And when a powerful culture and message is conveyed by the written word, it causes tidal waves throughout human lives and history.

Part Five: Necessities for the Future

"There is nothing more difficult to take in hand, more perilous to conduct, or more uncertain in its success, than to take the lead in the introduction of a new order of things."
— *Machiavelli*

Part Five: Necessities for the Future

A New State

I. A First Step

A child is born classless and without any privileges of the station, wealth, or importance of the parents. Only born with the right of an equal and fair chance to show skill and ability. In the case of orphans, they will either be adopted by other dutiful citizens or they will live in state-run boarding schools. These boarding schools should be at the same level as regular schools and should provide an environment that is safe and loving, yet strict. Much in the same way as the boarding schools for the superior will be, of which I will talk about later on. The schools of this society will be much stricter, but the mandatory years will be fewer. There will be advanced classes where the most intelligent of children are given more attentive schooling suited to them. Naturally, as it always is, these primary/elementary schools will not have the most gifted of faculty staffs, due to the priority of putting the best teachers to work in the schools of higher, and more important, education. These primary schools will be hampered in a number of ways by that fact, but this does not matter much because if the system proposed is in place, then everyone will get the best teacher and schooling available according to their ability and capacity. A problem in the primary schools, having these teachers of lower ability and intelligence, is the selection and finding of gifted children. There are a number of ways to tell exceptional performance, or capacity and intelligence, from the rest. I will start with the most obvious: These intelligent youngsters show a learning capacity that is above average. They will absorb larger amounts of information and will generally learn quicker. Their higher intelligence helps them understand things faster and more clearly. Doing well in school is not an indicator, though, because anyone who works at it will achieve good results, but these are not the gifted. Should they be rewarded? Yes, but not in the same way. They do not have the great potential we are looking for. The least obvious signs of these exceptional are that they may seem bored and uninterested. They may cause disturbances and may be otherwise unenthusiastic and disinterested in topics. This is repeatedly taken as being a problem today, and these children are usually treated as below par and hopeless, and by doing so they cause great harm. The actual reason for these children being this way is because they are not engaged. They do not care about these activities, because it is just not challenging. And one will quickly realize this when one talks to such children. They are very bright and intelligent, and they may have an insight and knowledge that goes far beyond even that of their teachers. Having standardized tests, and by designating the most intelligent and aware of the adults in a school to be an inspector or surveyor of these gifted, one can better find them. External inspectors may also help to check up on schools and students to see that there are no mistakes being done in the process of finding and selecting these gifted ones.

When the gifted are found they will be put in advanced classes. These advanced classes should be in every school and will help sift out the best and brightest. Obviously, the teachers of these advanced classes should be the best among their faculty, and they are therefore also awarded a status and higher pay accordingly. It is an important job, after all, to map the potential, and the areas of expertise and interests, in these advanced pupils. After they have finished primary school, these students will enrol in, and attend, advanced secondary schools. These advanced secondary schools will differ from regular secondary schools in the same way as advanced classes in primary school differed from the regular classes there. These advanced secondary schools will educate the upper middle classes of society.

Although, some may end up in the higher class tier. After the regular students from the normal secondary schools have graduated, they will no longer receive any education on behalf of the state. None whatsoever. Those who wish may continue further schooling, but it will be on their own expense. Will this be a detriment to society? Not at all. We see today—yes, even today in our advanced technological society—that the population is spending too much money and time on education. And then they end up in jobs that they are "overqualified" for (as this term being used today is called). Which is no wonder, really, as there are just too many low skill jobs in the world that are still needed to be done, and too few high skill ones. It is therefore a loss for the students because they waste a lot of their time and money, and accumulate large loans, on these worthless educations. Educations that they get from throwing money at private schools and programs, in order to get a job that they are ultimately wholly incapable and too incompetent to do in the first place. If they can get those jobs, that is. Much of the expense in the education of these people today are paid for by the state—yes, even those that are private. All of this ultimately equals a double loss for the state. First of all in the loss of productivity, which equals money, with having a smaller work force among the young. Secondly, the state spends a huge amount of money in the form of intuition money, school subsidies, and state school funding and the likes; which was what enabled that former loss to happen in the first place.

 A problem with schooling today is that when, and if, we are all left on equal terms, then one can only score so high. In doing so, there is really no academic way to tell the students apart, due to the extremely low ceiling on top grades, which is because of these very low standards set in order to include everyone. Also, with anyone and everyone getting in at schools, and everyone getting a degree, then we are left with no real way to discern the talented and exceptional from the mediocre; they all have the same degree and education. With the failure of measurement in academic ways, the gifted and the mediocre are left to be measured by other criteria. Which is social interaction and having connections. Yes, this corrupt practice—call it nepotism or whatever you like—is everywhere today. In the government, the job market, and the house/rent market. Everywhere, really. And when social interaction—how likable you are—is a criterion, it is then easy to lose out if you are not well liked, or not interested in being liked for that matter. But what do I mean by this? Am I saying that you should be preferred if you are socially stunted and weird? No. What I mean is that an intelligent man sees and interacts with mediocre men in the same way as these mediocre men would interact with one who is mentally impaired. Yes, that is what the great masses call those who are of lower intelligence. But as they see those less intelligent than them, because they can identify the failures in them, they cannot identify or see those who are smarter or more knowledgeable than them—you cannot identify a problem if you do not recognize or understand it, and because of this you will not be aware that there is a problem. This is why an intelligent man will have a problem relating with the masses, and vice versa. They are just too different. The great mediocrity is interested in, well...the very mediocre. They would have to, wouldn't they? And if we let the mediocre set the standards and criteria, then the mediocre will obviously be the ones who benefit the most.

II. Curricula and Duty

The curricula of the primary and secondary schools will have a greater focus on physical fitness and practical skills. Here the students will be prepared for a life of work and duty to each other. They will not get imprinted with such silly fantasies and beliefs that they are special or unique. They will learn that they have to do their part. And if they do well throughout school and life, they will be rewarded. For instance, the children who give an effort and do well may be sent to the advanced classes. And in any case, everyone will still have to maintain good grades if they want to get a better job after mandatory school, or if they want to apply for further education on their own expense. There is thus a continual gradation and hierarchy in society.

In this curriculum there will also be a great focus on opening the mind. We must try to build a learning mind early on. A mind that understands how and why to learn. By allowing the mind to see how things connect and where they fit, it will build a logical and intelligent cognizance that will see patterns and ways of doing things throughout life. It is not for nothing that such things as shape sorting boxes or Lego have become popular and are used as learning devices. They have a remarkable effect at young age, after all. A foundation of learning, that transcends the current standards, can therefore be achieved, but it will not only require devices such as these, but much more advanced ones, and also comprehensive learning plans that may or may not exist at this moment.

Enough with the old system of indoctrination. Honesty and truth will again be part of human life. We will show and tell what morality really is—the foundation of it, and understanding its purpose. We will teach religion from an atheistic viewpoint—why people made up religion, and what the purpose and function of it was, and also the psychological understanding of it. By which I mean the psychological need of having it for explaining how the world came to be and why it is so—answers we have today through science, but were earlier unable to obtain. And also how religion, and the institution of it, taught law and value through moral guidance, and created unity through commonality in knowing the story of people and persons. Similar to the building of national pride and patriotism today. Another important focus in education will be language. All citizens must be bilingual, and ideally all students should choose a third language to learn during their primary and secondary education. The use and practicality of language in this global and diverse world of today is very important, and a great strength. Just see how well some parts of the world that are very fluent or knowledgeable in English do, for instance. This is because the lingua franca helps them to integrate with the largest and most powerful parts of the world: the English speaking parts. It benefits trade and cooperation. Language is also the key to understanding a great deal of historical, cultural, and national points of view, and not to mention the various literature of said views. Language originated and operates in such a way that it reflects and reveals the inner workings of how culture and life influenced and formed language. We see an example of this in the Inuit and their many words for snow and ice.

Plato will be the philosophical foundation. He will teach us how to ask questions, and how to be true and idealistic. And we will teach Nietzsche, because of his magnificent worth as a poet and as a teacher of understanding morals, and everything else he has such great insights in. There will be no ban on books. We will not make it unlawful, or discourage anyone, to read, watch, and do whatever they want. Unlike most nations today, where the tyranny of political correctness turns society against you so that you not only lose your job and social life, but even your actual life. *Mein Kampf* by Adolf Hitler will be read and properly understood again for the first time in more than half a century. Books like *The Prince* by Niccolo Machiavelli will also be taught. As for fictional works, that are deep and filled with lessons, a few great ones worthy of mention are *Nineteen Eighty-four*, *Dune*, and *A Brave New World*. There are no evil books or opinions, and we will not be ruled by the hate and hypocrite labels of those guided by slave morality—a morality holding that evil is a thing, evoking pictures of hells and devils. Philosophy and difference of opinion will be celebrated, because with nuance and contrast the great truth will shine so much brighter. Even the pathetic and laughable *Communist Manifesto* will be read and discussed; all silliness and lies will be exposed thus. We will build a school and system of reflection and understanding, and not of dogmatic principles and political correctness. And the people will love the nobles, the state, and themselves for it, and take pride in it. In our country we will learn everything, and be taught to understand it. We will be a people of truthful and honest behaviour. We will not debase ourselves and sink to their level, where we forbid some information, and only tell partial truths. Or even worse: complete lies. We trust in our truths. So much that we will let anyone see and compare for themselves. We are not scared or shaken by information, because we have truth on our side. Every time someone researches and studies something, they will find that very information we adhere to and their respect for us will only deepen, and this way our ideology will grow unassailable and eternal. Truth does not harm those who are right, it only empowers them. This is why we will have an intellectually open school and society. And through having a better educational program than other nations, that include a more challenging physical and practical education, the people will have all the more pride in themselves and of the whole system. Part of this pride, and another source of unity and patriotism, will be the compulsory military service of every individual—every single man and woman. Even those with a physical disability will have to participate, and they will receive a job suited to their limitations. This service is a minimum of 1 year, but for more specialized positions there should be more, including military repetitions throughout life if required. The state is to take advantage of this as best it can. Conscription should not be a drain and economic loss to the state. Thus, it will use this labour force in any and all capacities, but the first and foremost duty is to make all men into capable soldiers. Or ideally, outstanding soldiers. This involves learning how to handle weaponry, radio, tech gadgets, and being given tactical and strategic theory training, and how to utilize and ration from what one has and what is available. This is not necessarily a great consumption of time, and that is why the conscript should and could be used for any service to the state—much like the Roman soldier was. This includes anything from road building, house building, factory and industrial work, or working at sea. Women in the service should generally be allocated lighter work, though. In military assignment, women and men will be housed, trained, and taught separately. Work assignment may be gender mixed, however. The work should be fitted as best as possible to every individual's skills and interests. A great plus in having this conscription, this service to the state, is that a person has now had work experience, and he will receive a certificate of his military service and the work he did there. They will also have a greater feeling of being part of the people and the state through this common service and duty that they have gone through; it builds loyalty and love.

III. The Formation of Nobility

In these advanced classes in primary school, there is one ultimate task. This is finding the genius and remarkable. These geniuses are naturally very, very few of. And there may not be any in an entire advanced class, as few schools may have these geniuses. But when they are found, they will be prioritized. They will get the option, at this very early age in primary school, to go beyond the advanced classes and be sent to superior schools. Another criterion, apart from that of the mental, is that those eligible for superior schools must be physically fit and healthy. They should, as a rule, be at least average or above normal children in fitness. These few superior schools are paid for and run by the state. They will be boarding schools that provide an environment that is, or should be, better than family life in every way. It is important that the children feel loved and cared for in their time there. However, if families want to move, or already live in a location around the superior schools, then board will not be needed, of course. It should be marked upon that for uniformity's sake there should be similar living arrangements so that there are no feelings of perceived preferential or privileged treatment by some. By having the best and most challenging of educations, and the most rigorous of physical programs, we will let these geniuses bloom to their full potential and become all that they can be. And as they rise to the challenge, they will take great pride in their opportunity and achievements. From the very outset, they will first enter a superior primary school, and then a superior secondary school. When their potentials have been mapped—any and all potentials—they will then proceed to a field of their choosing, and with the completion of college/university they are given status of nobility; they are the finest exemplars that the nation has to offer. This option to gain nobility is also open to other people in society. This will give the citizens something to strive for and a reason to better themselves. Although, the criteria should be that they have shown themselves mentally and physically superior just like the other nobles have.

These exceptional will form the basis of a nobility, a top tier of the upper class, which the people will rally around and the state will thrive on. These nobles will enrich the culture, and usher forth new political systems and practices and technological advances—the tools and means to the progress and advancement of the human mind and body, and for the value of society and the state, and thus to our evolution as a whole. They will have their nobility and rights for life, but this designation and title will not be able to be passed on. Their offspring will have to go through the same recognition process in school and life if they wish, and strive, to become nobles themselves. Once ennobled, they may do anything and everything. They can join politics, or they can live as hermits. They are beyond that of any other men, and their only duty is to advance mankind, and their only restriction is that they follow the law. If the law is Good that is, and not a detriment to our evolution or the state, or an obstacle to positive change.

IV. Free Enterprise and the State

Let us return to the common citizen. When in secondary school (which corresponds to high school), the student citizen will orientate toward what skills and interest he has, and therefore which profession to have. Not much orientation and specifics is needed, though, because with everyone being taught basics, such as mathematics and geometry, and various other skills needed for menial work, like the use of a great array of worker tools, then one has received the greatest schooling of all. The result is that everyone has the knowhow to become a carpenter, plumber, construction worker, etc. More in-depth professional education will be given by elders and co-workers while in that job, and one should read up on one's profession whenever one has the time. This is the most efficient way to educate people. This also makes for a very flexible work force. Wages should be set by the state and worker unions, although the state should have a final say, because of the need for a concerted and effective hierarchical leadership—having oversight and plans that take precedence. The commoner is, however, free to do anything he wants. He can get a job, in order to pay for further schooling, or he can take a loan, if he can get one, and start his own business of some kind. Or he can work and save up for any such. He can run a farm or a shop, or he can go to whatever school he can pay for. Free enterprise, that is the best system: one that emulates nature. There should be no restriction on how rich one can get or how high one can rise. It only depends on how skilled and gifted you are. We will have liberty. Freedom is not the ability to do whatever you want, however. Not at the expense of other citizen individuals, for example. And as the state is the expression and combine of the individuals, then a harm to the state is that same thing as harming an individual. Freedom is only applicable to yourself then. You will be free to start a business; to do as you please with what you own; read what you want and learn what you want; to express yourself; to have sexual relations with, and marry, who you like; and to have children. All of this, if it does not go against, and is detrimental to, the state. You can run a business, if it does not cost or harm the state in some way. Polluting the nation, for instance. Some pollution may be unavoidable, but if so, there has to be regulations. You are also free to express yourself, but not if it destroys cohesion of society. If you want to change the state, you should do it in a proper intellectual forum and argue your cause, and not by rabble rousing. And you may have children, if the state thinks you are a suitable specimen and then given permission, or if there is a general sanction in place. Always so that it does not harm the state as a whole.

The state will be of a mixed economy—it must be—which is the system most successful today, and was copied from the National Socialists. It was too successful and effective not to be copied, really. This gives the state the prerogative to run state businesses, which is usually based upon the largest resource of that particular country—the resource of largest wealth from a combination of value, quantity, and potential. Having such state run behemoths help prosper and stabilize a state economy greatly, due to a greater control and focus, and it will also help the state to employ citizens in need of work. That is not to say that the state businesses should not be run as efficiently and profitably as possible. However, the needs of the people, and their future, will and must outweigh the needs for profit and efficiency.

Some may be worried that if the citizens are completely free to get as rich as they can, it might lead us right back onto the track of corruptive political power games and practices. Still, keep in mind that all children will be classless and sent to the mandatory state run schools with everyone else, and with an (ideally) uncorrupted faculty in these schools throughout education, one will be graded and valued according to ability and achievement. As such, you will get the papers you deserve, and if you are given a job and position that you do not qualify for, then the people will know. This does not restrict privately owned businesses from hiring their own children and those from their family, though. And it will not restrict them from inheriting. We can thwart such behaviour, however, by making such nepotism a societal taboo. A taboo for children and family, who are undeserving of a control of companies and wealth, to inherit, or at least inherit a great part. This thinking should come about with the knowledge that the most important in a society and state are the superior ones—individuals of exceptional intelligence and physique. Therefore, the loyalty and love of those ideals should make individuals pass on their possessions to those most worthy, and in the case that one cannot find any some such, then one should will it to the state. The state may then continue the operations or put it up for sale domestically, letting investors and companies buy stocks and shares, or outright buy it. If an individual would make such clear headed decisions, such as willing his wealth and property back to the state, then one will be praised posthumously. With the notion of the importance of the superior, then the importance of the accomplished and successful citizen logically follows. Honouring the great in society will be a natural, and honouring them after they are gone will be even more glorious. These will then become the idols of the future, and everyone should strive to be better and noble in order to be venerated long after they are gone. A legacy will be the measure of a man's life and worth. Like the pharaohs and Caesars of old we will deify them when they are gone—the only gods worth believing in should be the most worthy and exalted of men that once lived.

The purpose of, and one of the reasons for, retaining inheritance and ownership is because it will serve as the identifier of the good bloodlines in a state. Meaning that if someone does well, then one can further allow one's blood to build on this previous success, and if there is continued success repeatedly, then one has shown that their breeding and blood is superior, and thus merits a higher status and position in society. This is also why surnames are retained. This may result in clannish and factional behaviour in society—where bloodlines and groups bond, and have tight connections—but as long as the loyalty to the state, and the people comprising it, take precedence, then this will ultimately be for the Good. Competition and grouping/working together is beneficial. It will strengthen the individual, the blood, and the state.

V. Breeding and Society

The mating and breeding in this society will be of the greatest importance, as it is the most important part of life—the continuation of life. The most essential thing is to breed the best with the best, and to breed as many of them as possible. The higher classes will therefore be heavily subsidized in order for them to have children without having any financial concerns. We will build a sense of duty among the best and superior in having children. Women who have a lot of children, and men and women who have a great number of exceptional children, will be rewarded and honoured, and given medals and awards. The upper middle class, and middle class in general, will also be treated in such a manner. However, the lower class will not be subsidized for having children, and if there is overpopulation, they will be discouraged and even forbidden to procreate. Other than that, they will be rewarded if they produce children who are exceptional. To facilitate a good fit of mates, one should preferably marry within one's own class. This can be by personal preference, but optimally it should be by having a good fit genetically and by intelligence, and thus by worth. Marriage, as an institution, should only be the indication of man and woman being linked to one another in some way—primarily for that purpose of children and mating. With the duty and need of man and woman to have many children, the state will both encourage and legalize polygamy. As such, for order and convenience, the citizen's middle name should come from maternal lines and the last name from paternal lines. The higher classes should, ideally, be the most prolific. The reproduction of man must be a continuous undertaking by the nobility and higher strata so that society will continue to rise, and not degenerate, thereby avoiding that fall of nation and civilization, which is always due to the gradual decay of the noble classes. And when these become less prolific, due to increased luxury and decadence and a soft living, then the lower classes will outbreed them quite swiftly. Eventually a revolution will happen, and if it fails, then another one, and another one, until successful. And with that upheaval, a slave morality will take hold again, which leads to nothing but the lessening of humankind.

We will not abandon the lower classes. Not even when it comes to the most insignificant of individuals. We will give them opportunities to work for their own existence and contribute to the state as everyone else. We will offer work and a place to live, in other

Part Five: Necessities for the Future

words. And if their mind and will is broken, we will fix it, or try as best we can. We will offer them female and male companionship of body and mind, which is the best medicine and cure for the malcontent, unhappy, and uncaring, and that of mental suffering and agony overall. With a position and importance in society, and the embrace and help of fellow man, it will give them a pride and purpose in their life. This will benefit the state as a whole.

Those who are beyond saving, and have criminal tendencies, must be allocated to reformation centres, which will serve as both a confinement centre for the detrimental elements of society, and as penal facilities for the criminal. This new penal system and the new reformation centres, with the new laws to accompany them, will focus on being productive; and not a financial drain on the citizen, society, and state. Another criterion for these reformation centres will be a focus on safety for the inmate, and also of his potential release after a service and obedience to the state that was shown when there. This means that all criminal activity is a no-go. You have already done something criminal and unwanted to get there, and if you persist in doing more of this, in a situation where you are supposed to atone for such behaviour, then you are beyond saving and of no use to your fellow citizen. Not only of no use, but you are a detrimental element of the state altogether. Criminal records will be examined closely, though, and if you have minor felonies, then leniency will be shown, but if you are thoroughly criminal and you persist in destructive and murderous activities, then you have sealed your fate. The punishment is execution. Swift and trouble-free execution. It cannot be said that it is unfair and that innocent people will be executed this way, because you have already done crime to get in, and then you persisted while incarcerated, and therefore all chances you have had are spent. A bad element is thus quickly eliminated, and it will serve as a great deterrence to other inmates and those on the outside, when faced with actual possibility of execution. As opposed to now, when very few are executed, and criminals sit on death row for years and years. It is not a threat as it is. It is merely seen as a chance to get away with doing bad things—a gamble worth taking, and not as a surefire way to end your days of freedom or life.

Society will be fair, and it will give equal opportunity to all no matter where one comes from. This is in accordance with Plato's Noble Lie, which explains a true society of meritocracy and nobility. The Germanic tribes, the Vikings, the Celts, etc., all had a system where the lowly could enter the higher strata, and where the nobles, or noble born, could be pushed to the lower strata. Each according to one's worth and ability, in other words. What fascism, or certain fascisms, tried to base itself on was the old Roman and Greek aristocratic systems. A system that had decayed and withered away, and fascism would fail because they ignored the factor that ultimately led to the downfall of those nations—the degeneration of the blood. National Socialism actually succeeded, however, by having the best of blood in charge from the outset. The smartest and most capable, which also resulted in the creation and use of a better system. A system of higher societal mobility, a socialist approach in enabling equal opportunity such as in school and work, and having the best specimens accorded a station and position by their merits. A very Germanic system, which we still see in Scandinavia today, and hardly anywhere else in the world.

One has to build society from the top down, and not the other way around. And one has to have good values and ideals altogether, born from a higher intelligence, which in turn comes from better blood. Which means that you cannot build a good society without making use of the best elements there and building on them. And the best elements in a society is, naturally, the best of humans. Society comprises humans foremost, and values and beliefs are nothing just by themselves. Yes, ideas, values, beliefs, and science—culture—may be transmitted, and are very powerful and important, and can even make or break a state, but that is not what I am arguing. What I am saying is that if those systems and practices are to be transmitted wholly and to best effect, then they have to be understood in accordance with how they were, or how they were intended. Meaning that one ought to have an equivalent or higher intelligence in society on average—comparable to the originators—for it to fully work. Intelligence is memory, in a sense, and information is memory based. So, if society is information, then increased intelligence and memory is the prerequisite for higher and higher forms of society. This concords with evolution, and we see this in the ladder steps from ape to man. These ladder steps are easily seen even today, with the still primitive peoples and their simple societies around the world. Most of which are in sub-Saharan Africa and the deep rainforests of South America and New Guinea. Which, incidentally, were also the places where they were most primitive when the European explorers found them. It is very obvious that this is due to genetics. Their evolution have been significantly slower, or they may have diverged and not taken the higher path that the Cro-Magnon, Neanderthal, and Denisova hybrids in Europe and Asia did.

VI. Should and Should Not

This new nation and society is one where we consider what is good and what is harmful to the people. We must avoid technology when not needed, but we must also embrace it when useful and when it betters our chances, production, technology, etc. We must be careful to avoid the perils and consequences of technology that we see today. Such as sedentary lifestyles, isolation, and being out of touch socially; and that of ignorance as a result of individualism and a catered information stream that does not educate the mind, but only entertains it. There should be public information posters and ads on TV regarding what one should and should not do. This helps to uniform opinion and also helps to educate and alert the masses on important matters. Yes, the use of propaganda—building nationalism and opinion. There is no problem in admitting that. In fact, all nations on Earth have used propaganda in some sense, or the successful ones have at least. And still today, the U.S., China, and Russia (mentioned as examples) all heavily use propaganda. In three different ways. American propaganda is more truthful and less obvious. Chinese propaganda is built around duty and nationalism. And the Russian one has turned into an historical absurdity—an absurdity only beaten by the predecessor the Soviet Union, and North Korea in present time. It does work, however. The prerequisite for doing this successfully is the total control of national media, and to have an incredibly dumb and uneducated population. As such, it also works on the weak elements of other nations.

We will use propaganda, and we will use rhetoric. We will not shy away from hammering in a message or picture about an enemy country or idea by using any association and notion we can. We will magnify events in history where we benefit, and we will diminish others where we do not. This is not lying. It is merely selecting a truth which we wish to promulgate. We will use the exact means that are used today, but in a more cunning and sophisticated manner. We cannot do otherwise in a world full of lies and deception. If we wish to survive in it, that is. We must be analytical and calculating. All steps and side-steps taken by the enemy must be predicted, known, and countered.

Part Five: Necessities for the Future

In this state of ours, we will think in terms of what is Good for the people, and not just what is good for ourselves as the hyper-individualism of today does. And certainly not in a communistic manner, where the only important thing is the state organ. No, we must consider what is Good for the people. Always the people, and the most important part of them, which are the best and brightest. We will have hierarchy, not equality. Or specifically, only equality of opportunity to become what one can be. The best of the people are the foundation and continuation of the people, and thus for the state. In thread with this Good of the people, we must re-evaluate a lot of things, such as technology, institutions, and societal structure. Technology, for instance, must be beneficial and symbiotic with man and his needs and limits. We cannot simply use technology to ease our lives just for that sake of doing so. If we were to automate society as a whole, then man would become obsolete, for one. This is the most extreme of situations, though. A better example would be the increasingly sedentary lifestyle of modern society. Today, we drive a car to work, when we could just as easily walk or take the bicycle for that 10 minute travel to and from. And we spend less time socially with each other, because of this ease of communicating through the computer and our smartphones. We must not depend on technology more than in the way that it helps our work to become more efficient, but not necessarily easier. The use of calculators, for example, will hamper a great portion of people, due to the convenience of its use, which results in people doing less math in mind and on paper. I am not actually proposing a ban on such items. I merely warn and highlight the effects of any and all of these. Some lifestyle problems are due to a convenient mode of living by and through the use of these apparatuses, after all. And in many cases, these gadgets and machines ease the living for people who are too weak and stupid to live, or survive, in the first place. One of these lifestyle problems is obesity and the many consequences of it: heart disease, diabetes 2, and so on. It is not a preposterous thought that if these lifestyles and their diseases cause a great many physiological changes, due to the body reacting and adapting, then these changes may also be passed on genetically. Why would they not? Everything from the use of drugs and alcohol—i.e., any chemicals that alter the body and causes an adaptation and/or decay—to that of the physical fitness, intelligence, and talents of the parents are again and again seen in the offspring in some or other manner. This is why we should guide or at least inform the public, in general. We should encourage people to stay healthy by exercising and eating healthy, and to moderate their alcohol intake and other detrimental quantities.

We want to educate the people whenever we can by having informative programs on radio and television. The individual should at least have that choice—that option to put on something educational—unlike today where we only get entertainment shows about the most inane things that one can imagine, and which only serve to dull the mind. There should be options to exercise at work, too, and to shower and stay clean and healthy there. If one can live in the workplace, as if it was a home, then one will be encouraged to be there, and this will help to keep the population motivated and interested in working. This way we can also implement work programs so that those who wish can work extended hours, and even making it a competition, of sorts, in the way that the most dedicated workers—the ones who work the most in a year or a given time—will be honoured and decorated, which may then also help them advance socially. As I said, if one feels comfortable and happy at work, and honoured and rewarded for it, then one will have no desire to be anywhere else. This way we can push wages down for everyone without it being a problem, and get an increased production per capita. Cost efficiency will become very great, in other words, and all without the workforce getting any less happy because of it, having made work a place for social interaction, i.e., making it the chief place to meet and be with people, and also by having great comfort there in a variety of ways, such as recreational rooms, proper wardrobes, and cantinas. Work must be made into a thing people want, and not something they need.

VII. The Military and a New Order

With such a well-educated and physically fit population, the military will have an excellent manpower pool to draw from. And to go hand in hand with this capable personnel will be a great and powerful military-industrial complex. A cutting edge military industry is reason enough itself for it to exist: it can drive a national economy, research & development, and create a lot of jobs and wealth. Having important, powerful, and friendly nations to sell to, and trade with, is a must for the existence of such an industry. Or just to have someone to sell to, in general. With having both the equipment and the men, we can start changing and shaping the world to our liking. The minorities in our lands, if there are any—and expectedly there should be a great many in most and any Western countries—will be the first line in any of their respective homelands in which a war is being waged. A war against any country will be conducted with as many minorities that have a similar ethnic, national, and cultural background to that country. Even if very distant in time and bloodlines. These minorities will have been educated and trained in the same manner as any of our citizens, and they would have been judged and given positions in our society like anyone else—according to ability and merit. These minorities do, however, have the important mission to institute change among the nations, and it is only natural that they should do that in the areas in which they would fit in, and adapt to, the easiest. They will not be unsupported, though. The entire might of the military will be behind them so that the war will be won, but the minorities will have to do their share. Once victory is complete, and order and a system has been instituted, our minorities will assume lordship and control over each of their respective areas. There they will merge with their long lost and now new found brethren, and they will form a culture and a new state based upon the principles of Third Alternative politics, such as is found in this book. This will preserve most of the races and cultures around the world, which are important and a part of us—we are done with multiculturalism and miscegeny. Piece by piece, little by little, a new order will emerge, and with a new system instituted, we will preserve the Earth and its resources, and this will ensure the survival of mankind; and with the genetic and cultural diversity of humanity still intact as well.

Art in this new state must take after the great empires and cultures of old and build on that. For us in the West, this entails the use of the most iconic of ancient structures like those of Roman and Greek architecture, and the ones in modern times, which are generally Art Deco and Neoclassical. Those should be the guidelines then, but there must also be a new, identifying, and unifying expression of the new state, and that is why we must encourage and welcome any and all powerful aesthetics. We must show ourselves different and unique in order to make sure that we are noticed. Therefore, we must create a new identity that others recognize, respect, and look up to—new symbols, flags, songs, mottos, etc. A new, ever growing, and strong culture.

Military matters have been the shaping hand of nations and empires. Anyone who is aware of history knows this. But a strong military is of no value if one does not know how and when to use it.

Part Five: Necessities for the Future

Even the greatest of military powers will buckle under the pressure of too many smaller enemies. We must employ realpolitik. We must be practical, and to exploit and plan for every situation. This is vital. That is why global consensus and support should be a main concern; we have repeatedly seen what happens to those who are too inconsiderate or arrogant toward other nations. The state must therefore always have justifiable reasons. Like a proper and recognized casus belli to engage in war, for instance. And we should not, as a rule, engage in wars that are unwinnable, and especially not wars that can result in total annihilation. However, a total annihilative war is usually only caused by a great want for it to happen, and if one is able to keep minds away from such thinking—the thought that the destruction of our state would do more good than harm—then one can be quite secure in a continued survival, no matter what the outcome of a war is. Yes, even when utterly lost. Many nations have survived by being perceived as having a place or function after their total defeat, and by posing no threat. With this in mind, we should therefore not compromise too lightly, or doubt and linger, when faced with war. Even if it is very difficult and hard won. If the menace is such that it directly or indirectly threatens the survival of our nation, then there is no alternative but war. In any case, try to avoid aggressive wars in order to appear righteous and just. A defender always elicits sympathy and can make demands of recompense and restitution much easier. And when wars are won, do not make too unreasonable demands and always try to include the global community—or the most powerful of said community—in order to legitimize the treaties and deals that are made.

The Third Position

Nordic Matters

I. A Common Nordic Language

The mutual intelligibility, and great similarity, of the Nordic languages of Swedish, Danish, and Norwegian in Scandinavia do not only follow along the lines of their respective standardizations, but also to a great degree between the dialects that branch below them. These branches are not distinct and separate, and they go across all three of these languages. Meaning that some dialects in these countries have as much in common with another Scandinavian language than they would have to their respective standardization. For instance, some Norwegian dialects have just as much in common with Swedish dialects than the Danish influenced standard of Norwegian called Bokmål, and some have as much in common with Danish. My point being that these standardizations are as artificial to the national dialects as other Scandinavian languages are. And in light of the ease of the implementation of the artificiality of Norwegian Bokmål—in the way that it changed the language across the country almost always to a great degree—it becomes clear to us how easy it is to adapt to languages and standardizations, how it binds us together and builds unity and cohesion, and how it influences speech over just a few generations—we also see this globally and throughout history. And since we already have mutual intelligibility and a strong cross-cultural tradition—a great learning of each other—it would only be natural to build on that and construct and implement a language that can be easily utilized and understood across the three nations of Scandinavia. This would serve as a bridge to bring and keep us together and help create a Pan-Scandinavian and Nordic state for the future. In order to do this, a Joint Nordic Language Council (Samnordisk Språkråd) should be established to create this Nordic language. The old Nordic Language Council (Nordisk Språkråd)—which I believe is now defunct—did put in an effort to smooth out and coordinate between the languages, but on a very miniscule and inefficient level. And it had no magnificent plans or goals, such as this intention to join the Nordic languages and people together.

II. A Nordic Empire

A unified Scandinavia has been a 500 year old dream going back all the way to the Kalmar Union of Denmark, Norway, and Sweden. Back then there was no real, palpable distinction of Scandinavian nationalities, as it is today. Sweden had the Geats in Gothenburg and Southwestern Sweden, and the actual Swedes were based around Uppsala and Ruslagen. Norway had the Trønder in Trøndelag, the Møring in Møre, and various other in the south and east. This was the same for Denmark, although that country is geographically smaller and therefore these differences were not too marked. The difference of people in Denmark is mainly between those in the Jylland (Jutland) peninsula and in the isles of Sjælland (Zealand). Historically, the demarcation—where a union of dialects took place to form Danish proper—was between Sjælland and Skåne (Scania)—the latter no longer being part of Denmark. The unitary measures that were taken back then is the reason why there is a national standard and widespread uniformity there today. As it is, and always have been, in all empires. But still today there are no great differences among the three Scandinavian countries. We largely look the same—not counting the hordes of immigrants—and there is mutual intelligibility between us. There is a reason why we call ourselves the Brethren People (Brødrefolket), after all. From the most ancient of times we have used that term for one another. So, why has there not been more effort or success in re-establishing the Kalmar Union? The reason for this is mostly because we have been at the mercy of power politics in Europe—that obviously did not want to see such a thing happen because that would have made it the most powerful country in Europe. The Swedish Empire, which comprised only Sweden and Finland, wreaked havoc in the years it still had territorial integrity. European powers were alarmed at, and outright deadly afraid of, this new scourge from the north, and the result was that Europe by and large turned against Sweden to dismantle her—succeeding in the end. Now imagine a country almost double that in size and even larger by population, and stretching across all of Northern Europe and into the Americas. Yes, they were right to fear such a union. Also, another preventive factor was the power and foothold that the monarchies had in each of the Scandinavian countries, which actively worked against this, or each blockaded any efforts.

So, why do we want a union today? Because it is more important than ever. Power blocks are forming around the world, and the power of smaller European countries are diminishing day by day. Russia has blatantly invaded a number of countries in modern times. It outright took Crimea in defiance of all treaties and amicability with Ukraine, or the entire world community and international law for that matter. Crimea, which was given as recompense to Ukraine from Russia for all the suffering and torment that the latter had—and still does, ironically—imposed on her and the people there throughout the years. Such as the Holodomor of the Ukrainians, or the expulsion and extermination of the Tatars on Crimea. And these are only a few of the things that happened during the Soviet era. It is a sad, sad thing that the world community was barely bothered when Russia invaded Ukraine in 2014.

Scandinavia with Finland, Iceland, the Faroe Islands, and even the Inuit of Greenland and the Sami of northern Scandinavia—the

Nordic countries—would do well to form an empire. This new written standard of Nordic based on the three Scandinavian languages of Swedish, Danish, and Norwegian will unify them, and over time will shape and join them together into a common Nordic language. This is not to say that Finnish, Icelandic, and the other small languages are to go away. Only that Nordic will be the unitary and working language. Doing away with the three largest and making them uniform is the logical choice, considering that a greater focus and need in the future will be for the citizen to learn foreign languages. We therefore need a unified and mutually intelligible working language for this empire of the north, this Nordic Empire (det Nordiske Rike). It sounds better in the Nordic languages. The meaning of the word *rike* encompass the words of empire, realm, and dominion. The word empire is thus used. Compare the translation Deutsches Reich into German Empire.

In economic matters we will benefit greatly from such a union. The Nordic countries are rich; and self-sufficient if need be. And we will also have much more pressure politically and globally with this Empire. We can dictate terms then, and not the other way around, as has been tried before. Such as with Norway after the completely independent Nobel Peace Prize Committee gave a Chinese dissident an award. The Chinese—in their usual ludicrous stupidity—in turn decided to punish Norway. Although, it did not have the effect the Chinese were hoping for, and it was overall only a minor setback in Norwegian economic growth, and the Norwegian populace certainly didn't notice anything. Such attempted bullying would not happen with a more united front. A Nordic Empire would be so powerful that we would dictate terms instead. Even against such giants as the U.S., China, and Russia. A combined GDP of all the Nordic countries combined would put us in the top ten of wealthiest countries on Earth. And a predicted economic and industrial boom from such a union would propel us even further. Perhaps even into the top five.

By combining our militaries, we will gain one of the most advanced and powerful militaries in the world. We will also have a more effective navy by gaining a large enough combined budget to invest in airplane carriers and other costly materials. A large navy being necessary, because a union of the Nordic countries would result in having one of the largest ocean economy zones on Earth. And with our political power, we may also enforce a takeover of the ocean zone called the Banana Hole and a number of other ones, closing all these holes of international waters in the middle of our territorial waters and in our vicinity as best we can, and extending our territorial water boundaries greatly, resulting in an economic boost. This will also enable us to enforce maritime jurisdiction more firmly. The military industries of the Nordic countries will—with economic growth and expansion, greater access to resources, greater political pressure, larger and more numerous foreign deals, military enlargement and uniformity, and larger areas of operation and duty—receive a great boost in the form of contracts, licenses, and tighter cooperation and coordination. In regards to the difficult matter of nuclear weapons, we would have to have a disposal of them, since the closest of our neighbours in the east has the world's largest supply and will thus leverage it against non-nuclear powers in every way they can. As they have always done, and still do. I doubt there would be any who would deny us nuclear armaments, given that we are, and have been, such civilized and trustworthy nations, and considering the fact that even North Korea has them now. But the goal should still be a total non-proliferation and refrained use of nuclear weapons. Once the world has dismantled theirs, we will dismantle ours.

Part Five: Necessities for the Future

Another great benefit of union would be that we would hopefully gain access to a greater pool of competent politicians and government employees through having a larger intelligentsia and population at disposal. Thus, avoiding such scandals as when Norway and Russia settled their border maritime dispute by giving the Russians half of their sector line claim. A compromise it was called. Yes, a compromise between a Russian claim that was purely fictional and out of proportion—although it did pay off greatly to them—and a Norwegian claim that followed the standard U.N. median line of normal practice. Consequently, Russia therefore got half of something she didn't have the right to have—a theft, in other words. And that half just happens to envelop one of the largest natural gas fields on Earth. After a Nordic Empire has been formed, one of the first orders of business is to declare that treaty null and void. This can be easily done by using Russian words and practices against them. The Russians, when dissolving/ignoring their former treaties with Ukraine regarding Ukrainian territorial integrity (Crimea) and then invaded them, justified it with saying that the Russian leader at the time, Nikita Khrushchev, was insane, and they even called him a traitor. Whatever the excuse, it was in pure violation of international rules. We will do the same thing and call Jonas Gahr Støre, Jens Stoltenberg, and the rest of that Norwegian Government traitors. This will not be as an absurd claim as the Russian ones, however, because what the Norwegian Government did was to go against internationally established rules and regulations when it deviated from the median rule and gave into the entirely fictitious rule of sector line. And in the process of giving away Norwegian land, they also failed to hold a referendum on such an important matter. They failed on all accounts; but primarily they failed the people and their country, and they will be trialled as the traitors they are. The Russians through their actions today—and one only needs to open a book and see that they have behaved this way throughout history—have shown that they do not care about treaties, and we will therefore not hold them to any forthwith. The nullification of this Barents Sea divide will be enforced through political and military pressure. A direct force of action leading to war should not be taken, however. And taking heed of our American and European allies is most important.

I see no difficulty or problem in a union between Nordic countries while retaining the monarchies. We do not need any of them as the head of state of our Empire—we will choose one of our own. The monarchies may exist for as long as they can endure, but make no mistake, when public opinion has finally turned against them and the time is ripe, we will finally abolish these dinosaur institutions. We will then send these families packing, and without a dime. All their assets and royal belongings will be appropriated by the state. Most castles and villas will be turned into museums, hotels, and attractions. Some will be retained and used for governmental purposes. All royal jewels and belongings will be placed in newly made museums, or put in old ones. These monarchies, once a drain on the state, will be turned into a source of profit instead. There will thus be greater accessibility to the people than before, and it will have a great impact on them as well. The citizens of this new empire can then learn about, and take pride in, all Nordic history and culture.

We will achieve this union through popular opinion and whatever opportune moments we are faced with. We should create a Nordic Union Party in every respective country. A political party that should be populist in the extreme to achieve the goal of unification. Better yet, we must detach the idea of union from any and all political wings and stances, and make it as if it was something that we couldn't live without—which, incidentally, we probably cannot. It must be such a popular movement that millions will march in the streets to achieve it. It should be such a popular idea that all political parties will embrace it and make it a part of their program in order to gain votes. We must assure that it's a perceived normality that it should be there, and a necessity obsessed over when not.

Anglo-American Combine

I. Preliminary Aims and Needs

The English speaking world is already quite united and solidary. Such are their feelings of, and for, each other that if any of them should visit each other's country, they would be treated as if one belonged and had a right to be there. Yes, it is first and foremost the language that is the reason for this, but through sharing this language, the culture among them spread and flourished, and in it there grew commonalities and eventually a familiarity. In the States, the Irish are known for their St. Patrick's Day, leprechauns, drinking, etc. The Australians also have their known traits, which are probably best left unmentioned. The Scots have their kilts and bagpipes. Both of which are widely used in the U.S. and Britain. In particular with law enforcement and the military. Canadian culture is basically American culture. Perhaps the least known people are the New Zealanders and the Welsh. In any case, all of these characteristics—whether through some much admired, or made fun of, trait that usually forms a stereotype—have ingrained themselves in society and are celebrated widely. A celebration that is most likely due to the commonality of language, as mentioned, but it has nevertheless helped to merge these cultures, centred in and on the U.S., into an Anglo-American culture. One that all these countries are a part of, and that they take to themselves and embrace.

A point of improvement for all these Anglosphere nations is to work towards greater uniformity. Not only with each other, but with the world, in general. Such as through the standardization of measurements, rules, and regulations. Metrication today has almost spread across the globe completely, but the U.S. has still not made the total conversion yet. They still cling to their traditional customary system, and the willingness to depart from this is quite meagre. Three states in the world are still not using the metric system: the U.S., Liberia, and Myanmar. This reflects rather poorly on the U.S., if you ask me. Liberia not having adopted it is due to them always following in the footsteps of their parent nation, the U.S., though. As the entire globe is using the metric system, this means that the U.S. has to focus on two systems, while the rest of the world only has to worry about one, really. For the U.S. this means a loss in production effectivity, and even quality. And for production efficiency and ease, the world thus excludes the U.S. and conduct their business elsewhere. It is just too worrisome to keep bothering with two systems when you only have to focus on one. Americans have to recognize that they are dependent on the world for trade and resources—as they have always been—and not to change and adapt is only a detriment. Another just as difficult topic, or even more so and of greater scope, is left-hand traffic. Even though this is the norm in countries that cover over a third of the globe, it only covers about 10% of global road length. The obvious problem with this system is that these countries need to have and produce cars that are built for this left-hand driving. And looking at the maps, and the countries and statistics, that have left-hand traffic, one can argue that these nations may be falling behind because of it. England, Scotland, Ireland, India, Japan, Australia, New Zealand, Thailand, Malaysia, Myanmar, Indonesia, Pakistan, South Africa, including greater parts of Southern Africa, and a number of other countries, drive on the left side of the road. Many of these countries are, or were, part of the Commonwealth of Nations—successor to the British Empire. It was different back then in the Imperial Era, when they were able to have and dictate their own rules and regulations because they were the number one power in the world. But today they ride the small ripple of that once large wave.

Their power and production is long gone and ever decreasing, and the ones who are not are those having natural growth that is due to catching up with the rest of the world community—meaning poor countries such as India. But their old customs are still holding them back, though. All these nations have to make cars and other accommodations for their left-hand driving. In doing so, they are focusing on, and limiting themselves to, a third of the world market. And even though Japan has been able to work around this before, they are now struggling immensely. Of course, they are blaming failing population growth, as is common in the globalist and multiculturalist agenda, but the fact is that they are not on the top in efficiency anymore. It is the same as the problem in the Western world. It is not efficiency that has dropped, nor is it that people have become lazier compared to earlier generations and other such nonsense. No, it is the entry of China and their billion strong slave worker army. The capitalists in the West wanted more profits, and the best way to do this was by cheaper labourers. Well, they had their way and profited immensely, and more than ever before, but in the process they destroyed much of the Western industrial base by moving it to the East. And when the industrial base vanished, so did the work and wages. The once glorious car industry town of Detroit is now a ghost town riddled with homelessness and crime. Not that there is any lack of homes, dirt cheap as they are. It is just that no one living there can afford them, due to unemployment and poverty, and most of these houses are therefore illegally occupied. The former car builders and workers of America have become squatters. That being said, the demographics and statistics of Detroit do tell us the primary reason why that city has become an above ground sewer, and the disappearance of the car industry was only a minor, contributory factor.

Part Five: Necessities for the Future

If all these countries that drive on the left side would convert to right-hand traffic, they would not only start a project that would initialize a new short-term growth and renewed investor interest in them, but they would also in the long-term be able to enter and compete effectively on the world market. This short-term growth is due to the new signs, road markings, and the labour needed—hopefully and preferably the people would see the importance of this and lend a free hand when able. The long-term growth would come from a number of things. It would first of all stimulate the need for all-new tools, machines, etc., that would be needed for factories. These can be produced at a home basis on the very outset of industrial reconfiguration that would boost, and hopefully establish new, companies and businesses. Secondly, it would also provide more competition and options in the Western world once the factories are up and running. Today, the labour costs in the West have dropped so sufficiently that producing locally, or continentally if you will, on a home basis would provide just as cheap products. Consider the fact that if not produced domestically, or by allies and in the vicinity, then one would suffer a great economic loss. A loss that far outweighs the costs of domestic production. This must be implemented, even if trade barriers have to be set up that result in a rise in prices for the consumer. Well, what are the options? First scenario, which is currently in place in the Western world, is: The consumer can buy cheaper goods, but he is unemployed and receives benefits from the state that drain, impoverish, and eventually bankrupts the state. A total collapse will ensue. Second scenario is: The consumer buys a bit more expensive goods, but he has money left over because he has employment, and he can pay rent or pay interest rates on his house loan. He can also get a good elementary education and health benefits for himself and his children, because the state can afford it through the taxes collected from a productive and economically prospering society. To me there really isn't an option, but it seems that this is apparently not true for everyone, since we already have that first and worst system in place. Whether this was forced upon the people, or chosen by them either through their own stupidity or a trickery by the profiteers, I cannot really say. Maybe it was a bit of both. Anyhow, the people need to wake up from their slumber if they want to have a decent life for their children and a prosperous future.

II. Unification and Federation

The first steps to a unified Anglo-American state are taken by resolving the various local/continental situations and finding workable solutions there.

In the region of Oceania, Australia and New Zealand should aim for a federation or a commonwealth of sorts. A Commonwealth of Oceania. With it, the numerous island groups of Polynesia, Melanesia, and Micronesia should join. One of the great powers in this region are the French, with their control of the large French Polynesian region, and they would probably offer quite some resistance to this idea, but with time and effort I am sure the French would eventually see a way to a transfer control. The incorporation of French Polynesia is not a thing of need for a federated Oceanic state, however, and it is therefore of no large immediate concern. This Oceanic Commonwealth would enable not only the dominance of, but a complete hegemony in, the whole of the South Pacific.

In the British Isles there are also some problems that need to be straightened out. The most glaring of these is the long tradition of the English monarchy. That is a stopper for most plans in the Isles and in the Anglosphere, in general. I have no solution for how to work with it or how to remove this obstacle, and I will therefore pass right over it, or work around it so to speak, and get to the most vital concern here.

First is the reunification of Ireland. This should have been done long ago and I solely blame the U.K. for actively sabotaging every effort and opportunity to make that happen. Sure, they talk about sectarian differences, but I have a problem seeing the argument that Irish people supposedly consider religion more important than national reunification. Yes, I know there have been outright wars between the Catholics and Protestants there, but I believe they are mostly a minority who are imposing their will on the rest. The story told is that people in Northern Ireland do not want reunification. Is it the loyalty to the English monarchy or an English lifestyle and a national feeling that make some of the Northern Irish supposedly not wanting to join Ireland? Dare I say then that they are not Irish at all? And if they are not Irish, then what say should they have in the matter? In any case, the bombings and insurrections in Northern Ireland are over. There is now peace between the Catholic and the Protestant. The religious conflict is no more, and it is very likely to stay that way after a joining of the two lands of Ireland. I say again, if they do not want to be part of Ireland, then they are most likely not Irish.

In Scotland there should be a secession. This may seem like it is going in the wrong direction, but a secession would be useful for Scotland to reinvigorate its national spirit and pride, and even the Gaelic language, and it would also serve to mark a split from the monarchy and the old institution. However, a secession of Scotland is not a necessity, and Great Britain may very well be just as it is, if it comes to that.

This also goes for Wales. They could also use a bolstering of their national pride and to find a new interest in themselves. An interest in their history and culture that is not linked to England. I do know of the close bond that is there between them, and I am not saying that their long shared history should be ignored or overlooked, but I only venture that a national revival is much wanted in Wales as well. And I extend that thought to the other small isles in Britain as well.

One might think that this fracturing will not do much good at all, and that it may only serve to split the countries further and distance them from each other. I see that, but it also serves a probably greater and more important purpose, which is to defuse all nationalist and cultural wants. As long as English is kept as primary language, or taught as a mandatory second language with widespread and equal use, then it does no harm. And if the English language should dominate completely, then I see no problem with that, either. Another reason for granting independence and general goodwill, such as the return of Northern Ireland, is that this will enable these countries to join a union without the misgivings that they would otherwise have. This in the case of Ireland, in particular. The Irish would only consider any inter-British cooperation, federation, and unification if Irish reunification happens first and without any interference and problems. If the rest of the U.K. remains intact, then only the joining of Ireland with the U.K. would be needed for a Commonwealth of Britain to materialize. However, with the monarchy still in place—this greatest of obstacles—Ireland, even after she has been given her lands back, will still be hesitant to join. It would thus be easiest to depose the monarchy of the U.K. before a joining with Ireland. Or perhaps Ireland will show herself the greater one and join, in the good faith that an eventual dissolution of the monarchy will take place.

The reason why I am so insistent on removing this monarchy is because with it in place a final unification with the rest of the

Anglosphere will be a tricky business. The U.S., just like Ireland, would have a difficulty, nay, perhaps a greater difficulty than Ireland, with the prospect of uniting with a monarchy. This is the reason. However, retaining the monarchy, this U.K., as long as possible is important, because it acts as a placeholder for the unity and cohesion of the great and small countries of the Commonwealth of Nations. With this structure in place, it helps facilitate a smooth transition of these states into an Anglo-American union, while retaining control over the largest possible number of nations and territories.

A union of the U.S. and Canada doesn't seem that difficult, really, and it is a bit strange that it has not occurred yet. Although, the Canadians do have quite a sense of national pride despite being so young a state. The Canadians also have bit more equality, income, and security in their lives, and so they are naturally distrustful of a union where they might end up with a lower standard of living. A higher crime rate and a number of other negatives in the U.S. is also a problem for the Canadian. There are a number of positives for such a union, however. First of all, the already rampant immigration that Canada is experiencing will be much lessened with a joining of the U.S. This may seem like quite a bold thing to state considering the status quo, but there is a reason why I do. First off, the immigration to the U.S. is simply unsustainable in the long run with the unemployment rates the U.S. has. What the U.S. is doing, and have been doing, is that it is compensating for a lack of economic boost, growth, and access to resources with this very unpopular immigration. There is not really much of a justification for it anymore, however, since the unemployment is now incredibly high. Yes, the unemployment rate may not seem that high in reports and on paper, but they are tricked out statistics. The truth is that the U.S., like a majority of countries in the Western world, has astonishing real unemployment rates. And just like those other Western countries, they therefore have no need of immigration. There is a reason why it exists, though. And that is to drive the labour costs down, and artificially boost the GDP per capita through the increase of population, and by increasing this you are adding on this GDP through having more people with a similar or equal living standard. An illusion of economic growth, in other words. What is really happening is just population growth, and with it comes the products that each life requires. The added products per capita that these immigrants supplement is thus only due to their life needs, i.e., more mouths to feed equals a necessity to produce and buy more food, housing, clothes, etc. The rise in state debts and domestic debts show us that it is inevitably the citizen who pays for these new countrymen and minorities as well. These immigrants themselves do much worse than the average citizen. Despite of this, the immigrant usually elope with more social benefits than he has been, or will be, worth in his lifetime through taxes, or just productivity for that matter. Which is not the case in regards to the citizen. Another problem with these immigrants is that they send the money they get from social benefits back to their family in their home countries, or even to religious and criminal organizations. If the argument is that the economy needs more workers, then it would be easier and less problematic to spend the money wasted on immigration on birth encouragement programs instead. Programs giving tax-breaks and benefits to a family for every child born.

It should be more important to enable the citizen to make a living than to drive labour costs down. We can drive labour costs down artificially if it is needed, but providing useful work and a living for everyone is not always that easy. State work programs can only do so much in the very long run. There has to be private initiative and growth, too. Closer cooperation and unification in North America can provide this, with an access to more natural resources, removal of trade and border barriers, a merger of interests, and a larger work pool throughout a much greater area. That is why, in the event of a unification with the U.S., Canada can also end their immigration, because there should then be a flood of Americans willing to go to Canada for work, even if social benefits have to be cut or removed in the U.S. in order to facilitate a need among the people to seek out work there. It would be better for Canada to have Americans working in their lands than foreigners that cause cultural and linguistic problems. Canada and the U.S. already have a brotherly bond that is closer than that of any other countries. A Canadian in the U.S. is seen as quite an ordinary, common, and expected thing. Furthermore, the U.S. and Canada already have tight economic bonds, and a military cooperation that is also of the closest nature. In other words, the two are already co-dependant. Uniting these two nations in a North American Union is just a tiny push and small step beyond what is already in place. This Union will exert its influence much more strongly and assertively throughout the Americas, and it will be able to stretch out further throughout the Caribbean, Mexico, and Central America. Naturally, Greenland will be retained by Denmark, as it serves no great purpose economically, and the military cooperation and status of ally with the Nordic countries will be continued as before, in any case.

III. An Anglo-American World

What comes of all of this is a tighter bond and cooperation, and ultimately a union or federation, between these three hypothetical powers—the North American Union, the Commonwealth of Britain, and the Commonwealth of Oceania. Once these are all uniform in industrial and societal regulations and standards, and the three blocks have formed, then all the pieces are in place for an Anglo-American

Combine. Such a supranational union will be self-preferential and will continue the English hegemony of the world. And not only in the foreseeable future, but seemingly perpetually, due to the unparalleled uniformity and the sheer geographical extent and locations. With this Combine comes the creation of a new currency that will take over for the dollar as the world leading currency. Or perhaps I should say take over for the euro as a leading currency, because the American dollar lost out years ago and only retains its power through being the standard measure of goods and services. This new currency—let us call it the dollar pound, as a compromise and amalgam of the widespread and well-known dollar and British pound—will be as unparalleled in strength and dominance as its issuer will be. No other supranational entities would come close to such a union for a very, very long time. If ever. A continued English dominance in the world is thus secured. For the good of all.

Part Five: Necessities for the Future

Potentialities

I. A Stabilized World

The two most potent threats to the world community today are Russia and China. These states are sable-rattling in a number of directions around their borders, and they seem to be greatly undeterred by any threats or consequences. It doesn't help that they are nuclear armed nations, either. Russia has shown herself quite warmongering these last years. She has had a number of conflicts in both the Caucasus and in Eastern Europe with the Russian invasion and annexation of Crimea and the war in Ukraine. It is certain that Russia will refuse to give up her dominance in both Central Asia and Eastern Europe. And I have no problem with it, really. Let Russia have her hegemony in Central Asia. Let Russia keep her mastery in the Caucasus. Let her even keep her sphere of influence over both Ukraine and Belarus. But those three allowances will come at a price. A price that has to be paid, or else the deal is off. The terms are: Firstly, the island of Karafuto (Sakhalin) and all of the Chishima Islands (the Kuril Islands) will be returned and given to Japan at a set price. Secondly, the old Finnish lands of Karelia, Salla, Petsamo, and the islands in the Gulf of Finland should be returned to Finland, also at a set price. There will be established a neutral council of nations that will determine the price for the return of these lands. A third demand is that Russia will work to help variously around in her spheres of influence to resolve certain issues. High on this list is the reunification of Transnistria, Moldova, and Ukrainian Bessarabia with Romania. Russia must also help Armenia and Nagorno-Karabakh unite. It is due to Russian power politics that these problems have not been resolved yet, and with Russian help, these conflicts can finally end. They must also agree to renegotiate the maritime border treaty with Norway, and thus also with Finland when Petsamo is returned. Finally, the Russians should help end nuclear proliferation. When concluded, this Russian cooperation will be rewarded and they will be given a free hand in the areas promised. There will be no involvement in their internal affairs, either. Such as critique of their violent and oppressive handling of the ethnic and Muslim conflict in and around the Caucasian countries of Dagestan, Chechnya, etc. Central Asia and other parts of the former Soviet Union is therefore guaranteed to them when they have rightfully given back the aforementioned areas in the first two points and having finalized the rest. Areas that were for the most part stolen and gained by deceit, treachery, and crime in the first place. Russian cooperation and the following mutual agreement will net them more lands, power, and control than they could ever hope to gain otherwise. All for the loss of lands that are a lot smaller than those they would gain. And the goodwill alone will net them a huge profit through increased trust and inclusion in the Western economy—one that is not there due to sanctions, mistrust, and exclusion. This is not counting the profit they will receive from the economic compensation for the lands they will return.

China is an ambitious country, but their greed has been blurring their vision of reality these last years. Their greed for land has grown in proportion to their greed for money and material goods. There is nothing like the greed of a commie; even worse than a capitalist that is. The hypocrisy knows no bounds it seems, but it is what it is. And as they are a nuclear power, an economic power, and having a seventh of the world population, it is therefore better to work with them than against them to resolve the issues at hand. But they, too, must compromise in order for this to work. And if they do not, then let it be known that it was they who caused a destabilization and possibly even a war. China's disputes are primarily with India in South Tibet, and India in turn has a dispute with China regarding the Aksai Chin area. The easiest solution here would be to agree upon a complete compromise from both parts and just forfeit their claims and keep the status quo. The next dispute in order of size is the island of Taiwan (ruled by the separate Republic of China, or Kuomintang). This is going to be deadlocked until the People's Republic of China rids itself of all communism. Only then will the Republic of China be interested in talks of unification. The rest of the Chinese disputes that are had with a number of states are just smaller and trivial ones concerning smaller islands. These states are Vietnam, Malaysia, and the Philippines in the South China Sea, and then there is also a pure grudge dispute with Japan over a few islands outside Taiwan that the People's Republic do not even have any proper justification for claiming, given that these islands are in Taiwan's territorial vicinity, i.e., closer to Taiwan, and that there is not an unresolved issue there in first place. The Senkaku Islands have been Japanese for hundreds of years, after all. And they have international recognition of them as well. In behaving as they do, China is souring the relationship with all her neighbours. But in the one place that the Chinese should press their claims, they do not. Which is in Outer Manchuria (Primorye)—the whole coastline from Vladivostok and upwards, which the Russians took in the Amur Annexation and was cemented by the Convention of Peking in 1860. A convention that made for a number of unfair treaties, of which all have been rectified by the Western European powers today, with the recent and final return of Hong Kong and Macao. All that remains of the Convention are the lands along the east and north of the Amur River and their ownership by Russia. I find it strange that China has no problem with this. These huge areas of lands in Outer Manchuria dwarf these petty disputes that China has in the south—in any and all ways. But if they don't want to press these claims, then so be it. What is unacceptable is their bullying and threatening of their other neighbours. The annexation of Tibet is still fresh in memory despite the decades gone by. Where China should be the trusted big brother and driving force in the region, they instead quarrel with everyone around them and make little or no efforts of reconciliation and cooperation. First of their tasks in the area should be North Korea. China needs to pressure and outright back the collapse of that rogue state. China is the only reason that it is still alive, and the rest of the world is fully behind South Korea and their way. South Korea has proven herself as a true inspiration to the world through her model society and economic power. It is worth to note that she has had a population growth that has made her population double to that of their northern brethren. A reunification of Korea is of highest importance, and China's ball play on the wrong side of the field is the only thing hindering it. Furthermore, a better relationship with Japan must be worked at. Even between South Korea, or a potentially unified Korea, and Japan. The war hatchet and grudges that have been held since the Second World War have to be buried and forgotten. In the South China Sea, the maritime disputes regarding the Spratly Islands, and others such as these, should be resolved by applying the principle of closest vicinity. This gives the Philippines control of all but the Riflemen Bank and the islands west of there, which should be given to Malaysia. The Scarborough Reef should be awarded to the Philippines given its closer vicinity. But whatever the case, a compromise has to be reached, because no one would ever accept a complete control over all the disputed areas by China.

The People's Republic is the natural leader and great power in this area. If greater autonomy would be granted to Tibet, and the communist worm is finally rooted out, then China would be seen as a place where one might want to be, or a nation to cooperate with, instead of that dubious neighbour it is today. With a friendlier tone

Part Five: Necessities for the Future

and outlook, China may find herself not only gaining a unification with Taiwan much quicker, but perhaps even in a federative union with Mongolia and others as well. This is only achieved with neighbours, and a global community, who see a trustworthy, free, and open China, though.

There are a number of other small disputes and conflicts that should be resolved once there is a will and initiative to do so. In Europe there should be a unification of states that are largely artificial or purely of a regional nature with states of similar nationality, ethnicity, language, and culture. Montenegro should be joined with Serbia. The large Albanian part of Kosovo should join Albania, and the rest with Serbia. In Macedonia, the smaller Albanian parts should join Albania, while the large remaining part should be joined with their Bulgarian brothers in the east, and perhaps a third part should join Serbia as well. Moldova should join Romania. Hungary should be given back Transylvania and various other parts on her border. Turkey should finally leave Cyprus and allow for her unification with her brothers in Greece. These smaller entities can, in exchange for joining with their seniors, be given a higher autonomy if need be. There should be efforts in standardizing languages and dialects for the future, though. As is normal everywhere. Northern Ireland should join Ireland. Belgium is to be dissolved and Flanders should join the Netherlands, while Wallonia should join France. In exchange for this, France should open for referendums in Corsica on a secession and unification with Italy. Austria and Germany should finally be allowed to reunite. Luxembourg should be joined with Germany. Switzerland should be divided into a German part in the north, a French part in the southwest, and an Italian one in the southeast. More or less following linguistic lines, that is. The Romansh part should preferably join the German lands due to their dispersal there, and the connectivity issues. The microstate of Andorra will be annexed by

Spain, Monaco by France, San Marino by Italy, and Liechtenstein by Austria. Their days as tax shelters and whatnot are numbered. The hope and goal in all of this is that the most common element—meaning the Spanish, French, German, Italian, and the Flemish with the Dutch—is to form as large an entity as possible and finally unite. This will also help to further stabilize and cement the respective regions.

There are some global matters that need to be attended as well. All the small nations in Central America—now also including Belize, and extending down to and including Panama—should federate into a version of that formerly tried Federal Republic of Central America. A Gran Colombia should also be resurrected from the grave and built on those formerly united states of Colombia, Venezuela, and Ecuador, as well as some smaller parts of Brazil and Peru. In the Middle East there should be efforts toward creating a large Kurdistan homeland for the Kurds. This is almost a reality, but it is a Kurdistan that is confined to the small province in Iraq which it currently comprises. There are plenty more Kurdish lands in Iraq and Syria to free, but independence for the Kurds and their lands in Turkey and Iran seems a bit more complicated, though. Armenia should be united with Nagorno-Karabakh. Azerbaijani parts of Iran should join Azerbaijan. Balochistan should become independent from Iran. The Pashtuns of Afghanistan and Pakistan should form a state, while the Sindh and Punjab may be better off forming their own ones. The states of Central Asia also have a number of displaced people that warrants a reconfiguration of borders. Such as the Tajiks and Uzbeks, with quite a lot of them located in Afghanistan, which is all the more reason for dissolving that state. There is also a bit unevenness in Southeast Asia. Brunei, for one, should be annexed by Malaysia. Actually, the entire island of Borneo should be transferred to Malaysia. The islands of Sumatra and Sulawesi should become independent. The western part of New Guinea Island should be given to Papua New Guinea, and as such all of New Guinea (Papua/Irian) Island and the smaller islands in the vicinity should be governed by that state. In Indo-China there only needs to be small adjustments, if any at all.

The overall aim of all these territorial changes and various treaties is to resolve as many conflicts as possible, and to create contentment within and among the nations and states. To resolve the disputes between the states, the rules are clear: either reach a compromise or be subject to, and at the mercy of, an arbitration.

The U.N. Security Council needs to be restructured and reorganized to avoid the extreme, disproportionate, and unjustified power those few nations have today, and also so that it is always the most powerful nations—using a combined measure of population, size, and primarily economic power—that hold seats there. The stronger should move in, and thus the weaker out, and on a term basis of half a decade or even more. We must let the U.N. structure change and adapt with the times, otherwise it will eventually become completely ineffectual and useless.

II. A New Homeland

The Western world today, by which I mean the Anglosphere and Europe, is being destroyed by immigration. The original people and culture there, this Celto-Latin-Germanic mix, is slowly being supplanted by foreign elements from Africa, the Middle East, and Asia. These immigrants usually have higher birth rates and they also miscegenate with the original population, which in the case of the Anglosphere and Scandinavia is predominantly of a Germanic stock and descent. We need to start calling ourselves the native people of our respective countries. In Norway, the Sami are classified as native inhabitants (*urfolk* in Norwegian, which translates to English as original/ancient people). However, in historical sources the Germanic man is repeatedly mentioned early on, while the Finnish, for example, are only first mentioned after the death of Christ. In Norway, Sweden, and Denmark proper, excluding some of this north that is designated to the Sami, Germanic man has lived for at least 4500 years, and there are no signs of any other extant cultures being there before him. This makes the Germanic man the actual *urfolk* of Scandinavia proper. And therefore the Sami should only be called this when Germanic man has received this status as well, and the place to where the Sami will be designated as original inhabitants must exclude these areas to which Germanic man is designated. Which leaves only the very north of Scandinavia, and maybe a larger part of Finland. The Finnish and the Sami have the same origin. The word Finn and Sami were actually used interchangeably until the formation of Finland as a state. The word Suomi, which is what the Finnish call their country, has the same root as the word Sami. They are both Finno-Ugric, which the Hungarians are also a part of, albeit very distant. However, due to the prevalence of Germanic traits in the Finnish, they are most likely of a Germanic-Ugric mix who took to using a Finno-Ugric language—perhaps due to invasion or lordship of some such, or a cultural hegemony and prevalent use of that language in this area. We have repeatedly seen in history how quickly a language and culture can be replaced without having much impact on the blood of the people there.

In Northern Europe then, or certainly the largest part of it, the Germanic man is the native inhabitant and he must be treated as such. Since ancient times we have been here, and we have remained the most unmixed of all the peoples of humanity for the longest time. And some of us hold that title still—easily seen in our characteristics of having fair hair and eyes. Yes, we are the natives, yet we are not treated or termed accordingly. We have a right to self-determination and self-preservation like all else. And even if a majority of our inhabitants, which includes the imported voter cattle, now vote for or back up the current agenda, then the minority of us should be protected against it if we wish to. Also, there have been no referendums regarding immigration, and immigration is a topic avoided by most of the politicians and political parties; and those parties that may have it in their political program may not appeal to voters in other aspects. Immigration is thus an unresolved, and unsolvable, issue due to this. At least until a referendum is held.

All other ethnicities, nationalities, and religions today are being protected as if sacred, even though their importance and contribution to the world is, and have been, rather minimal. Meanwhile, an intended demographic war is waged against the most successful of the human races—the most successful genetic elements of man in history—and against our world, the Western world. I say intended because the consequence is well known, and even wanted. So brainwashed are we today, that not only do we believe that genetics—these genes of ours that made the modern, advanced world—somehow had nothing to do with our success, but even that our culture and heritage is not important anymore. Yes, let us import cultures and bloodlines that have not merited their worth in coming here at all—absurdity. What is it that makes them think that these people, who come from broken countries—these same people who are the creators and the foundation of these failed nations—would do any good here at all? They will only turn their new homeland into a cesspool like the one they came from. As we are already witnessing today in full.

A much peddled notion today is that all of what the West has accomplished and worked extremely hard for—all of our advancements that elevated us so greatly above the rest—was just handed out to us randomly. It must be of great comfort to non-Westerners to believe that they were just unlucky—rationalization always soothe the inadequate. Why this notion and belief is so bizarre is because we do not assess individuals this way—that they were just lucky. We do, after all, believe that the intelligent and strong man will do better and achieve success, wealth, and a prosperous existence, and that a lazy, stupid man will get all the misery he had coming to him for his efforts, or lack thereof. We believe in individual differences and that one has to work at it to produce results. This is how it was with the Western world as well. There was hard work, and there was massive competition. But alas the slave mentality, or morality, of today has reached proportions that have resulted in total insanity.

I will speak no more of these underlying foundations and causes. They should be quite evident at this point. Instead, I will focus on the future. The future of the Celto-Germanic race. Do we not have the right to continue our survival on Earth as other people do? These people who are deemed endangered and threatened, precious and important, and are given any and all opportunities. Heck, even the Jews were given a new homeland—or perhaps it would be better to say that they outright stole and took it. They have defended it with tooth and nail ever since, though—shedding much blood for it—and for that they are to be admired. They had to work and lobby for it, and so should we. We, too, can create a country designated to our own kind. If we are not able to stop the democide in our native lands—if we are unable to stop this takeover by political means, or by violent and aggressive force—then we have no other choice but to seek lands elsewhere. It is a matter of the survival of our blood—a blood that has shown itself as the most advanced expression of

Part Five: Necessities for the Future

humankind to date. A place to settle must to be found. Fortunately, there are still some areas of opportunity left on Earth.

A place such as this can be located in South America on the northern shores along the Caribbean in the Guiana Shield. Here the three states of Guyana, Suriname, and French Guiana form a large part. Earlier called the British, Dutch, and French Guiana, respectively. These three states, which I will collectively call the Guianas, are some of the least populated, yet richest, in the world. It is lush with virgin forest and rivers, and the biodiversity in this region is one of the highest in the world. And so small is the human population in this trinity of states that they count just 1.55 million people. This in a combined land area of 460 000 km2 (square kilometres). Which is about the size of Papua New Guinea, or slightly larger than Sweden, and comparatively the Guianas have a population that is 1/6 than that of Sweden. One of the smallest population densities in the world, in other words. This in a climate zone that usually sustain populations in the several tens and even hundreds of millions. To put it in even clearer perspective: The countries of Germany, U.K., Italy, or Poland are each of them smaller than the Guianas! And these countries have quite large populations. Germany, for instance, has a population of 80 million people. The small population already in the Guianas is very mixed—of Indian, African, and Native American origins—and they are therefore not very uniform and solidary, or even very indigenous for that matter. There is very little justification for their own preservation then, and thus offer little sympathetic value to the outside world, and this would facilitate a much smoother process of settlement. But what of resources then? The Guianas is literally an Eldorado. It has a great quantity of gold, which is also the main export. And it has one of the largest bauxite reserves on the planet, which is needed to produce aluminium. Couple this with the great quantity of rivers there, and hydroelectric dams, and you have the potential of becoming a top global producer of aluminium. There are also diamonds and large oil reserves. The tropical climate with an invariable median of about 28 degrees Celsius and a decent amount of rainfall and moisture all year around—yes, it is extremely warm and hot—offer enormous opportunities for agriculture. There is already a lot of sugar, rice, and banana cultivation. The rivers and the coastal shoreline also provide a lot of fish and crustaceans. The largest features, the forests, have a lot of valuable hardwood trees for loggers to take advantage of. All in all, it is a land of plenty. Of course, the most important thing is energy, and with oil, and plenty of rivers and hydroelectricity, this shouldn't be a problem. With proper investments and a workforce—there is already the native population there that can be taken advantage of in the meanwhile—it can be turned into a tiger economy in no time. The most difficult thing would be to get Celto-Germanics from around the globe to come there. A number of help organizations should be set up to provide travel and settlement assistance for those who wish to immigrate. Naturally, the priority of settlement should first be the most populated British Guiana (Guyana), then Dutch Guiana (Suriname), and then the least populated French Guiana. This in order to gain a majority faster, and consequently a democratic majority faster, but I will get to that in a moment.

The largest obstacle of all will be to get open visas and a right to stay/citizenship for any and all of us who wish to move there. We should go there en masse and organize ourselves early on so that we cannot be ousted so easily. We could even form militias and buy our own military material. Those natives already there have to give way to another people. A greater and much larger people. After all, the "world" told the Arabs in Palestine that they had to make way for the Jews—a very small people. If we can lobby and present our case, and play most cynically on sympathy and political correct notions to the fullest, then we may get the global acceptance we need. We do not even need that, though. Again, Israel has survived thus far, and this despite the fact that much of the world can't stand them. They did this mostly by appealing to the military-industrial complex and the economic powers in the U.S. (of which they were, and are, a great part themselves). So should we. If we can get the U.S. capitalists and politicians on our side, we can achieve our goals. Easiest way to do this is to convince them that there is great opportunity for profit in our endeavour for them. If they realize that, then they will do most of the work for us, such as lobbying for our cause to U.S. politicians, and putting up most of the investments needed throughout.

Once we have built up an industry to provide jobs and wealth to the people, and finally achieved a population majority, we will democratically come to power by winning elections to get the seats needed for legal constitutional changes and referendums for a unification with the other Guiana states. Preferably, everything should be done with legal means so that we may be righteous in our cause and have the validity required for attaining a favourable global opinion and consent.

It is either the Guianas or finding some other attractive plot of land somewhere else in the world. This seems like the best bet at the moment, though.

III. Cosmic Survival

We take the world for granted. Just like life. Life is fragile, however. Many times throughout the existence of life on Earth have there been massive cataclysmic events that caused profound changes. Not catastrophic for the survival of all life, obviously, otherwise we wouldn't be here today, but it was catastrophic for many of the species that lived then. We must assume that we have only been fortunate to survive; and as well situated as we are between the main asteroid belt and a number of planets that shield us, we should nevertheless not take it for granted that no cosmic threats will slip by. The asteroids of the past only devastated the surface of the Earth so much that it altered the conditions for life, which would be quite catastrophic even for humans today, but there are no reasons for why one large enough would not just as easily find its way here as those previous ones and cause a definite end of all conditions for life to exist, once and for all. Another problem is that we are well on our way to destroy ourselves in the way of pollution and global warming, and the dire consequences this brings. We should do as we have done on Earth then: seek out and spread to new habitats and environments for the continuation and survival of our kind.

It is not as easy as that, however. Not on a cosmic scale, and not even on an interplanetary one. There are no other truly habitable planets or celestial bodies really suited to us in our Solar System, and very few are well situated and factored for terraforming. Mars may be our best bet. We should and must attempt a terraforming and/or colonization in habitats there. Sadly, there is just no will to spend resources on such projects at the moment. Public opinion, intoxicated by slave morality as it is today, conjure up any and all reasons not to. For instance, they are much too concerned with the potential safety of astronauts, which is not an issue, really, because there are thousands upon thousands of people who would want nothing else but to be a part of this and will volunteer despite the risk. After all, for many it is their life's dream and ambition to see a colonization of Mars happen. Other possible places for colonization in our solar system are Europa, Venus, or Titan, but there are even greater problems and obstacles to be overcome there if any success is to be had.

Part Five: Necessities for the Future

The last possibility is interstellar travel and exploration. This is also the most difficult option. While the vast distances between planets in our solar system are enormous and almost insurmountable themselves in terms of human physiology or resources, the distances to other solar systems are overwhelming in most aspects. It would take a great many human lifetimes to reach any other solar systems with our current technology. Hence, there would have to be a continuous cycle of life on board the spacecraft, with whole generations living and dying on them. These spaceships would have to be so huge—on account of needing a massive amount of stocks and supplies, and the self-sufficiency and amenities required—that the resources to get such a project completed would have to be supplied by all nations on Earth. This will obviously have to impact the global population. Population growth needs to not only stop, but the population needs to be greatly reduced as a whole, if we are to conserve and spend resources on this most important mission: the cosmic continuation and survival of man. New technologies are our best bet for interstellar success. Like a propulsion system or some other means of travel. Is such a thing only fantasy and fiction? It may seem so, but our technological progress have accelerated at such a pace and achieved heights that man could not even have dreamt of before. The people living 300 years ago in the pre-industrial world would think us gods if they saw our contemporary achievements. For instance, the electronic miniaturization which allows for music, movie projection, communication over distances, calculators, etc., all in our tiny, mobile smartphones. Or just the much, much older inventions of cars, airplanes, and other such things, for that matter. What holds us back today is energy. Efficient energy in terms of how much space it occupies and what it weighs. If we were able to build viable fusion power reactors—harnessing the power of the processes in the sun—it would help us greatly. We would then have massive amounts of energy for propulsion, life support, and hydroponics, while needing only extremely small amounts of fuel. Someday we may even get good enough space telescopes to find the habitable planets we need from the safety of our homeworld, and that way we don't actually have to explore space by travel. This would be much better, as we could just send ships on a one-way mission to viable planets instead of worrying about the risk and gamble of fumbling about in the dark and wasting time and resources. Space exploration and colonization of whatever kind—anything is better than nothing—only requires a bit of will and initiative and a reallocation of a few resources, and therefore it's the general ignorance of the wastrel population that is the largest obstacle. Their mindless, selfish wants and that constant search for happiness—that is the great hindrance.

Conclusion

This is my analysis of the world. My truth. How we came to where we are. The inversion and reaction that the mind is capable of has triggered on all possible factors. We now live in a time where the great masses have taken over all areas of society. They have instituted a dictatorship of mediocrity, and everyone must be pulled down to their level. All but the most mediocre, or even those more inferior than the masses themselves, will be embraced by them as idols and epitomes. A tyranny of normality has been established thus—normal being the better sounding version of mediocre. They think it's better to be normal than intelligent, strong, or to have the will to do anything great and glorious.

There can be a reversal, however, and that is primarily by information. One fights fire with fire—indoctrination and propaganda is information, and one combats it with the same means—and nature, science, and atheism are the fires and flames that burn the brightest. The naphtha of truth will always seep through the chinks in the armour. When truth and reality corresponds, people will recognize it and they will not be able to continue lying to themselves. They will then have to own up to the fact that the current falsehoods have done them no good at all and will feel compelled to walk down the path of truth instead. And when they finally know that the avoidance of pain and suffering for themselves and others was a mantra contradictory to life itself, they will grow up to become humans instead of animals that worship gods and cling to other fantastical beliefs. Animals obeying laws of heaven to gain godly approval and entry to some afterlife. In doing so, they voluntarily cast moral shackles upon themselves. One has to have laws, yes, but these have to be based on a need and justification, and not derived from some supposed millennia year old stone tablets or the newly carved, modern additions called individualism and altruism, whereby contemporary man has become apolitical, individualistic, and selfish. Selfish in the way that he helps others only to satisfy his own indoctrinated sense of being good; and that he will be rewarded in matters of the soul and afterlife for it. This is the path to becoming the Last Man. The fastest way to awaken or to get rid of such men is to break the structure completely. Information alone may not be enough, but it is certainly the primary weapon. The problem today in this mass media world is that there is not much interest or room for anything that is not shallow and careless fun. What is digested is entertainment and fiction, all due to the endless search of feeling good and happy—this hunt for constant stimulation, and alleviation of suffering. They all look for eternal bliss, yet no one finds it, and in the pursuit they end up being more lost than ever. Stop listening to the quacks! Stop listening to that square screen! Stop listening to the politicians!—why bother and why care, when there is so much ignorance that one is not even able to tell truth from lies?

Information first, and then understanding. First learn about the truth of the world yourself, and then teach others. Start reading. Read all the books they do not want you to read: The ones that are avoided or deemed uninteresting, and especially the controversial ones. And the ones that are not only deemed bad, but the ones they call evil. If one considers society faulty and corrupt, then the best place to search for answers is where society tells you not to. Any sources and beliefs that are polar opposites of what is believed today, in other words. We need to convince people to start reading and reflecting seriously about the realities of our world again, i.e., learning and thinking for themselves. Break free from the terror of political correctness. Revive freedom of speech. Reignite political interest, and start organizing and make yourselves heard.

Conclusion

If you can feel the power of events that led you to where you are today—what we call fate and destiny—then you can also feel the power of the present and foresee the shaping of the future taking place at every moment. Through this learned analytical prescience, we cognize that the smallest of occurrences and events, and even the most powerless of men, can have a profound impact. Little by little the brooks converge into rivers, and rivers into floods. Know, then, that the power of the few is strong when combined: The bundle of sticks (fasces) are much more resilient and effective, and almost unbreakable, when together, but one by one they can be easily broken. Therefore, join in cause and stand together, brothers, and you will then be able to bend and break the world to your will.

www.ingramcontent.com/pod-product-compliance
Lightning Source LLC
Chambersburg PA
CBHW030516230426
43665CB00010B/642